Remember,
when finding your Dream Job . . .

Any Dream Will Do.

How to Find Your Dream Job
And
Make it a Reality.

Solutions for
A Meaningful and Rewarding Career

By
Jason McClure

National Library of Canada Cataloguing in Publication Data

McClure, Jason, 1972-
    How to find your dream job and make it a reality : solutions for a
meaningful and rewarding career / Jason McClure.
Edited by Sarah K. McClure.
ISBN 1-4120-0538-8
    I. McClure, Sarah K., 1978-   II. Title.
HF5381.M33 2003   331.7'02   C2003-903347-3

This book was published *on-demand* in cooperation with Trafford Publishing.
On-demand publishing is a unique process and service of making a book available for retail sale to the public taking advantage of on-demand manufacturing and Internet marketing. **On-demand publishing** includes promotions, retail sales, manufacturing, order fulfilment, accounting and collecting royalties on behalf of the author.

Suite 6E, 2333 Government St., Victoria, B.C. V8T 4P4, CANADA
Phone   250-383-6864   Toll-free 1-888-232-4444 (Canada & US)
Fax   250-383-6804   E-mail sales@trafford.com
Web site www.trafford.com   TRAFFORD PUBLISHING IS A DIVISION OF TRAFFORD HOLDINGS LTD.
Trafford Catalogue #03-0907   www.trafford.com/robots/03-0907.html

10   9   8   7   6   5   4   3   2   1

Acknowledgements

A book of this magnitude and influence cannot be written without the assistance of others. I have the following individuals to thank:

My wife Sarah McClure, for her careful editing of this manuscript. I also thank her for choosing to be my life long companion, constant supporter, and best friend.

The Schwager family, for their support, love and friendship.

Judge Jesse Ferrell, my first mentor, for taking the time not only to notice my potential but also to develop that potential.

Norith Ellison, for his constant work in the field of motivation and his ongoing support and sound advice.

Todd Bermont, for sharing insights into the field of training and for sharing business notes.

My mother Sara Richardson, for demonstrating that entrepreneurship is still alive and that it is a reasonable career pursuit.

Finally, I would like to acknowledge you the reader for making a difference in the world. By finding your dream job and making it a reality you are making a positive difference in your world and the world around you. Thank you for sharing this book with those you come in contact with and for realizing the importance of finding that dream job, making it a meaningful career, living with passion, purpose and making a positive difference in the world that we live in.

Authors Note

The Guiding Principle

Myth: *"The human race is faced with a cruel choice: work or daytime television."* –**Unknown**

Fact: *"The law of compensation seems utterly unfair. But fair it is. The higher the joy, play, and satisfaction a worker gets from his job the more the worker is compensated for the job. The lower the joy, play, and satisfaction a worker gets from his job the less the worker is compensated for the job."* –**Mark Twain**

Far too many people buy into the myth that work equals misery. I do not believe that work should be something people dread. I believe that work should be something you enjoy. I believe what Mark Twain said about the law of compensation. This book is designed to destroy the myth that work is a cruel choice. After reading this book you will see that Mark Twain was right.

The guiding principle behind this book is to equip you to find not just a job, but a meaningful career that is high in joy, play, and satisfaction. This book is built on the fact that the more an individual enjoys their job the more they will be compensated for the job. Notice I did not said paid, but I said compensated. The reason is work should be more than what you do for a paycheck. Work should be what you do to make a difference in the world. Work should be an activity that you enjoy. This is why I believe that life is too valuable to spend in a job that you hate.

This book has two purposes. The first purpose is to teach you the secrets of job-hunting success. The second purpose is to provide you the motivation and information necessary to live your dreams. I believe that by using the information found in this book you will be able to find your dream job and make it a reality.

Table of Contents

How To Find Your Dream Job
And make it A Reality

It is not often that I have had the opportunity to write the forward to a book. The invitation to be part of *How to Find Your Dream Job And Make it A Reality*, however, was one I could not turn down because of the two parties involved: Jason McClure and his wife Sarah.

I first met Jason at a Toastmaster's meeting in Little Rock, Arkansas. After being introduced to Jason, we immediately engaged in a discussion about the possibilities of teaching people how to get what they really want out of life.

That was several years ago, and the excitement of that conversation and my respect for Jason has only increased. I have great anticipation for the readers of *How to Find Your Dream Job and Make it A Reality* because this book can only be a positive change in your life.

Jason and I have since shared the speaker's platform for a host of organizations and public seminars. He continues to be a powerful, dynamic, and wise presence. I admire him principally because his life's work has been to help individuals grasp the significance of their lives and to use their courage and creativity to face challenges, handle adversity, and grow as individuals.

How to Find Your Dream Job And Make it A Reality is a guide to finding your dream job, making it a meaningful career, living with passion and purpose and doing it in a way that resembles children at play—intensely, while learning, having fun, and relating to other people.

The "playground," if you will, that most of us have chosen is the world of work. Helping you enter into and thrive in that playground are the important elements in *How to Find Your Dream Job And Make it A Reality*. So if you've been outside peering through the fence struggling with ideas on how you will get your successful career started—read this book! Otherwise you might quickly get left behind.

How to Find Your Dream Job And Make it A Reality will give you the insights and tools to be better able to deal successfully with the permanent whitewater of job searching. The ideas are simply presented and easy to use with exercises that will make a profound difference in the way you see yourself as a job candidate.

In this insightful book, Jason skillfully presents the fundamentals for finding, landing, and succeeding in the career you have dreamed of living. If you have ever wondered how you would make it happen for you, this book will give you the keys to success. The great thing about success is that it isn't complicated, nor is it magical or mysterious. It is a simple process: Success is merely the natural consequence of consistently applying proven fundamentals to your life. In *How to Find Your Dream Job And Make it A Reality*, Jason has masterfully taken the seemingly complex and made it simple and doable for the reader.

I'm excited by this book and by the potential it creates for thousands of readers. It represents the distillation of five years of work, thinking, and creation in the pursuit of helping people get what they want. Read, learn, apply, and enjoy the results.

Norith L. Ellison, CEO
HuCom Training Solutions

What This Resource Will Do For You

In every chapter of this book you will find practical, useful, and proven methods, ideas, techniques, and principles that will equip you to find your dream job and make it a reality. Through the pages of this book you will discover the keys to career success, happiness, and satisfaction that you not only desire, but that you deserve. You will discover not only what you can or want to do, but more importantly, you will see exactly how to attain it. Here is what this book will do for you:

Chapter 1

It Could Happen to You!

This could happen to you. For a moment, pretend you are at work. While at work you are in the break-room, water-cooler, or wherever you go to take a break. You finish your break and you walk back to your office. When returning to your office you see a yellow piece of paper thumb tacked to your door. When you get to your door, you see that the note is an urgent message from your boss saying that he wants to speak to you as soon as possible.

Then you ask yourself "I wonder if this has anything to do with the million dollars I cost the company last quarter?" The note says, "Tracy, we need to talk. There is a situation that needs immediate attention. As soon as you get this memo come see me quickly." You sense the urgency and you think you have a good idea of why your boss wants to talk you. You sit down behind your unorganized oak desk. You look at your certificates of achievement. Then you look over the skyline of the city, taking a moment to look at the park where you like to go eat lunch when the office is hectic, and you begin to formulate reasons why the loss of money was not your fault. You say to yourself that the loss could have happened to anybody. You make a list of people to blame. You do not want to lose your corner office and you do not want to re-enter the job market. You have worked long and hard to make a name for yourself here, and you think one bad quarter should not be grounds for termination. Then you ask yourself the following question: "Suppose one bad quarter *is* grounds for termination?"

You get in the elevator push the button for the 13th floor. The music is playing the elevator version of "Another One Bites the Dust." The elevator stops with a slight jar and the music seems to do the same. You step off the elevator and walk towards to the receptionist. At this moment, the receptionist looks up, sees you coming towards her, and pushes a button to tell the boss you are here. Before you can say anything to the receptionist, she says, "He's been waiting on you." Then she smiles like a stock trader with inside information.

Feeling like a kid who has been caught cheating on a test and sent to the principal's office, you walk up to two huge, overpowering wooden doors. You grab the handle, turn it, and then push your shoulder against the door to help open it. Framed covers from Business Week, Forbes, and Fortune decorate the walls. All of them have your boss on the cover. The boss invites you in. He tells you to have a seat.

He then says, "Tracy, I have been hearing great things about you. I hear you have promise, and you are a person of vision. I just wanted to meet you and find out if what I've heard is true." You thank him for the compliment. The boss then goes into the story of how he started the company from scratch and the long hours he put in. He also tells you that he feels you have those same qualities. You then wonder if the boss has even gotten the latest figures. You believe if he had received the latest figures for your department you would not be right here right now listening to this compliment. You believe that you would be out the door and on your way to the unemployment line.

The boss then gets up and leans over his desk, as if he has a secret to tell. He says, "Tracy we have a new position opening up, and it is up to me to find the right person to fill it. Are you interested in a career change?" You think to yourself "Oh great, he has not heard about what I have cost the company." Thinking quickly, you say, "Yes I am interested; please tell me more."

He says, "Okay this new position will be a position of great responsibility, and as you know with great responsibility comes great risk, but with great risk comes great reward. This position will push the limits of human achievement. This position will take our company and your life to the next level. This new position will require creativity, leadership, perseverance, and the ability to create a vision for yourself and our company.

It also requires the ability to develop a strategy on how to get it. Are you *still* interested?" You realize it is official he has not heard about you losing the million dollars. What will happen if you take the position and he finds out? What will happen if you take the position and you cannot handle it? What will happen if you decline to take the new position? You are afraid if you say no, he will want to know why. You will have to tell him the truth because he will find out anyway.

The boss then says, "Tracy, this may be your only opportunity to stay with the company. I have reviewed your performance review for the past quarter and frankly, it was not as good as it has been. As matter of fact, it was terrible. For six years, you have done excellent work. I do not know what happened last quarter, but I want to give you one more chance.

Now are you interested, Tracy?" Seeing your options clearly, and after one second of thought you say, "Yes I am. What can I do to secure my employment with the organization?" With a family, a mortgage, car payments and other bills to pay, anything is better than unemployment.

The boss says, "Good, I would hate to lose you. Especially after the million-dollar investment we just made in your education. Over the years, you have been a great asset. This is what I want you to do. I want you to take a week off. During the next week, I want you to write out a detailed job description for yourself. In that job description, I want you to include your job duties, your rate of pay, and relate how your job will benefit the company. Then I want you to write how your job will benefit you. I want you to tell me how your job will benefit society. Write a job description for a job that you will find financially and emotionally rewarding.

Then write a mission statement for your life. Include what you want to accomplish professionally and personally. What awards or achievements do you want? Take an inventory of your personal assets and find out what you are good at and where you need to improve. Make a list of skills, both technical and non-technical that you need to acquire to accomplish your job. Then determine the amount of time that it will take you to acquire those skills. Do you think you can do this, Tracy?" To this Tracy replies, "Yes, I can do this."

If you were Tracy, could you do this? If you were given the opportunity to create a job at any rate of pay, doing what you wanted to do when you wanted to do it, would you be able to clearly define that job? Remember the following criteria:
- ➢ Your job will have to benefit society.
- ➢ Your job will have to benefit the organization.
- ➢ Your job will have to make a difference in the lives of others.
- ➢ Your job will have to benefit you.

After all it is not realistic to write a job description for sleeping all day or watching your favorite TV Show for 8 hours a day. It has to provide a valuable product or valuable service that can help people by improving lives and/or solving problems. Right now, you have that opportunity. By reading this book, you are in the process of creating that job. In this book, you will learn how to find your dream job and make it a reality. The purpose of this book is to do more than teach you some basic job-hunting skills. While it will do that, what sets this book apart is it will encourage you to find and pursue work that you find meaningful.

KAPS
Key Action Points

> - Start taking inventory of yourself and your current situation.
> - Read the rest of this book.
> - Realize that it really can happen to you.

Note: "It could happen to you" is inspired by a real life event. The story comes from the IBM Corporation and was originally reported in *Fortune* magazine on August 31, 1987. Since then it has been retold a number of times by motivational speakers and authors everywhere. The story goes like this:

A vice-president took the lead on the development of a new product that was both risky and expensive. The project was a total failure and cost the company millions of dollars. The vice-president was sure he was going to lose his job, but he did not. The surprise came when Thomas Watson, CEO of IBM, told the vice-president that he was not being fired because the company had just spent millions educating him on what does not work. "Now," the CEO said, "it is time for you to put that education to use."

I confess that I was not at the meeting with the vice-president and Mr. Watson, but I have studied successful people and I do know how successful respond to adversity. This is why I believe that the meeting would be surprisingly similar to the description in "it could happen to you." That is why I also believe it could *truly* happen to *you.*

Chapter 2

How Decisions Shape Your Life

Not long ago, I was talking to a friend of mine who is in the recruiting business. We were having a conversation about people's resumes and applications. My friend told me of a person who recently sent her an application with a resume attached. This person recently graduated from a good college, and he participated in a few internships. The problem was this person was applying for two positions. He was applying for both an entry-level administrative position and a middle management position. The recruiter told me that on paper this individual look great, but by applying for these two very different positions he revealed that he did not have clear career goals, and as a result he was never interviewed. This is a real life example that indicates clearly that employers are looking for individuals who have clear goals and a vision for what they want in a career.

Your circumstances may be similar to the young man in the previous example that sent my recruiter friend a resume for two different positions. It may be that you may have many job ideas, and you may be well qualified for all of them, but it takes more than being qualified for a job for you to get a job. In order to get a job you have to be the best job seeker. This is why getting your dream job means you must *become* the best job seeker. When you do this you will be able to turn your job idea into your ideal job.

What's Your Preference?

Most people go through life stating preferences or as Brian Tracy has said, living life as a "*wandering generality*," but only a few individuals ever make the firm and definite decision to become a "*meaningful specific.*" The world is designed for us to state preferences. When you go to a restaurant, you are expected to state a preference for what is on the menu. If you wanted a hamburger, but found yourself in a restaurant that only sold tacos, you have only stated a preference if you stay at that restaurant and eat a taco. But if you left that restaurant and went to get a hamburger no matter the obstacle, you have made a definite decision to get a hamburger. I say that to illustrate that we are all conditioned to state preferences. The world around us is created that way. The good news is we do not have to continue through life only stating preferences. We can take charge of our life and make definite decisions about who and what we choose to become.

Your Moments of Decision

In his book <u>Awaken the Giant Within</u>, Anthony Robbins tells his readers, **"*It is in your moments of decision that your destiny is shaped.*"** I agree with that. I also believe that *YOU* are in such a moment right now. You may not realize that this is one of those moments, but it *is*. I believe you are facing a life changing decision that could change the direction you are headed and the results you are currently getting out of life. That decision is a career decision. At this moment, you are being asked the following questions:

➢ Are you willing to settle for less than what you deserve?
➢ Are you willing to settle for less than what you can become?
➢ Are you willing to settle for less than you desire?
➢ Are you going to continue to "*just go with the flow*"?

➢ Are you going to let the forces in the environment and the people around you tell you what you can and cannot do or accomplish?

For your sake, I hope you answered **NO** to these questions. You should say NO to these questions. I hope you have the courage to say to yourself and to the world "This is my moment of decision, and at this moment I will decide to do the following . . .
➢ From this moment forward I have decided that I will make the most of my abilities, talents, skills and education.
➢ From this moment forward I have decided that I can do what I want to do in my professional life.
➢ From this moment forward I have decided that I will to take charge of my professional life.
➢ From this moment forward I have decided that I will have the job I want to have.
➢ From this moment forward I have decided that I can add value to my life and the lives of those around me.
➢ From this moment forward I have decided that I will start living my dreams one moment at a time.

Notice that the word try is not used. When people say they will try something, they have already set themselves up for failure by giving themselves a way out. I hope you choose not to try and instead choose to *do*. To reinforce this point, take a moment and write the previous statement out in your own words, put it in a visible place, and repeat it aloud several times a day until you have it committed to your memory.

Instead of giving yourself an easy out by saying you will try, be like the ancient general who, when he had to face an awesome enemy on the enemy's shore, immediately ordered all of the ships burned. He said to his men, "Men, see the boats in flames. That means if we want to leave here alive, we must win!" They were victorious. They were victorious because they totally cut off retreat as an option. If you want to win the battles you face in life, retreat cannot be an option.

Focus Determines Results

Another way that our decisions shape our lives is what we decide to focus on. It is more than a cliché to say that we get what we focus on. The human mind is much like a magnet. As you know a magnet attracts or repels objects depending on the object. The human mind is a magnet, but it is a magnet for ideas, both good and bad. Your focus determines what your mind attracts. To be successful your mind must focus on solutions and opportunities in life and not the obstacles that stand in the way of success. This is why it so important that you diligently develop a Positive Mental Attitude (PMA). Once you have a PMA you will see that great ideas will come and not only will they come, but also they will come in abundance in the form of inspiration and intuition.

The primary sources for inspiration and intuition are the subconscious mind, prayer and meditation. Your focus directs all of these sources of inspiration and intuition. In addition, focus nurtures the human experience. When you focus your conscious thoughts on getting the job you want, it will turn that job idea into a burning desire. Then it becomes more than a wish; it becomes a *possibility*.

Do not think that you can fool the subconscious because it is foolproof. Equally important, prayer and mediation only work for what you really want and only if you believe you can achieve it. The fact is if you do not really want the job, believe you do not deserve the job, or believe you cannot obtain the position, the subconscious mind will keep you from getting it. If you really want the job, your subconscious will go to work and help you get it.

When you develop a burning desire for a job, or anything else, your conscious mind will paint a partial picture and the subconscious mind will go to work to complete the picture. For example, if it you want to be an entrepreneur first you must see yourself as an entrepreneur, think of yourself as an entrepreneur and use words like "I am an entrepreneur." At this point I should warn you to not underestimate the power of language. The words you choose to use will shape your world, the words you choose to use will shape your destiny, and the words you choose to use will shape who you will become.

Right now, it is not important to know *how* to get to where you want to go, it is only important to know *where* you want to go. The only thing you need to do now is to make the decision on what you should be focusing on and why. Let your words reflect your life's focus in terms of accomplishment. Remember when you hold the thought of where you want to go in your conscious mind long enough and hard enough, the subconscious mind will fill in the gaps for you.

You Determine Meanings

What things, choices, or events mean depend on what you want them to mean or what you decide for them to mean. This decision is critical in shaping your life. I will admit that at first glance, it would be easy to say things mean what they mean, but I do not think this is the case. In 1936, Ivor Armstrong Richards wrote the book *The Philosophy of Rhetoric*, in which he claims that meanings are in people, not in words. According to Richards, meanings are not in words, symbols, situations, circumstances, or in other people; the meanings are in you.

Richards believes that meaning begins with our perception of an event, circumstance, or outcome, and in order to connect meaning and perception, we develop a context in which to develop meaning, which he defines as "a cluster of events that occur together." Meaning is created by how we organize those events together. We often cluster independent events together in a linear fashion as if one directly causes the other, when in reality they may not be related. Then we use this context, which may be inaccurately based on previous experiences, situations, and future expectations, as a way to categorize new events.

I believe that there are two things that are happening here that may be holding many people back. The first thing that is occurring is when people have experienced an extremely negative event, circumstance, or outcome and they continue to cluster that event with other unrelated occurrences. By doing this, this they are subconsciously creating a pattern of failure and defeat that will continue to hold them back and that will keep them from being successful.

The second thing that happens in this process is the subtle way the process itself works. The fact is many people are totally unaware of this process. When you are unaware of this process the following things can happen. First, you can assign inappropriate meaning to an "event cluster." Then you group unrelated events together.

Either way may cause the same adverse results. The key is to understand that this happens so you can decide to consciously assign meanings to events that will help you become more successful. **I like to say it this way: it's not what happens to you, it's how you see it and it's the meaning you assign to it.**

The key to assigning meaning is becoming aware of the context in which you put the situation. This has to do with the words, symbols, and meanings that you assign to describe things. It also has to do with the meanings that you assign to events, circumstances, and situations that happen in your life. All too often when people experience temporary defeat, they assign the wrong meaning to the event. A self-defeating person will label the event as just one more reason they should not succeed.

In my opinion, this is one of the greatest tragedies of life immediately behind living life without purpose. When it comes to assigning meaning to events I believe that Napoleon Hill has a great way to assign meaning to temporary defeat when he says, ***"Every adversity, every failure and every unpleasant experience carries with it the seed of an equivalent benefit, which may prove to be a blessing in disguise."***

Notice that I have not told you that getting your dream job would be easy. I am not going to say that. I personally believe that ***success is not easy, but success is rewarding.*** Success is rewarding because successful people do not live paycheck to paycheck. Success is rewarding because it eliminates the stress of having to provide for the individuals who are dependent on you. Success is rewarding because success brings more and better choices for the individuals experiencing success. Success is rewarding because successful individuals are living life to the fullest.

On the other hand I believe that life is much more difficult for the unsuccessful person. Life is more difficult for the unsuccessful person because unsuccessful people have to worry about paying their bills on time. Life is more difficult for unsuccessful people because they have to worry about being able to purchase new clothes for their kids. Life is more difficult for unsuccessful people because they live from paycheck to paycheck. Life is more difficult for unsuccessful people because they get "*stuck*" in day-to-day survival and the result of this is they can see no other choices for their lives other than what they have experienced.

The good news is you can be successful and repeat the rewards of success. One reward is when you get your dream job, you may enjoy the work so much that you do not think of it as work. I believe that the road to success is full of obstacles. You will find that you may be moving along at 100 miles per hour on a smooth and straight road only to be derailed by a huge pothole. You will find that there will be obstacles so large you must build a bridge to pass it, but I promise in the end you will say one of two things: "I'm glad I did" or "I wish I had."

I believe that the potholes, detours, and bridges in my life have prepared me for a greater level of success. Looking back, I can now see how these obstacles were nothing more than ***learning experiences*** that have taught me what doesn't work. The older I get the more I look forward to these "learning experiences." I now know that when I have these experiences I am closer to being able to use only what works for me. Like many people, I used to believe that these so called obstacles on the road to success were holding me back, but now I believe that they were stepping stones that are now lifting me to a higher level of success.

Just Do It...

A third way that decisions shape your life is making the decision to take action. Many people have the knowledge, skill, expertise, and education to be successful but they never act. You have to act; I am giving you the information necessary to identify and find the job you desire. I have done everything I can do to help you get your dream job and to make it a reality. I wrote a book that you can use as your personal job-hunting manual, but the rest is up to you. With the information in this book, I can lift some of your obstacles and I can lower some of your hurdles, but you still have to run the course. To do this follow the advice of the Nike and just do it.

I know this from experience. I know a 32-year-old waitress who hates her current job. Her dream job was to become an emergency medical technician. To do this she would have to spend a few months to get her GED and then she would need to train as an EMT. It would take her just over two years to complete the process. For a period of three years, I would eat at the restaurant were she worked and she would wait on me. I would ask if she had gotten her GED and she would say, "I haven't done it yet because I haven't been able to afford the book."

After a year of her not being able to afford the book, I made a twenty-dollar investment in her and I bought her the book. I gave it to her, and she thanked me and said it was one of the nicest things anyone had ever done for her. Three months later, I asked if she had taken the GED test. She said, "Jason, I don't know where to go to take it. I have been studying real hard and I think I'm ready." I went home that day and made a few phone calls to find out where and when she could take the GED. I found out the answers, called my friend, and gave her the information. She thanked me for the information, and a month later, I asked her if she had taken the test. She had not taken the test because she could not afford to take off work to take it.

Even though she had all of her perceived obstacles removed, she never made the decision to act. I bought this bright young lady a GED book, helped her study, and offered to pay her test fees. I lifted every obstacle or excuse she presented me. I did everything but the one thing she had to do for herself and that is to take action. No matter how much I did for her I could never act for her, and until she makes the decision to act, nothing will change and she will keep getting the same results. Her life will still be miserable, and she will continue to be unhappy.

I believe in our own unique way we all are like this girl. We all have obstacles that are nothing more than invisible walls that we have set up in our mind. Instead of facing our obstacles, we make the decision not to try and we follow that decision with the decision to give up our dreams. That is why I believe that the biggest obstacle between us and what we want out of life is a lack of belief as indicated in this next illustration.

In his autobiography, Chuck Yeager says, "After all the anxiety and all the anticipation, breaking the sound barrier was a real let down." He went on to describe it as a poke through Jell-O because the only obstacle to breaking the sound barrier was in the minds of people. You see getting your dream job is just like breaking the sound barrier because the only barrier keeping you from your dream job is the barrier in your mind.

It Takes Practice to get it Right

To get decisions right you will need to practice making decisions. I think one of the biggest reasons we do not feel comfortable making decision is we lack practice. Start making little decisions and quit saying "I don't know." Start practicing with the small decisions. For example when you go out to eat do not spend too much time thinking about the menu. When the server asks what you want to order, make a quick decision by picking the first thing that comes to mind.

When you do this, you might get some food you do not like. But the next time you will know in an instant not order that item and over time you will become skilled at picking out what you like and avoiding what you do not like. Apply this example and process to other decisions you have to make in your life, and you will see that this process will work in everything you do. I should remind you that it is important to weigh your options and analyze the outcomes, but at the same time do not debate or wait too long to make a decision.

Confucius Says Stop the Insanity...

The final decision you need to make is the decision to try something different. The Chinese say that the definition of insanity is doing the same thing repeatedly and expecting different results. I agree. If something does not work it does not mean that your goal was bad, it just means that your approach did not work. The good news is now you know what doesn't work and you are more prepared for success because you are now able to try something new and different that just might do the trick.

It is okay to try something different because by trying something different and persevering, you are sure to find the one thing that will work. I believe this to be true because Thomas Edison practiced this principle by sitting through 10,000 experiments trying to get the light bulb to work before he was successful. When asked why he did not quit he said, "I knew that if I kept on trying I would run out of things that didn't work so eventually I would find the one thing that would work."

I know some people reading this may need something different to try and if you are one of those people, try following this 8-step outline for success:

1. Define your mission, purpose, or chief aim in life.
2. Decide what you are willing to do and how you will successfully fulfill your life's mission.
3. Decide to acquire all the knowledge, skills, and expertise about what you want to accomplish.
4. Decide to take that knowledge and put it into action.
5. Decide to take personal responsibility for the outcome of your actions.
6. Decide to take notice of what is working and what is not working.
7. Decide to constantly change your approach, not your mission, until you achieve your goals.
8. Decide to be persistent.

Knowing how to make decisions is as important as knowing what decisions to make. You need to practice decision making so you can make good decisions. The reason for this is simple: your decisions are the forces that shape your life. To begin shaping your life in the right direction, you need to make a decision that you are no longer going to be a creature of circumstance, but rather you will consciously create your circumstances by remembering that the decisions of today influence the choices of tomorrow.

In this chapter, I have focused on decisions. Please remember that your decisions will shape your life. Because of your decisions, you can become a great success or a miserable failure. Many people never realize this. The fact is it is the little decisions that have the biggest impact on our outcomes. That is why when you make decisions those decisions must support what you want to accomplish. When you do this you will find success will be much easier to attain and as a result you be able to enjoy the rewards of success.

KAPS

- ➤ Decisions determine outcomes.
- ➤ Decide what you want to focus on because the human mind is like a magnet and you attract what you focus on.
- ➤ Make a conscious decision on what events and circumstances mean.
- ➤ Make a decision to act.
- ➤ Make a decision to do something different if what you are doing is not working.
- ➤ Start practicing little decisions so you can more easily make big decisions.

Chapter 3

Values:
The Building blocks of Reality
and Compass Points

Have you ever thought about the meaning that is behind the little word *values*? Webster Dictionary defines this word in two parts: 1) the desirability or worth of a thing; merit. An example of this is *the value of self-discipline*. The second part of this word is defined as: 2) something regarded as desirable, worthy, right, as a belief, or ideal. An example of this is *a situation that you want to create for your life*. Therefore, when I talk about values in this book I will refer to these two aspects and how they can be applied to your life.

If you were to survey the job hunting/career books on the market today, you would wonder if this is important. After all, hardly any other author addresses this issue, but I believe values are important in finding your dream job. The fact is until you retire, you will spend more time working than engaged in any other activity. I believe that is reason enough to address this issue.

Also, I believe no matter how much money you make you will not be happy with your job when it forces you to compromise your values. The best way to know if your job compromises your values is to have a clear understanding of what your values are. Until you are clear about what you value, it may be extremely difficult to identify the right job for you. I believe this is one reason why so many people are dissatisfied with their current vocation.

Many people never clearly define their values and as a result, they end up in a job they do not like. There are two primary reasons for this. The first reason is without a clear set of values it is much more difficult to find a cause to fight for or a job that will make use of your values. The second reason is when you clearly define your values you are able to see if what you are currently doing supports or conflicts with your values . . . for the same reason you are also able to see job choices that you did not know existed before.

What Are You Selling?

When you go to work are you selling your values or are you selling your labor? I believe that when you do not clearly define your values, you may become like a friend of mine who is responsible for purchasing merchandise for his employer who complains that he hates his job. He likes the money and the responsibility that goes along with the job, however, he hates the hours, and he often feels like he is in the business of ripping people off. He tries to rationalize this aspect by saying things like, "In the business world it is either you or them." I believe that my friend is selling his values. I also believe that he doesn't believe that he is doing this.

I believe two things are creating this situation. The first thing is my friend has not clearly defined his values. He is operating on what is called "*automatic pilot*." Automatic pilot is what you do when you are not mindful of your actions or circumstances. He has not made a decision to define his values. I believe he values both honesty and free time.

The problem is his job is not providing him with either one. As a result, he is miserable. Instead of clearly defining his values, he is doing what many people do. He is constructing a perception of reality that is supported by unclear values, wants, and desires.

Creating Your Reality
Like many people he doesn't realize that reality is not about what is happing in the world around you. Reality is about the way you process information about what is happening in the world around you. Reality is based on your perception of things and what you decide those things mean to you. What you value determines the type of information you absorb and process. The fact is it is impossible to process all the information in the world around you. Since it is impossible to take in all of the information, we take in information that supports our pre-existing ideas and ways of living. That is why our values determine what information we take in and what information we ignore.

Think about my friend for a moment. How could a guy who values honesty really enjoy a job where he feels like he is ripping people off? How can a guy who values his time with friends and family be happy in a job that encourages him to work 60 hours a week? (I used the word encourage because he does have a choice. The truth is we all have choices though we may not see them.)

When he interviewed for the job he was in the process of getting married and he valued the role of being a providing husband. He stays in the position because he currently has student loans, a car payment, and a mortgage. Since he values his good credit, he needs to make money to maintain his credit rating. It is these values that have shaped and continues to shape his perception of his job. He has filtered out all other aspects of the job and continues in that job based on those two values. I am not judging these two values. However, I am saying there are more than two values that should be considered when making a career decision.

The second reason we need to clearly define our values is that often our job becomes a major aspect of our identity. If you don't believe me, think about when you first meet someone. After you exchange names, one of the next pieces of information exchanged is usually career related information. The problem occurs when you find yourself in a job that causes a major conflict between your actions and your behaviors at work with your core values.

There are many people who are quick to point out to me that there are many jobs that require a clear set of values such as being a doctor, lawyer, fireperson, law officer, teacher, and consultant (of course this is just a partial list.). I agree with that, but it does not change the fact that we need to develop a clear set of values.

The fact is you may be initially attracted to a job that has clearly defined values, but unless you clearly define your values, and they match the values of that job, a perfect match has not yet been made. I believe we all want clearly defined values. I also believe that sometimes people mistakenly believe that if they get a job with clearly defined values then their values will have been clearly defined. This is not always the case.

Defining Your Values
Lionel Kendrick says, "***Values are the foundation of our character and of our confidence. A person who does not know what he stands for or what he should stand for will never enjoy true happiness and success.***" I agree with this statement,

and I would also like to add this: values are your life's compass. Having clear and well-defined values will cause you to experience happiness and success. If you think of your life as a ship, your values will be the compass that will direct the ship and your dreams will be the stars you use to chart the course.

I would like to dissect that quote to get more meaning out of it. "Values are the foundation of our character and of our confidence." I think everybody would agree that character without confidence is no good. I really like the second part of the statement: "A person who does not know what he stands for or **what he/she should stand for** will never enjoy true happiness and success." I agree with that because most people experience life never knowing what they *should* stand for. Many people go through life acting on everybody else's values and not their own.

Two Types of Values

To start defining your values, I would like to make a distinction between two types of values. The first type of values is macro-values. I believe these values are fundamental and everyone should adhere to them even if they may not agree with them. John Locke says these values are all part of the social contract. An example of these values would be freedom of speech and other unalienable rights. The other type of values is micro-values. These are the values that you hold and are unique to you. An example of these values is your choice of religion or no religion and other values that are of a personal nature.

I think we should start defining our own values in terms of how they fit into the realm of *macro-values*. Everyone in our society should agree on some basic values. I believe these values should include but not be limited to honesty, freedom, security, love, hard work, family, country, loyalty, achievement, persistence, free speech, and freedom from cruel and unusual punishment, and the freedom to follow the religion of your choice. As you can see these are the basic values behind the American dream and our country's Constitution.

What Macro-Values Can Do For You

What can you expect to accomplish from having these fundamental values? To answer that question let me tell you a story of a man who held these values. It is a story of a man who started from poverty and rose to greatness. This man's father was an unsuccessful businessman who gave up at business and decided to try to make it as a farmer. Working on the farm is where this man learned the value of hard work. At an early age, this boy learned if he wanted to succeed in life, it would take effort. Along with hard work, he learned that it would take persistence.

As a young man, he worked on the farm barely getting by. In an effort to get ahead and live the American dream he began to try other things such as land speculating and oil leases, all of which left him bankrupt at 38 when he decided to try politics. At the age 38, he put everything he had monetarily into running for the senate. Rising early and working hard well into the night, he won his first senate seat. Knowing this was his last chance to live the American dream, he would arrive early and stay late. This is why he became the first senator to ever be issued a key to the building. During WWII his committee on War Production inspired major improvements in defense industries, and as a result saved millions of taxpayer dollars. He did all of this with only a high school diploma.

In the 1948 election he decided he would run for President. During the presidential race against Thomas E. Dewey, he was told that he would not and could not win, but he won. President Harry Truman is the man I am talking about and he believed in these macro-values. He also had the faith and courage to believe that if he worked hard enough and long enough the nation would elect him as their president. He was right. Truman's hard fought campaign inspired millions of Americans to vote for him. As a matter of fact many of the people voting for him expected him to lose, but they voted for him because they admired his determination. Everybody was so confidant that he would not win the newspapers had already printed the headlines for the next day declaring Dewey the victor.

Harry Truman lived by the macro-values that we are taking about. His macro values were honesty, freedom, security, love, hard work, family, country, the individual, honor, loyalty, achievement, persistence, free speech, and freedom from cruel and unusual punishment, and the freedom to follow the religion of your choice. I believe his micro-values or personal values would have included self-reliance, taking responsibility for his actions, and developing a burning desire for what he wanted.

Defining Your Micro-Values

Until now, the discussion has focused on the big values we all should share, but you also need to clearly define your own values or your **micro-values**. These values are a little more complex because they are more personal. This is where you break the macro-values down into bite-sized pieces so you can digest them. In this section, you will also have the opportunity to prioritize and analyze your micro-values.

This step is necessary before you find your dream job and it is necessary to create the life of your dreams. These values help you to become what author Grace Cirocco calls the "authentic self." When you develop your "authentic self" two amazing things happen. You decide who and what you are going to become and you decide what you really want out of life.

I am sure that there is someone reading this book saying, "You can't tell me what is right or wrong for me and I can't tell you what is right or wrong for you." I agree with that statement to a point. That point is this: I believe that we all should do things that are legal, do not infringe on the rights of others, or create an unfair circumstance that may cause a significant loss to another person for our own personal gain. To clearly define your micro-values I have some questions that you can ask yourself. Answer them honestly, taking time to clearly articulate your answers.

Value Determining Questions

The first question is this: **What are your religious beliefs?** There may be occupations that you may not be able to pursue if a vocation goes against the teaching of your religion or is religious itself. You need to know that before you start pursuing that vocation. You need to have an understanding of your religious beliefs. For example, if you are a Christian and you want to own an adult novelty store it just would not work because the two industries have totally different values. On the same hand if you are an atheist, you should not go into the ministry. Of course, these examples are extreme but it clearly illustrates the point I am making.

The point is your religious beliefs cannot conflict with your job. I believe that humans are made up of three parts: body, mind, and soul. All three of these parts need to be able to operate in a spirit of harmony. Acting in ways that conflict with one or two of these components may cause harm to the other component. I also believe that many people do not realize that a major source of stress is the result of the body, mind and soul going in different directions.

The second question is this: **What do you want most out of life?** This seemingly easy question is a trick question. The obvious answer is a million dollars, a loving spouse, and a new car. I do not think that it is bad to want a million dollars, a nice house, a new car, and other things. I do think it is wrong to expect those things without effort. Wanting those things may help you stay motivated, but when answering this question think in terms of accomplishment. When answering this question think of the process that you need to go through to get the things you want.

For most people this is the hardest question. When I ask people this, I get all kinds of answers. One common answer is "I just want to be happy." I think of course you want to be happy, we all want to be happy, but what is being happy? Is it an end or means? Is being happy a state of mind? If you want to answer this question with that phrase, you need to be able to describe the behaviors, events, and circumstances that will create true happiness for yourself.

I will not say being happy is the wrong answer, but it may not be the right answer. The right answer will clearly define what makes up happiness for you. I think we would agree that people want to be happy. Therefore, we need to define what will determine our happiness. It can be cars, toys, or other material objects; it can be better relationships with the people you care about; or it can be both.

Your definition will greatly determine the type of job you need to pursue. Some people want material wealth. Other people want to leave a legacy. Then there are some people who just want to be famous. Some people do not want anything out of life. I cannot tell you what you should want out of life. You must decide that for yourself. This reminds me of a story I once heard about a prominent doctor who was a high school drop out during WWII.

His first battle taught him a valuable lesson. He was only 17 at the time. The same age most people are getting their first job, first car, first kiss, and still rebelling against their parents. Like most people his age, he felt invincible. But he was fighting in the Battle of the Bulge, and the battle raged all night. The only thing that broke the darkness was exploding bombs and bullets that flared in the air.

He spent that night shooting aimlessly in the dark while in a foxhole that he had to dig with his friend while the enemy was shooting at them. The night seemed to go on forever. He could not look around without seeing someone he knew, dead on the ground. The smell of burnt flesh and death was unavoidable. It was at that point he made a decision of what he wanted the most out of life. At that moment he wanted nothing more than to save the men around him from death. This is why he decided if he made it back to America alive he would dedicate his life to saving lives, and that is what he did.

The third micro-value-defining question is **what would you do if you were invisible?** This question usually gets some interesting responses. People tell me they would go to Fort Knox and get all the gold. Others say they would open doors for people and pick people up when they fall. Other people say they would slam doors on people and trip them. Other people lie and say they would not change their behavior. This question is made up of two questions. First, what would you do if you if you knew you could avoid punishment? Secondly, what would you do if you knew that no matter what you did you would never get a reward for it? When you are invisible, these two things tend to happen.

What do you do when no one is looking? What do you look at on the Internet? What books do you read? What movies do you watch? What thoughts do you have? Answering these questions indicates what you really value, and if you do not like your answers remember the greatest thing about human behavior and character is its ability to change. If you decide you do not like the values you came up with on this question or any other question, you can change.

This next question is the hardest one to lie about. ***Where does your money go?*** I used to say I valued success. Then I looked at my spending habits. I had habits I was supporting but the habits I was supporting were not helping me to become successful. Instead of buying resources and tools to be more successful, I was buying beer, fashionable clothes, and other items designed to help me impress people I did not even know. Then I asked myself this question, "What do I value? Achievement or social popularity?" What is more important? I decided that achievement was more important than social popularity and as a result, I changed the way I was spending my money and I started spending money on what I decided I wanted to value.

This is because money represents the value we place on a product or service. When we spend our money on something we are saying, "This is what I really value." I changed my values by buying motivation books, going to success seminars, and taking more classes. I was no longer the person who would buy things to impress people I did not know. I also found out that true friends like you no matter what you drive or wear. I discovered that once you start becoming more successful, people you thought would be the most proud of the positive change were the same people that were the most resistant to the positive change.

Time Really Is...

Another question that will help you clearly define your values is this: ***How do you spend your time?*** How do you spend your time at work or away from work? When you are at work, are you putting everything you can into those hours? When you are away from work, are you trying to improve yourself? Henry Ford said, "When the whistle sounds to end the work day, it is really sounding the start of the thinking day."

If you really want your dream job chances are great that you will need to spend time studying the industry or gaining additional skills or knowledge to be qualified for the job. In the beginning, it may not be enough to work forty hours a week; a forty-hour week may just be the beginning. Remember time is your scarcest resource. You must always use your time wisely, because time is more than money. I believe that it is a mistake to think of time as money; it is more accurate to think of time as your life because how you spend your time is how you spend your life.

The last question that I will ask is ***if you were to die today, what would people say about you?*** When you die, people will be honest about what they really think about you. There is a training exercise where people are asked to write their own obituary as a way to answer this question. I do not know what you would like for your obituary to say, and if you do not know, try writing one sometime. Perhaps if you are lucky your town paper will do for it you like it did for this person.

This story is about a chemist who had an explosive career inventing and marketing weapons. That is until his brother passed away. The town newspaper received inaccurate information that the chemist had passed on and that his brother was still alive. A reporter seized this opportunity to voice what he and the rest of the world thought of this man. The headline for the paper read "Dr. Death dies!"

Could you imagine the surprise of this man dressed in slippers and bathrobe when he stepped outside to pick up that day's paper? Could you image what he thought as he came back inside, sat down at his kitchen table, and poured a cup of black coffee? I have a hard time imagining how I would react if I read that about me.

I wonder what his initial reaction was when he realized the paper was talking about him? Picture this old man with gray hair and reading glasses as he looked over the top of his glasses and read *his* name in the article. I can picture his raised eyebrows as he put the paper down on the table. Could you imagine what you would be thinking if you read that about yourself in the morning paper? What would you think?

This man had the opportunity to experience the true reality of this question when he discovered what the world thought of him. The whole world thought of this man as Dr. Death. They viewed him as the inventor of explosives that enabled armies around the world to wreak havoc onto innocent people everywhere. He thought about the article all that day and decided that he did not want the world to remember him as Dr. Death.

He knew if he wanted to change the way people would remember him, *he* must change. But what could he do at this point? He spent his whole life and career developing these explosives and he could not un-invent them. He decided it was time for a career change. It was at that point Alfred Nobel created the Nobel Foundation, which would award six international prizes for outstanding achievements in the fields of physics, chemistry, physiology, literature, economics, and the promotion of world peace.

He did this because he wanted to change the way world would remember him. The good news is you do not have to wait for an event like that to happen in your life. The good news is you can learn from the lesson of Alfred Nobel, and you can start living the way you want to be remembered. When you do that you will be living your values.

Values Determines Needs

I would like to end this chapter by reminding you of the words of Earl Nightingale. "*Values determines our needs; needs determine our goals.*" For many people their basic goal is getting the job they want. It should be more than that. It should be pursuing a meaningful career and creating success so you can make a positive difference in your life and in the lives of those around you. That is why I believe your dream job should be more than what you do for a paycheck. I believe dream jobs come in all forms such as the job of a good parent, spouse, sales professional, librarian, doctor, lawyer, or anything else that has a positive impact on the world.

No matter what job or role you want out of life, if you do not have clear values you will not be able to get what you want. It is up to you to develop and clarify your values right now. This is too important to put off. Without values, you will not have a compass to direct your ship, and without goals, you will not have a chart to guide your ship. With values, you will have a compass to direct your ship, and with goals, you will have a chart to guide your ship.

➤ Having a clear set of values is a must if you are going to accurately define your dream job.
➤ Macro-values are based on our fundamental ways of life.
➤ Micro-values are your individual values based on what you want to accomplish.
➤ Values are the building blocks of reality because your values play a major role in determining what events and circumstances mean to you.

Develop Your Compass Points
An exercise in building values

I hope by now you realize that values are compass points in life. Here is an exercise that you can do that will do two things. First it will help you to clarify your values and secondly it will help you to reinforce your values. In this exercise, you will create "compass points" for yourself and put them in a place where you can refer to them often.

The first thing you need to do is list all of your values. Then examine those values and determine why those values are meaningful to you. Then list that value, what it means to you, and a quote about that value. The quote can be your own or it can be from someone else. If you need some quotes, visit your local library or go to my web site (www.jasonmcclure.com) and under free resources I have an online database of quotes that may be helpful to you. Once you do this, write out at least one specific behavior that you can do that will demonstrate that value.

For example, let's say you value accomplishment. On a note card, write the word accomplishment. Then you can write something like, "I value accomplishment since it allows me to become the person I want to become." Then you can put a quote that supports that value like the following, ***"Don't let what you cannot do interfere with what you can do."*** –John Wooden. Then write out something to the effect of "Today I will plan, act, and perform to the best of my abilities." Then go out and do it. Your note card might look like this:

Value: I value accomplishment.
Why: I value accomplishment because without accomplishment there can be no reward.
Quote: "I will not let what I cannot do interfere with what I can do." -John Wooden
Action: Today I will do the following activities to help me accomplish my goals.

Note: Of course your note card can look any way you want. There is no right or wrong way as long as you do it. If you do not like this particular technique, it may help trigger an original idea of your own.

Chapter 4

Getting and Maintaining Direction
What Kind of Job do You Really Want?

Up to now, we have talked about decisions and values. Now it is time to answer the following question, "What job/career do you really want?" Examine this question closely. It does not ask what kind of job do your parents want you to have. It does not ask what others say you can and cannot do. It does not ask what others say you should do. It does not ask what your friends and acquaintances do for a living. The question at hand is *what kind of job do you really want?* You have to be able to answer this question if you want to get and maintain direction.

It is important for you to answer that question for yourself because there are many people who have taken a vocation at someone else's suggestion, only to find themselves in a job where they feel like they are stuck in a rut. I am sure you know someone like that or perhaps that person is you. I believe that everybody who wants to have his or her dream job must be willing and able to answer the question: *what kind of job do you really want?*

For some people this is a difficult question because they see too many job choices. They may be qualified for many jobs, and they may have many skills, or they may just have a lot of job ideas. Other people have difficulty answering this question because they do not see enough choices. If you have too many choices, this information will help you to narrow those choices. If you have too few choices this information will help you to create more career choices and at the same time it will reveal choices that you did not even know existed.

What's Your Excuse?

In order to be successful and make your dream job a reality, you will need to make clear choices, clear decisions, and clear career goals. This will give you clear direction. Many people admit they have a lack of direction. The good news for these people is they have identified what is holding them back, and this is the first step to overcoming that obstacle. However, if they replace that excuse with excuses like the ones listed below, they will never gain the direction needed for sustainable success.

➢ I do not have the time to get the skills to be successful in that career.
➢ I am too old.
➢ I am too young.
➢ I have the wrong degree to do or be…
➢ I don't have the same talents or skills as…
➢ I will go back to school when I find an employer to pay my tuition.
➢ I will go back to school when I have saved enough money.
➢ I will go back to school when I have more time.
➢ I am not smart enough.
➢ I have been in this job or company for too long to change positions.
➢ I am waiting for the right time.
➢ I don't know what I want to do.
➢ If I did the work I love, I could never make as much money as I could as a…

Many people use these excuses and other similar excuses that have a socially desirable message to them as reasons to stay in their current circumstances. I believe the reason that people continue to use these excuses is because they lack direction. Failure is not the result of a lack of time, money, or other resources. Failure occurs because the individual experiencing failure has a lack of *direction*. Hannibal said it this way, **"We will either find a way or make one.** " When you have direction mixed with the right motivation, the right information, the right decisions, and a commitment to persistence, then Hannibal's statement becomes true.

People with direction do not put their success in the hands of other people. They do not wait for changes in the external environment to make internal decisions and commitments. They do not look for organizations to pay for their tuition. They choose to value education over things and to spend their money accordingly. They realize that waiting on the external environment to change is the pathway to failure. So instead of waiting on the external environment to change they change internally.

People without direction invest more time in finding and making excuses. They look for reasons why they should not be successful and why they cannot be successful. The result is they go through life with less than desirable results. On the other hand, people with direction invest more time in finding and making solutions. As a result these fortunate people are able to see choices and pathways that the other group of people never see. Because of this, these people go through life getting desirable results.

I Will Put Gas in My Car When…

Remember in order to get you have to give. Life is like a computer because you have to have input in order to get output. That is in order to get something out of life you have to put something into life. This should not be a surprise to anyone reading this book. However, I mention it because I am often reminded of a person who I once heard about. While driving, this person's car ran out of gas. They pulled over to the side of road and said "Car, if you want some gas you have to get me to the gas station."

What would you say to a person who is waiting for the car to get them to gas station before they give the car gas? How does this relate to your career and turning your dream job into a reality? Please do not wait on external events to occur before deciding to take action. When you take action the world will notice and respond appropriately.

4 Ways Decisions Impact Your Life

A major aspect of maintaining direction is the decisions you make. That is why in this section I will discuss the 4 ways decisions impact your life. Many people never fully realize that the decisions they make determine the results they get. The first way decisions impact you is by the meanings that you assign to events and circumstances that happen in your life. The only meaning anything has in life is the meaning that you assign to it. Meanings are not in words, symbols, or actions, but meaning is in you. If you want to be successful, you need to make sure you assign a positive meaning to the events or circumstances in your life.

The second way decisions will impact you is by the outcomes that are related to the decisions you make. That is why it is important to set your agenda. If you go through life without deciding what you want out of life, someone else will come up with something for you. Your life is too valuable to spend it accomplishing someone else's goals without you ever living your dreams. I believe it is important to invest in other people, but at the same time, you need to remember if you do not set your own agenda someone else will do it for you. I can also tell you that the agenda they set most likely will not be in your best interest.

When setting your own agenda remember to consider all the options that you have. You may notice at this point in the process that many options and outcomes are not clear. That is okay, and this is just another reason why you should be prepared to make quick decisions, because the quicker you can make a decision the more time you have to fix the decision if the decision was flawed. In addition, by making quick decisions when an opportunity arises and there is not much time to consider it, you will be able to make the right decision quickly.

The third way decisions impact what you do is to influence the results you get in the future. When making a decision you should try to visualize the possible outcomes of that decision. You should make decisions so that even the worst-case scenario is not that bad, and the best-case scenario is the ideal situation. To do this you will need a clear vision of your long-term career goals. When you have long-term career goals you can insure that your short-term decisions will directly influence the results you get today and the choices you will be able to make in the future.

The fourth way decisions impact you is making definite decisions with a clear purpose changes you from what some motivational speakers call a "wandering generality" and into a "meaningful specific." When you make decisions about what you want to accomplish in life and then focus your other decisions on that accomplishment, amazing things will happen and you will get unlimited results in everything you do.

What Interests You?

In order to maintain direction you need to know what interests you. Most people never really answer this question. However, the answer to this question may be the key that unlocks the door to defining your dream job. When you really, and I mean really, know what you are interested in, chances are great that you will find a career that is out of this world just like these two young men did.

As a young boy, this person was extremely interested in aviation. At the time, it was a new science. His interest led him to dream about becoming a great pilot one-day. This tiny interest in a small boy grew until it led the same grown man, Neil Armstrong, to be the first man to walk on the moon. Another young boy had the same interest. John Glen dreamed of flight, and this dream stayed with him into what would be retirement years for most people. However, instead of retiring like most people, he decided to become the oldest man to orbit the earth. These men both had careers that were literally out of this world because they were able to turn their interests into a full time vocation. The good news is you can do this too.

As adults we often forget what it was we enjoyed most as children. I admit that it is easy to be consumed with trying to survive. The result is we forget about the dreams we had. We forget about the possibilities we once had for ourselves when we were younger. This was not the case with Neil Armstrong and John Glen. They held onto their childhood dreams. I personally believe that just like them and thousands of other people who are currently living their dreams, your childhood dreams can and in many cases do hold the key to your future career. Dennis Waitley claims that many adults return to childhood activities, dreams, or desires either in the form of a major hobby or as their vocation. This is why I believe it is important for people to ask themselves the following question, "*What did I do as a child that I really enjoyed?*"

For example, another young boy had an interest in music. This boy got himself a beaten up, broken down, second hand guitar that he could not tune. He then taught himself how to tune the guitar and he began practicing. After months of practicing hours a day, he finally got the hang of it. After many years of trying, he turned that interest into one of the most influential musical careers ever. Elvis Presley is a wonderful example of an individual who turned a childhood interest into a career that not only made him rich but also outlived him.

Another way to define your interests is to look at your hobbies. Many people turn their hobbies into their vocation. If you think about it, you probably know someone who has done this. I know a guy who would fix computers as a hobby. He would help his friends whenever they had problems and could not afford an expert. He was extremely good at fixing computers. His name is Jim Doppelhammer and he turned this part time hobby into Double-Hammer, a web design company that specializes in designing websites for the dental industry.

You may have a hobby that could become your vocation if you worked hard enough for the goal. Do you think Bill Dance went to the unemployment office and applied for a fishing job? Then do think the person at the unemployment said, "Bill, the only fishing job opening we can find for you is on a TV show, would you be interested?" Then do you think Bill said, "I'm not sure, can I think about it? I was hoping for a job on a hot ship in the middle of the ocean making one-tenth of the money." Perhaps he just turned his hobby into a vocation.

Seven Questions That Uncover Your Interests

In addition to childhood interests and hobbies, here are seven questions that you can ask yourself that will help you define what you are interested in.

1. What excites or motivates you?
2. What would you do right now if money did not matter?
3. Where would you like to go? What would you like to do there?
4. What is one fun thing that you used to enjoy but have not done in a while?
5. What was your favorite and least favorite subject in school?
6. What hobbies do you enjoy, and what hobbies would you like to pursue?
7. What are your favorite TV shows, movies, or books?

If you do this, you should start to get a clearer picture of what your interests are. Most people go through life saying, "I would like to do this or that." You do not have to be one of them. To keep from being one of them, develop a keen sense of what you are interested in. This way you can be one of those lucky individuals who go through life doing exactly what they enjoy. Understanding your interests mixed with taking charge of your life are essential if you are going to get and maintain direction.

Taking Charge of Your Life

Without taking charge of our lives, we cannot expect to get or maintain direction. Without proper direction, we cannot get the results we need, we desire, or we deserve. The fact is everybody has an agenda, and the only person who has your best interest at heart and the best agenda for you is you. A classic example of this is the parent who wants their son or daughter to go to medical school because they want a doctor in the family.

What parent would not want his or her child to grow up and become a doctor? This is a socially desirable goal. The problem is all too often the parents set the goal before the child was even born. They set the goal for the child before they could possibly know what the best career path would be for the child. Since the parents have their own agenda for the child the result is they give the child advice and direction that will support their agenda and not the child's.

To take charge of your life you need goals. Along with setting goals, you will need to develop discipline, and you will need to build your self-confidence. I would like to take a moment to discuss why people do not take control of their lives. I believe that there are three primary reasons people do not take charge of their life. The first reason is they have not clearly defined what it is what they want to accomplish. The second reason is they do not realize that they have a choice. The third reason is they are constantly doing things that are keeping them from getting what they want out of life.

I personally believe that not having goals is the most common roadblock in finding your dream job and turning it into a reality. The fact is many people spend far too much time focusing on the rewards that come with success but not on the process of becoming successful. You do not have to be that person. When you start setting goals, you will find that extraordinary things will start to happen. Later in the book, I have a detailed section on goal setting. So, for right now I will just give a couple of guidelines to get you started. When setting goals remember to do the following:

➢ Put goals in writing.
➢ Put a time limit on achieving that goal.
➢ Include sub-goals that will act as measuring sticks for bigger goals.
➢ Complete an honest self-assessment of yourself.

Equally as important as goals is self-discipline. Self-discipline is nothing more than doing what you should be doing right now, so that one day you will be able to do the things you want to do when you want to do them. It should be no secret that in order to accomplish your goals you will need a certain amount of self-discipline. Self-discipline is a powerful force in becoming successful. Without self-discipline, you will be stuck getting the same results you have been getting.

This brings us to this question, "What can you do today to build more discipline into your life?" The simplest way to become disciplined is to become more dedicated to what you want to accomplish. It also means that you need to develop a more realistic view of the world around you. I know these two things are abstract. To make this point more real here are some key action points that create discipline.

If you want to be more disciplined you need to set deadlines. These deadlines need to be realistic. That is why you need an accurate view of the world. You need two types of deadlines. The first type of deadline is long-term. This is where you would like your career to be one year, two years, five years, and ten years from now. To accomplish this you need short-term deadlines as a way to measure your progress. These deadlines can be daily, weekly, monthly, or quarterly. When you reach these deadlines analyze your progress, analyze your actions, and analyze yourself.

The second thing you need to do when becoming more disciplined is to avoid procrastination. I love what Brain Tracy says about procrastination. He says, "Eat your frog first thing in the morning." The point is to do the most dreaded thing in your day as soon as you wake up. By eating that frog for breakfast, the rest of your day will not seem that bad, and as matter of fact the rest of your day will seem quite wonderful. In his book Success is a Choice, Rick Patino gives this advice on the subject. Rick says that you should schedule your day so that you do the things you do not want to do first. That way you will look forward to the rest of your day and as a result, you will have more energy and enthusiasm.

Another way to avoid procrastination is to do something. Even if it is wrong, doing something is always better than doing nothing. If things go terribly, at least you have found out what will not work. What I have found is that once you have started doing something and you make a daily habit of doing something, you will have beaten procrastination. The two hardest elements of any task is starting and finishing, but you can never finish until you start. That is why you should start now, and do something everyday until you have reached your goal.

The third and last thought about creating discipline is to increase your ability to say no. I understand that it is difficult to say no. One reason is the person we are saying no to takes it personally. Let them know it is not personal. Reassure them that you are just saying no to the current offer, and you are not rejecting them. To let them know that you are not saying no to them, try scheduling an alternative activity for another time. Just remember if you do the things you need to do today and do this everyday, then one day you be able to do the things you want to do when you want to do them.

Developing a Personal Mission & Vision Statement
Successful businesses have mission and vision statements so why shouldn't you? Most people do not have a mission in life or a vision for the future. Many people believe the two are the same. In many cases, they are similar. The difference is a mission is what you are going to do, and how you are going to do it. A vision defines what the future will be like after you accomplish your mission.

For example, after the attack on the World Trade Center in New York, the military had a mission to capture Bin Laden. This is a mission because there is a specific objective whereas the vision was and still is to wipe out terrorism. If you notice, the vision gives us a clear description of what the world should look like. The mission gives us a specific task to accomplish in order to make that vision a reality.

If you want to be successful, it is important for you to have a mission statement because you will need objectives to accomplish. You will also need a vision statement that will give a description of how you are going to live in the future. They work together to chart a long-term path to follow. They also should be written or designed in a way that inspires, excites, and motivates you to follow them through to completion.

When designing your mission and vision statements you need to include the following elements.

- ➤ Define where you are now and where you want to go.
- ➤ Define how you are going to get where you are going.
- ➤ Define SMART objectives (specific, measurable, attainable, realistic, and timely).
- ➤ Define your mission and vision in a way that is inspiring, exciting, and motivating for you.
- ➤ Define your core values, beliefs, and philosophies.

After you have clearly defined these things put them in writing. If possible, make it short, easy to read, and easy to remember. There is no rule on how long or short a mission statement can or should be. I have seen mission statements that are just a few words, and I have seen mission statements that were several pages. The most important thing about your mission and vision statement is that they should clearly define what you want to accomplish.

Taking Inventory of Yourself

In order to write a mission statement, create a vision, set goals, and turn your dream job into a reality, you have to take inventory of yourself. Many people never take the time to take an honest inventory of themselves. They just assume that because they spend more time with themselves than they do with any other person in the world they have complete understanding and knowledge about themselves. This is not always the case. As we go through life we get caught up with the here and now, and as a result we forget who we once were and who we once wanted to be. This section will help you to recapture that.

To do this I will ask a series of questions that are designed to get your mind thinking in terms of the person you really are and in terms of the person you really want to be. There are no right or wrong answers to the questions, and you do not have to share the results with anybody. This is just an exercise to get you to take an inventory of yourself.

1. My proudest moment in grade school was when _____
2. My proudest moment in middle school was when_____
3. My proudest moment in junior high was when _____
4. My proudest moment in high school was when_____
5. My proudest moment in college was when _____
6. My proudest moment on the job was when_____
7. My proudest moment ever was when I _____
8. My confidence comes from my ability to_____
9. My favorite teacher was _____ because _____
10. My favorite class was _____because _____
11. My greatest accomplishment was when I _____
12. My favorite type of people to associate with is ____ because_____
13. My favorite type of people to work with are
    _____because_____
14. The person who had the greatest positive impact on me was
    _____ because _____
15. The person who had the greatest negative impact on me was
    _____ because _____

16. The event that has had the greatest positive influence in my life is _____ because _____
17. The event that has had the greatest negative influence in my life is _____ because _____
18. My most embarrassing moment in grade school was when _____
19. My most embarrassing moment in middle school was when _____
20. My most embarrassing moment in junior high was when   _____
21. My most embarrassing moment in high school was when _____
22. My most embarrassing moment in college was when   _____
23. My most embarrassing moment on the job was when _____
24. My most embarrassing moment ever was when I _____
25. My insecurity comes from my inability to   _____
26. My least favorite teacher was _____ because _____
27. My least favorite class was _____because _____
28. My biggest failure was when I tried to _____
29. My least favorite type of people to associate with is _____ because _____
30. When I was in grade school I wanted to be _____
31. When I was in middle school I wanted to be _____
32. When I was in junior high school I wanted to be _____
33. When I was in high school I wanted to be _____
34. When I was in college I wanted to be_____
35. Now I would like to be _____
36. Life would be perfect if I were more _____
37. Life is difficult because _____
38. If I had more time I would do the following _____
39. If I had more money I would buy _____
40. Who or what is holding me back _____

These are the questions that you should ask yourself when you are taking an inventory of yourself. Notice questions include both positive and negative experiences. The reason for this is because both types of experiences make up our personalities. We often try to forget the bad and pretend as if it does not affect us. The truth is it does impact us, and it is better to come to terms with both experiences so that you can make them work for you instead of them working against you.

Take a moment now and look at your answer for the last question. What was your answer? Unlike the other questions, there is a right answer to that question. The answer to that question is YOU. You have control over what you do and what you think. If you put another person's name as an answer you have given that person control over your success. Don't do that. Never let a person who wants to see you fail be in charge of your life. You may have released the power over yourself to someone or something else for so long that you have forgotten that the power to succeed is within *you*. If you have forgotten, this is your wake up call. Reclaim the power from whatever or whoever is holding you back. Reclaim that power from your circumstances.

When you realize that you have complete control over your circumstances even if it means adjusting your mental attitude to an attitude of accepting the things you cannot control or change. When you set your mind to work on changing the things you can change, you will begin to make things work for you instead of against you. When you have unleashed the power from within, you have unleashed the ultimate power to win!

I would like to encourage you to make this self-discovery an on-going process. This is a major element of the success process. The more you take inventory of yourself, the more self-improvement will occur. The more self-improvement you experience the more opportunities you have. The more opportunities you have the more career choices you have. I believe that we can all live our dreams if we do this. As you get more comfortable with this self-discovery process, you may want to ask other people what they really think of you, and let them know that it is okay to be brutally honest. If they are totally honest with you it may hurt, but it will help more than it will hurt.

In this chapter I discussed the importance of maintaining and keeping direction. Now you should be able to determine your interests and relate these interests to job options. I hope that because of this chapter you are able to see more job choices then you saw before reading it. In addition, I hope you will be able to take greater control of your life by writing a mission and vision statement for your life because your success is dependent upon it.

KAPS

- In order to be successful you have to be able to get and to maintain direction.
- Realize that most time problems are direction problems.
- If you do not have direction, someone else will provide direction for you, and it will not be in your best interest.
- Focus on solutions and not problems.
- Decisions influence the meaning you assign to things, the results you get, the choices you make, and decisions enable you to become a meaningful specific.
- Your dream job may be turning a hobby into a full time vocation.
- Take charge of your life by developing a personal and professional mission statement.
- Avoid procrastination by eating that frog.
- Take constant inventory of yourself.

Chapter 5

SWOT Your Way to Success

Questions are the answers. That is questions provide us with answers. I believe that without the right questions, you can never get the right answers. The questions that I am talking about are the questions that you should be asking yourself. Asking yourself the right questions will help you define what kind of job you want to get. The questions that we ask ourselves should help us to do what I call a personal SWOT analysis. This SWOT analysis is something that should be done at least every 3-4 months.

The term SWOT is an acronym for strengths, weaknesses, opportunities, and threats. The strengths are an area of our life where we feel we are living up to the best of our abilities. It could be your natural gifts or a talent you have worked long and hard to develop. It can also be a degree or specialized training. Weakness is an area that we need to develop. Examples of this are areas of our lives, things in our lives and/or events in our lives such as a lack of education, lack of direction, or lack of experience that are holding us back.

The opportunity can be two things. The first thing it can be is what we are going to do to "fix" or improve our weakness. The second thing that it can be is a position that we can fill or create for ourselves. Threats can be both external and internal. External threats are negative events that are happening in our world, such as down sizing, recessions, or other external struggles. Internal threats are beliefs, attitudes, or thoughts that typically hold people back.

Let me explain this a little more. Strengths and weaknesses are primarily internal issues. These things are totally about us. They are a reflection of our individual talents, gifts, and shortcomings. We have control over these two areas by what we decide to improve or ignore.

Opportunities can exist internally or externally. If we are improving a weakness, it is internal. An external opportunity is when we show an organization that they need to create a new position or open a closed position and then show them how we can best fill that position. External threats are things that happen that we may have no control over. While we have no control over whether or not a threat occurs, we do have control over how we respond or plan to respond to a threat.

Questions Are the Answers

With all of this in mind, I developed three sets of questions and statements that will help you analyze yourself. The first set is designed as a way to check your job performance. Answer the following statements by rating yourself on a scale from one to five, with one being no improvement is needed and five being much improvement is needed.

1. In past/current jobs, I take initiative at work.
2. In past/current jobs, I set and achieved measurable goals.
3. In past/current jobs, I have found ways to improve professionally.
4. In past/current jobs, I have found ways to improve personally.
5. In past/current jobs, I have found ways to improve my organization.

6. In past/current jobs, I have made an effort to get along with my co-workers and leader(s).
7. In past/current jobs, I have made an effort to complete all assignments on time.
8. In past/current jobs, I have made an effort to maintain a positive attitude.
9. In past/current jobs, I have exercised self-control in my actions.
10. In past/current jobs, I have made an effort to use proper time management techniques.
11. In past/current jobs, I have made an effort to spend the majority of time engaged in profitable work.
12. In past/current jobs, I have made an effort to solve problems with workable solutions.
13. In past/current jobs, I have made an effort to go the extra-mile.
14. In past/current jobs, I have made an effort to volunteer for special projects when given the opportunity.
15. In past/current jobs, I have made an effort to give and take proper credit for work completed.
16. In past/current jobs, I have made an effort to take responsibility for my actions at work.
17. In past/current jobs, I have made an effort to take care of the little things.
18. In past/current jobs, I have made an effort to accept criticism when offered.
19. In past/current jobs, I have made an effort to understand the differences between my co-workers and me.
20. In past/current jobs, I have made an effort to take advantage of the opportunities that are offered.
21. In past/current jobs, I have made an effort to be the kind of person I would want to employ.
22. In past/current jobs, I have worked in a vocation that makes use of my talents, abilities, skills, and education.
23. Based on these statements, how would I rate myself on these traits?
24. Based on these statements, how would my current or past employer(s) rate me on these traits?

Now the next set of questions is designed to help you identify specific qualities about yourself. Qualities such as actions you have or have not taken in the past. Qualities such as actions that you should take or should not take in the future that will help you become more successful on and off the job.

1. What are my best skills?
2. What are my worst skills?
3. What am I doing to improve those skills?
4. What are my best personality traits?
5. What are my worst personality traits?
6. What am I doing to improve those traits?
7. What do I want to pursue for a career?

8. Why am I interested in this career?
9. How much time do I currently devote to self-improvement?
10. How much more time do I need to devote to self-improvement?
11. Who is in charge of promotions, the employer or me?
12. In the past, have I been passive in taking immediate and decisive action?
13. In the past, have I been overly aggressive in taking immediate and decisive action?
14. What are my most destructive habits?
15. Do I really want to change these habits and if so what am I going to do to change those habits?
16. What do I do to develop positive relationships with my co-workers?
17. What do I do to build trust with those around me?
18. What have I done to improve my job performance?
19. What have I done to improve my creativity?
20. What have I done in the past that was effective on the job?
21. What could I have done in the past to be a more effective worker?
22. What will I do in the future to be a more effective worker?

Here is the last set of questions that you should ask yourself when trying to find your dream job. These questions should help you quantify what you want out of your next job.

1. What aspects of your previous job(s) did you like most?
2. What aspects of your previous job(s) did you dislike the most?
3. What aspects of your previous job(s) did you not like but could tolerate?
4. What aspects of your previous job(s) would you not tolerate under any conditions?
5. What aspects of your previous job(s) made you feel good about yourself?
6. What aspects of your previous job(s) made you feel bad about yourself?
7. What hours and days of the week do you want to work?
8. What kind of vacation and time off do you want?
9. What rate of pay do you desire? Why do you deserve that rate of pay?
10. What benefits are you looking for?
11. What kinds of positions would you like to have in the future?
12. Are you qualified for those positions?
13. If you are not qualified for these positions, what do you need to do get qualified for those positions?
14. Do you want to continue in your present career path or would you prefer a new career?
15. If you want to enter a new career, have you identified the steps needed to start that new career?
16. Do you want to continue to work with your current employer, new employer, or start your own business?
17. If you want to continue to work with your current employer, do you want to continue in the same position, new position, new location, same position and new location, new position and new location, or some other combination?
18. If you are looking for the same career but a new employer, do you want to work part-time, flextime, or full-time?

19. If you are entering a new career, are you willing to go back to school or seek out appropriate training?
20. If you are entering a new career, are you willing to take a part-time position?
21. If you are entering a new career, are you willing to take an internship or do volunteer work?
22. Do you have the financial resources required to change careers?
23. If you want to work for yourself, what have you done to identify the steps to self-employment?
24. Would you want to work at home?
25. What type of business would you want to start?
26. If you are starting a new business in a new industry are you willing to accept work from an established organization in that industry as way to educate yourself about the industry?
27. What do you want to accomplish professionally and personally?
28. What action steps are you taking to accomplish that?
29. What are you doing that is preventing you from accomplishing that?

Did you do it? Did you answer those questions? If not stop and do it now, if you do not want to stop now make sure you come back and do it. The result of the previous section should help you identify your dream job, and it should help you to make it a reality. Although there are many questions in this assessment, I think it is important to perform a self-analysis of yourself if you are going to answer the important questions.

The Importance of Doing What You Enjoy

It is important to answer the previous assessment so you can more effectively answer the following question, "***What type of work do you or would you really enjoy doing?***" This question is harder than it sounds. Some people, musicians for example, love their work so much they never think of it as work. Perhaps you may be like that and have something you enjoy doing so much that the thought of it being work dose not even occur to you. It could be anything from working on computers or cars, drawing, working on lawns, photography, or perhaps helping people with their hair or makeup. All of these things along with many other activities can lead to a career.

I heard about a young girl who was a skilled piano player. At the age of five, she would play for her family friends as well as anyone who would listen to her play. As the years went by, she began acting and was on a couple of TV shows. As a TV show was canceled, she would fall back on her skills singing and playing the piano and she also became a skilled guitar player.

When she was still in high school, she had reached national fame with some of her music. A few more years went by and she could not sell a record. She moved from one place to another, but it did not really matter because she really enjoyed what she did. It did not matter that she could not sell records; what mattered to her was she could still perform. One night at a club, she met a man and they started writing music together. The album they wrote and produced became a huge hit. The album was *Jagged Little Pill* and the singer is Alanis Morissette. Like Alanis Morissette, you too can become a big hit when you work at what you really enjoy doing.

The Truth About Natural Talent

Along with doing what you really enjoy be sure to take inventory of natural gifts and abilities. Ask yourself what gifts, talents, and strengths you currently have. Then ask yourself what you can do to refine them so that they can become a source of income. I would be lying if I said that everybody has the same talents. On the other hand, I am not saying you cannot develop certain talents if you are willing to put in the time and effort. It is true that some people are born with certain natural and societal advantages. It is also true with about ten years practice you can become the best in any chosen field. At least that is what Mazoyer Ericsson claims.

Mazoyer Ericsson has spent 20 years studying expert ability. During this time, he has become convinced that geniuses have no more natural ability than the average person does. The difference between a genius and the average person is motivation. According to his research, you can reach the top of your chosen field with deliberate daily practice. With deliberate daily practice, it should take no more than ten years to reach the highest level of performance in any field.

Although we all have the potential, I do not think we all should develop the same gifts. We need diversity in the world if the world is going to operate properly. The problem is many people feel guilty when they use their natural talents. Do not feel guilty. It is okay to use your natural talents. I implore you to use or develop your talents no matter what they are. If you do not, what happened in this next story could happen to you.

The animals of the world had a meeting and decided that they needed to make some changes. They decided they needed a school and they would do away with "natural talent." They figured it was a good idea for everybody to be equal and being equal meant everybody could do the same things. They also wanted the school to be fair so everybody had to take the same courses. Here is what happened.

Mother Goose got a B in swimming and flying. She may have gotten an A, but she spent too much time in tree climbing and running in which she made a D and C respectively. However, she passed and passing was all that mattered. Of course the real problem was she was too old to learn, every one knows the older you get the harder it is for you to learn.

Peter Cottontail, who before this would hop down the bunny trail, was no longer able to do so. He now majored in climbing trees, learning to fly, and swimming. As a result, he was on the bunny trail one day and The Big Bad Wolf, who was skipping school, was there. Peter was unable to hop as fast as he used to and The Big Bad Wolf ate Peter Cottontail.

Consequently, The Big Bad Wolf was sent to detention and forced to go to school on Saturdays. He started out doing great in pouncing, but he lost his ability to pounce, because he was learning how to climb trees. The Big Bad Wolf eventually starved to death, because he could no longer pounce fast enough to catch his food. At least this kept him out of detention.

Charlie Horse was in school too. He was a great runner. In fact, at the beginning of the school year he could run farther and faster than most everyone, except for Tony the Tiger and The Cowardly Lion. However, Charlie was held back in school one year because he did not learn how to fly. The instructor, a Bald Eagle spent many extra hours working with Charlie, but he could not grasp the concept of flapping his wings or in his case his front legs. He would insist on running where he needed to go. This got poor

Charlie nowhere in the academic world and they even warned him how hard life would really be after he got in the "*real world*." He was told that he could not be successful because he ran and could not fly. So he dropped of school and was last seen living in a van down by the river with the rest of his classmates.

What does this have to do with using your natural abilities? Quite a bit. No matter your age, social status, or intelligence in a given area, if you focus on your natural abilities, you will develop them. You should focus on your natural abilities and learn how to strengthen them. I believe if you are built to fly, you should fly; if you are built to run, you should run. I do know that you were built for accomplishment so accomplish your dream no matter what your dream is. No matter what your talents are or no matter what you are good at you should take the advice of Nike and just do it.

Determining the Job Characteristics You Want

By now you should be gaining a better understanding of different things you can excel in. Now ask yourself, "**What job characteristics do you want?**" You need to know if you prefer working alone or on a team. Do you like stress and/or can you handle stress? When do you want to work? Do you want weekends off? Do you want to work early in the morning, or late in the evening? Do you like to research new procedures?

If you like research and are good at compiling statistics, maybe a career in marketing research is in your future. Are you good at troubleshooting? If you are, you might want to think about a career in computer repair. Would you be good at training people and instructing people? The world can always use more teachers to touch the lives of the future. Are you good at persuading? If so you may consider a job in sales.

Of course, this list is only a partial list, and it is only limited by your imagination. If you want more job titles or ideas, the US Department of Labor, Bureau of Labor Statistics publishes a book called *The Occupational Outlook Handbook*. In this book, you will find job descriptions for jobs in which 85% of the American workforce is employed. The U.S. Department of Labor publishes a resource called *America's Top Jobs*, which is a book and CD-ROM. You can go to any public library and look at these books or other related books. If the library does not have them, see if they can order them through interlibrary loan. If you are in college or recently graduated from college, go by and see the career services department at your school, and they should have these resources as well as many others.

Where is Your Dream Job?

Another question to ask that will help determine your dream job is, "**Where would I like to work?**" This next statement shouldn't be a shock to anyone. There has to be jobs in the geographic area of the world in which you wish to work. For example what if you moved to the South Pole and you wanted to drive an ice cream truck? Do you think you would be successful? You would not be successful for two reasons. It is too cold in the South Pole to sell Ice Cream, and secondly there are not enough individuals living in that area to support that profession. This example should illustrate a point. The point is the economy of the geographic area where you want to live has to be able to support what you want to do. If it does not, you need to decide what is more important to you. Is where you live more important, or is the job you want more important?

What would have happened to John Cougar Mellencamp if he had never left his small town? I am sure he would have written all his songs, but we would have never heard them. John Cougar left his small town to pursue his dream. Did this mean that he forgot about the people who lived there? No, some of most popular songs are about that small town. Did it mean that he could never return? No, he has moved back there and when he is not on tour, he is living in that small town. You see it really is okay to go where you need to go so that you can do what you need to do.

What Are You Going to Accomplish?

This last question is the most important question and it is "**What do you want to accomplish both professionally and personally?**" To put it another way, what can you envision yourself doing for a living? Having a clear understanding of what you want to accomplish will go a long way in helping you get it. Knowing what you want to accomplish will help you overcome obstacles and it will manufacture persistence into your character much like it did for the person in this story.

This story is about a man who was born into poverty and who was failure in business. His mother died when he was young boy and he had to work to provide for his family. He started a business and failed. The next year he ran for state legislature and lost. He knew he wanted to hold office and to shape his country. This led him to law school, but he could not get in. He was told he was not smart enough.

It was during this same period in his life that he lost another job. He struggled for food and shelter all year and the following year he was able to borrow some money and begin another business. This time he was bankrupt by the end of the year. He then spent the next 17 years of his life paying off that debt. It was election time again, and he ran for state legislature again. This time he won.

While he was in the Senate things seemed to be going well for this man. He had a position of respect, but soon tragedy struck him again when his fiancé died. This caused this man to have a nervous breakdown, and he was in bed for six months. After he regained his health, he decided to run for speaker of the state legislature. He was defeated. Then three years later he decided he could have more of an impact in Congress so he ran for a seat. In a hard fought race, he lost. Three years later, he ran for Congress and this time he won and not only did he win, he did a great job. Feeling confident enough to run for a second term, he ran. He felt confidence because not only was he experienced, but also he was good at what he was doing. However, this was not enough to win the election. He lost his run for re-election.

With all this experience with public affairs, he was surely qualified to be state land officer. This man applied for the job he was the most qualified and he deserved to get it. He did not get it. The good news is it gave the man time to run for U.S. Senate. After a long campaign, he lost. You would think by now he would quit, but he did not.

Instead of quitting, he sought the vice-presidential nomination at his party's national convention. He was experienced. He was a hard worker, but he lacked the votes. When the votes were counted, this man received less than 100 votes. Being in a position at least to lose the vice-presidential nomination, he was doing something right. He figured he had the support to get a seat in the Senate.

He ran for U.S. Senate again. I wish I could tell you he won but he did not. What he did do was to wait two more years. This time he decided he was getting too old to run for things like state legislature, land officer, and U.S. Senate. He knew if he was going to accomplish what he wanted to accomplish both personally and professionally, he had to do something extraordinary.

That is precisely what Abraham Lincoln did. In 1860, he ran for and was elected President of the United States. Not only did he become President of the United States, he kept our country together through one of its toughest times. According to some scholars, this man was the greatest President of our country.

What did he have to say about his path to the presidency? He was quoted as saying, *"The path was worn and slippery. My foot slipped from under me, knocking the other out of the way, but I recovered and said to myself, it's a slip and not a fall."* Let me ask you this question. Do you think Abraham Lincoln had a clear vision of what he wanted to do personally and professionally?

I think he did. I also think we can all take a lesson from this great American and forge a vision for what we want to accomplish personally and professionally. Then we can go out and fulfill our vision by remembering when we meet temporary defeat or failure that it is only a slip and not a fall.

Conclusion

I would like to close out this chapter the same way I started it by asking you some questions. I hope that by answering all the questions in this section you are able to get some insights on some job ideas.

1. What aspects of your previous jobs did you like or dislike?
2. What types of work would you like to do?
3. What skills do you possess--technical, non-technical, tangible, and non-tangible?
4. What are your natural talents?
5. What job characteristics do you most treasure?
6. Where would you like to work?
7. What would you most like to do?
8. What motivates you?
9. What would you do if money did not matter?
10. What do you want to accomplish professionally and personally or what is your mission in life?

KAPS

- ➢ A SWOT analysis is a tool to gain a better understanding of your strengths, weaknesses, opportunities, and threats.
- ➢ You have to ask yourself the right questions to get the right answers.
- ➢ Doing what you love is more rewarding than doing a job only for money.
- ➢ You need to understand your natural talents and gifts if you want to use them.
- ➢ It takes ten years to become an overnight success.

Exercises: At this point, if you do not have a clear idea of what type of job you want, read the want ads and surf job-hunting sites. When you come across a job title or job description you find interesting, write it down. After you do this for a while start narrowing down your job selections.

In this chapter, I introduced the idea of a SWOT analysis. Using the chart below for a model make your own SWOT chart and list all of your strengths, weaknesses, opportunities, and threats.

Strength	Weakness	Opportunities	Threats

Once you have filled out your chart. Ask yourself the following the questions about your chart:

➤ How are my strengths moving me forward?
➤ How are my strengths holding me back?
➤ How are my weaknesses holding me back?
➤ What can I do to keep my strengths from becoming weaknesses?
➤ What do I need to do to turn my weaknesses into strengths?
➤ What I am doing that is keeping me from taking advantage of my opportunities.
➤ What can I do to create more opportunity?
➤ What opportunities can I act on today?
➤ What opportunities can I act on in the near future?
➤ What opportunities can I act on in the more distant future?
➤ What opportunities have I missed because of inaction?
➤ How I going to make use of my opportunities?
➤ What threats are internal and external?
➤ What can I do to eliminate that threat?
➤ How can I turn that threat into an opportunity?

Chapter 6

How to Find out if Your
Job Idea is the Ideal Job

Now that we have discussed decisions, values, and maintaining direction, you may have a number of job ideas. If you do not, that is okay. I promise you if you continue to read this book and ones like it more job ideas will come. What is important is to look at a number of career choices and then take the advice of Peter Lowe when he says, "*survey the job field, but forge your own destiny.*"

This brings us to the obvious question, "How do you survey the job field?" Here are five ways you can generate more job ideas. First, try spending a day on the job. Second, read trade magazines or books about your job choice. Third, attend seminars and interview people who have the position or a position similar to what you want. Fourth, if you are in college or a recent graduate, go by the Career Services department at your school and take advantage of the services they have to offer. Fifth, look at the want ads in the local and national newspapers.

How Shadowing Others Can Help

Perhaps one of the best ways to determine if your job idea is an ideal job is to spend a day on the job. This is sometimes referred to as shadowing. I did this once with a friend of mine, Kevan Krestel. Kevan is a sales rep for Abbot pharmaceuticals. I spent a day with him doing what pharmaceuticals sales reps do. We visited clinics, took people to lunch, and bought tickets for a ball game. It was an interesting day. I had the opportunity to talk with reps from other companies and interact with the staff at various clinics. While he enjoyed his job and many other people in that field enjoy their jobs, it just was not for me.

However, by spending another day on the job I was able to find a job that was for me. Norith Ellison introduced me to the world of training and development. I first met Norith at Toastmasters. After a few conversations, we found out that we had a lot in common. We both wanted to be motivational speakers and both wanted to own our own business. The only difference between us was I was a complete novice, and he wasn't.

The only experience I had up to that point was attending a Peter Lowe Success Seminar in Memphis, Tennessee. I heard some great speakers get up and talk about success and what it took to be successful. Watching them, I knew for the first time what I really wanted to do. I wanted to do what they do were doing. They looked like they were having fun. People were having fun watching them. To top it all off they were making money at it.

Shadowing Norith was great for me. I realized that getting in the speaking field was a little more difficult than I had anticipated. Although it was a little more difficult and the financial rewards would be a few years off, I still enjoyed it. I knew that this was the right for job for me because I did not mind the effort I would have to expend in order to get to where I wanted to go.

I mention these two things because of the learning involved in the process. The learning comes in two forms. The first and most obvious form is finding out first hand that you would really enjoy that job. The second and most taken for granted learning experience came in the form of finding out what you would not like to do for a career.

Knowing what does not work can help a lot when you are trying to figure out what will work for you.

Do not be afraid to ask to shadow someone for a day. People will take it as a compliment. When I have shadowed people, I thought it was fun. I love to see what people do in their everyday life. I am sure you would love it to. Believe me when I say it is exciting to know what people do to make money and to make a difference. The biggest benefit from shadowing is it takes less time than a wrong career choice.

Expand Your Experience By Reading

If you are unable to shadow someone, the second best way to know if your job idea is the ideal job is to read about the job. In a college essay about why she was an English major, my wife wrote, *"My experiences are limited by what I know, and what I know is limited by what I read."* That really is true. We all are all limited by what we know. I believe I am as far as I can go in my career with what I currently know. I also believe that to go to the next level I need to learn to do something I am not currently doing. I believe that holds true for everyone, not just me. I also know that the one thing we can all do to expand what we know is to expand what we read.

When you read you can get into another person's head. It is as if you have a window to that person's innermost self. You know what they feel, they think, and experience. When people write they tend to be more open and honest. Take advantage of that and learn from them. The fact is you can learn from their successes and failures just like they were your own experiences.

Most bookstores and libraries have shelves of books about careers. Look in this section for books, but do not forget about biographies because these are stories about real people doing real things. That is what makes them so exciting. Biographies may be even more helpful than the career books, because you can read and experience first hand what it took to make those people successful. By doing this you will find out if what they have experienced is the same thing you want to experience for yourself.

Attend Trade Shows and Seminars

If you have been reading about the vocation that you wish to enter, I am sure that you have found a few trade magazines. In these magazines, you will undoubtedly come across advertisements for an industry meeting or seminar. Go to one of these events. You will get the opportunity to meet people who work in the industry. You can hear the latest advancements in the industry. You will hear speakers that will educate you on how to be successful in that industry. This will give you an edge on your competition when applying for a job. Employers want people who take initiative, who are ambitious, and confident. Doing this will show that you are that type of person.

This has one of the same benefits of shadowing because it will give you the opportunity for some valuable networking. When you go to an industry meeting or seminar, make sure you have copies of your resume with you, and I would even suggest getting business cards to distribute. If you want to really stand out have ink pens or other products printed with your name, address, and telephone number.

Dr. Markham, a marketing professor from the University of Central Arkansas, gave me this advice when I started my career. He told me to go to seminars and make some small talk about what these people did daily at their jobs. Then say, "That's sounds very interesting would you mind if I visited your office?" Usually, they will say yes. Go and visit them and check out first hand what they do. Then give them your card and tell them what you do. Now you have not only made a business contact, but a friend as well, and friends like to help friends. If they do not have an opening in their company, they may be more willing to help you in your job search.

This will also help in the next principle of finding out if your job idea is the ideal job, which is interviewing people. Call people, buy them lunch, and talk to them, earnestly seeking insights about their profession. You would be amazed at how well this works. I have been able to meet some high profile individuals using this technique. Even when I was a college student waiting tables, I would have lunch with mayors, judges, publishers, authors, and multimillionaires.

I never used this as a way to hand someone my resume or ask a person for a job. I think that could tear down any trust or friendship you have established. I did this to expand my network of people who could help me achieve my goals. I started receiving invitations to events and I began getting involved on projects that only successful people were asked to do, although at the time I was just getting started and was not established. It didn't matter because these people liked my attitude and willingness to try. If you follow this advice you will be asked your opinion on issues you never imagined that you would be involved in.

Volunteering or Interning for Experience

The last principle of determining if your job idea is the ideal job is by volunteering or taking internships. These usually involve little or no pay. Mostly no pay, although there are some internships that do pay. If you really want a specific job, I would not worry about money; you can always find ways to make extra money when you need to. It might mean that you have to work more than forty hours a week, but *if something is worth doing it is worth working for.*

The internship can be a valuable tool because it gets your foot in the door. It will teach you how an industry works. It should also tell you if you have picked the right employer. Sometimes we put our ships in the right sea (industry), but we are at the wrong port (organization). After doing an internship you should be able to tell if you like the industry. If you like the industry but not the employer, when your internship is over you are free to go. Until then, **it is your obligation to yourself, not the employer, to do a great job**.

If you do sub-standard work because the boss dose not like you, they will give you a bad reference. If the boss does not care for you and you do good work, they should give you a good reference. If they do not, that is okay because you were the one who acted with integrity. Having a bad boss or working in a negative environment is not a reason for doing sub-standard work.

Along with internships, volunteering can be an exceptional way to open doors and to gain valuable experience. The benefit of volunteering for a non-profit organization in my estimation is that you are helping yourself by helping others. The reward will be substantial even if is not financial at this point.

Typically, when you volunteer most of these organizations are thankful to have a helping hand. The fact is most non-profit organizations will have the same or similar position you would be applying for in the for-profit sector. As you get involved with these groups, you will realize they have a similar corporate structure as most for-profit businesses, yet with less money and manpower. You will learn the same skills needed to succeed in the profit world, and you may even learn better skills because in many cases you will learn to be more efficient, and perhaps you will discover you would prefer to work for a non-profit.

Whether you get an internship or a volunteer position, the biggest benefit is you have your foot in the door. Once your foot is in the door, it is up to you where you go. If you plan properly, you should be able to turn a volunteer assignment or an internship into a full time job.

Turning an Internship or Volunteer Position into a Career

The most important thing is the attitude you display. People treasure people with good attitudes. Think about it, have you ever really enjoyed being around a person with a bad attitude? Of course not, we all like people with good attitudes. Keep a positive attitude that says I can do it, I will do it, and I want to do it. Remember you want to show these people that you are an extremely capable individual. The attitude you display in the small assignments will get you the big assignments, even if you feel ready for big tasks and they keep giving you little ones. You owe it to yourself to keep doing great work on the little jobs. Just keep reminding yourself of what W.W. Ziege once said, *"Nothing can stop the man with the right mental attitude from achieving his goal; nothing on earth can help the man with the wrong mental attitude."*

That quotation is so true. If you are like this man and believe those words to be true, then what happened to him will happen to you. This man was committed to his dream job. He dreamed of being in radio broadcasting. He went to a radio station and talked to the station manager about a job. The manager told this man they did not have any openings. This man really wanted to be in radio so he came back the next day, but there were still no job openings. He figured that if he went to the radio station everyday, as soon as there was an opening he would be there to fill it.

It worked. After seeing the station manager everyday for a week, he received his break into the radio industry. He did not get the job he wanted of being a well paid on air personality; he became an errand boy with no pay. However, he knew he had his foot in the door.

At first, he would just get coffee, pick up lunches, and clean the bathrooms. Although some of the people he idolized would abuse him in his current position, he still made it to work and kept a close grasp on the vision he had for his life. He had a great attitude and a great love for broadcasting. As a result, he began to get more and more responsibility.

When he was not running errands, he was hanging out in a control room learning how the equipment worked. He made it a point to learn everything he could about the station. He was like a sponge that soaked up every bit of information while he was at work. At night when he went home he would practice speaking into a hairbrush and playing his records.

One day he was at the station and the personality on the air had been drinking before work. This man knew the station manager would be calling any minute with orders to get this guy off the air. The station manager did call, and he gave Les Brown the authorization to take over the show, because of his attitude and willingness to do what was asked of him. That helped to make this man successful not only in radio, but in TV, politics, and public speaking. Not bad for a man who started in poverty, mowed lawns for food, and worked for free in the beginning.

I told you this to illustrate that your attitude may be the only thing you can control about a situation. There may be aspects of your internship that you really dislike. The workers of the radio station hazed Les Brown in the beginning. He had coworkers that would take advantage of his zeal for radio. Just like Les Brown, there may be co-workers who do everything in their power to upset you. Guess what? When you let that person get you angry, frustrated, or depressed you have given control of your life over to that person. Do you want to give your success over to a person who wants to abuse you? Are you going to trust your success to a person who wants to see you fail? **When you let others control your attitude you are granting them permission to control your destiny.**

Attitudes and Behaviors

Once you develop the right attitude the next of these steps will be easy. They are easy because they are the result of having the right attitude. If you do not have the right attitude, do them anyway. William Glasser says, *"If you want to change attitudes, start with a change in behavior."* If you do not believe that is true try being mad and laughing at the same time and you will find it will not work.

The right behavior with the right attitude on the job will go a long way in turning your internship or volunteer job into a full time position. This will involve a demonstration of good social skills. It also includes going the extra mile. Going the extra mile is one thing that all winners have in common. Going the extra mile helps because of the concept of compare and contrast. Most people never go the first mile. You will set yourself apart by going the extra mile.

The right behavior is learning everything you can about the job you are doing and the organization in which you are employed. It is demonstrating leadership by helping your coworkers perform their jobs better. Going the extra mile involves offering to lead a group, working on new projects and taking calculated risk. It is admitting your mistakes. It is the building up of your skills both technical and non-technical. Above all, it is behaving like a professional.

You Can't Get What You Don't Ask For

The third way to turn your internship or volunteer position into a fulltime vocation is to ask. Let your intentions be known. Les Brown made it abundantly clear that he wanted to be in radio broadcasting, just as you should make it clear that you want to be in an industry. If you have been displaying a positive attitude and if you have been going the extra mile and acting like a professional, they would be foolish not to hire you.

If they are foolish enough not to hire you, then you should sell your labor to another employer. I would like to say that every employer is rational and makes good decisions but that is not always the case. You owe it to yourself to find an employer that encourages hard work, innovation, and risk taking. These are the things that will keep the business alive. It is your job and security at stake, and if the business doses not succeed, you will not succeed.

The key point to remember is they may not offer you a position because they may not realize you want to work for them. For many people these positions are just stepping-stones and the organization knows that. It is because of this reason they may not offer you a job. They may think you are such a great worker that you have bigger and better plans.

To sum up this chapter in one phrase it would be this: **It is up to you to secure your ideal job**. Unfortunately, too many people have a misconception that it will just come to them. The fact is it will not. Knowing what you do, desire is an important first step in finding your dream job and making it a reality. However, it is only the first step. You still have to prepare for the job, and you still have to market yourself to the people that will be able to help you get that job.

KAPS

➤ Remember to survey the job field, but forge your own destiny.
➤ Shadowing is a great way to determine if a job idea is the ideal job.
➤ Reading trade magazines is a great way to determine if a job idea is the ideal job.
➤ Reading books about your chosen vocation or industry is a great way to determine if a job idea is the ideal job.
➤ Interviewing people who have the position or a similar position to the one you want is a great way to determine if a job idea is the ideal job.
➤ An internship is a great way to determine if a job idea is the ideal job.
➤ It is possible to turn an internship into a full time job if you know how.

Chapter 7

Put it in Writing: Making a Contract With Yourself

Yale University did a study and at random they picked a graduating class. What they found was at graduation only 3% of that class had clear, written, and well-defined goals. Twenty years later Yale did a study of the same graduating class and found that the 3% who put their dreams in writing accomplished more than the 97% combined who did not commit their dreams to writing.

The reason is by writing down your dreams, you can see for yourself what it really takes to get it. By writing down your dreams, it reinforces what you want to accomplish. By writing down your dreams, you are clarifying your dreams. By writing down your dreams, you are able to identify the obstacles that are standing in your way. By writing down your dreams with a time frame and action plan, you are transmuting your dreams from an abstract thought into realistic and attainable goals. By writing down your dreams you are making a contract with yourself.

Contracting with yourself is taking control of your life. You are taking control by writing down what you want to accomplish. You might be asking, "How do I write down my goals?" I will answer that question for you by giving you a list of things to include and a model to follow.

Nine questions you should ask yourself when putting your dream job into writing:

1. ***What would I love about this job?*** Make a list of everything you can think of about your job idea that will give you both tangible and non-tangible rewards. Will this job give you prestige? Will this job cause you to be looked up to as an authority figure? Will you be a leader? Will it be challenging? Will you enjoy the work? Will you be making a lot of money? Remember *taking a job for money is the fastest way to hate your job, and the fastest way to make money is to love your job.* Mark Twain said it this way, "The law of compensation is utterly unfair. The more one enjoys his job the more he is paid and the less he enjoys his job the less he is paid."

2. ***Why would this job be right for me?*** Is this job going to make use of your natural abilities, gifts, experiences, and desires? Is this job going to help you accomplish your mission in life? Is this company willing to promote you if you are willing to put out the effort? Will you be able to use your degree? Do you want to use your degree? It is important to answer these questions because it will intensify your desire for the job. At this point it does not matter how big or insignificant the reasons are for you wanting this job. It is simply important to have reasons for wanting the job.

3. ***Can I make a commitment out of this job?*** A career is a long-term commitment and reaching the top in any career will take time. (Remember it takes about ten years to become an overnight success.) Ask yourself if the amount of your life that you are going to invest in the job is worth the job. I

believe that when you have a job, you are giving part of your life to that vocation. You need to make sure it is worth it. Employers want people who are willing to commit themselves to the work. If you want to be an entrepreneur, you have to commit yourself to your business. As you can see either way you must be willing to make a commitment.

4. ***How will I benefit personally and professionally from this job?*** It is okay to ask questions like how much will I be paid? What benefits will I have? What benefits do I want? Will I have job security? Is there long-term growth in this field? How much vacation time do you want to have? Is this job a stepping-stone for something better? Remember for a job idea to become the ideal job it needs to benefit you. Tune in to your personal radio station WIFM (What's In it For Me.) I am not saying to embrace a what's is in it for me attitude, but on the other hand you need to remember your self-interest. I recommend that you seek to find a balance. After all, your success is dependent upon it. Just do not get the wrong idea of what self-interest really is. Most people have gotten self-interest confused with selfishness. They are not the same. Selfishness is short-term and does not take into account cause and effect. Selfishness leads to greed and greed leads to poverty. I know greedy people who are poor because they are greedy. They are constantly looking for ways to take advantage of people. As a result, other people do not want to do business with them. Self-interest, on the other hand is treating people the way you want to be treated. It is understanding that the way you treat people influences the way you are treated. As a result, they are honest, dependable, loyal, and try to do the best for everybody involved. They are not greedy, and as matter of fact, most of these people are not afraid to give. So when you are tempted to be selfish, ask yourself if the action is in your self-interest or if it is selfish. Sometimes it can be both, but if not remember it is always best to strive for self-interest and to resist the temptation to be selfish.

5. ***What can I bring to this job/career to make it better?*** Being able to make a measurable and positive impact will not only help you get a job, but it will help you keep a job. When you bring something new to a job, you are increasing your employment security. Ask yourself some of the following questions. What level of education do I possess? What certifications do I hold? What organizations do I currently belong to or have I belonged to in the past, and what offices have I held in these organizations?

6. ***Will I be proud of the work I will be doing?*** Will the work you do outlast you? Look at the work of Martin Luther King Jr., the work of George Washington, the work of Plato, or the work of Jesus. These men and countless others have left a lasting impact on our world. With this in mind, how do you want history to remember you? Can you say I want to be remembered for being a _____? Being able to fill in the blank with your chosen job title is important if you want to find your dream job and make it a reality. Is your job something your children can respect when they are grown? Think about it this way. Would you want your daughter or son to be in your position? If not, you are probably in the wrong vocation. The job you have should promote your values. It is impossible to be proud of a job

that will make you cheat, lie, or slander. If your job is forcing you to sell your values then you need to look at what you really value. If this is the case, you have two choices. First, you can stand up for what you believe in and get out of that profession, or you can remain in that vocation and continue to suffer. Remember what you do will make a difference. It is up to you to make a good or bad difference.

7. ***What would excite me the most about having this job?*** There has to be something about your job that will get your adrenaline flowing. What is it about this job that is fun? What is it about this job that you would do for free? There has to be something whether it is closing a deal, climbing a tree to save a cat, or helping someone pick out the right shirt to go with a suit. It does not matter what it is, just find something.   When you find a job you can be excited about then money and advancement will come. I believe that society rewards people for being excited about their jobs. If you do not believe me, watch a professional sporting event, go to a concert, or attend a motivational seminar. When you do this, you will see people excited about their jobs. Not only are they excited about their jobs, but in many cases they are millionaires. Do you think Bill Gates thought computer programming was a boring pastime or do you think he found it exciting? Use examples like these to keep you motivated.

8. ***What are the skills, experiences, and knowledge needed for this job?*** Sometimes this question is easy to answer especially if you want to be a CPA, professor, or a doctor. These professions and many others require a certain amount of education. Once you have identified the skills, the next step is acquiring the skills, experience, and knowledge needed for your job.
If you want to become a lawyer, scientist, or systems engineer, you can. The education is available; you just have to develop the discipline to get that education no matter the obstacle. Some jobs may not have a clear educational requirement. This is one reason why you need to become well educated about the profession you want to enter. Believe me when I say that education will pay off. If you lack knowledge about your chosen profession and you want to know what the education requirements are ask someone who has the job. If you cannot do this look in the classified section of the paper and find out what employers are looking for.

9. ***Set a deadline for accomplishment.*** By setting a deadline, you are giving yourself a time frame in which to get your job. This time frame needs to be realistic. If you have to get a degree or other certification, check with the learning institution you are going to attend and look at when the classes are scheduled. For example, my graduate degree in Interpersonal and Organizational Communication has a strict policy. You enter in the fall and take two classes each semester year round for two years. You have to pass every class because the next class is built on the information you learned in the previous class. If you fail a class or miss a semester, you have to wait a whole year before it is offered again. In my case, it would be unrealistic to think I could have taken three classes a term and finished in a year or year and a half, because the classes were not offered. Also when setting your time frame you should be aware that many businesses have a probationary period

of 30, 60, 90 days or more and during your probation you can't transfer departments or change jobs. If you are in the military, you are assigned to a job for the length of your contract. These are just a few of things to think about when setting your time frame. By the way, do not let a long time frame discourage you. If you have to wait a year or two to get out of the military or to change your current job then do it. In the interim, use your time wisely by remembering that there are always things you can be doing to move closer towards your dream job. You can use this time to volunteer and gain experience. You can use this time to learn more about your job idea. The fact is the years are coming and they will continue to come with or without your dream job. The world is full of under achievers and people who are not living up to their potential. I do not want you to be one of them, and I know you do not want to be one of them.

The vast majority of people never dare to dream, let alone pursue big dreams and the hope for a better future. This is where you are different. Dreaming big is what you and I can do to change our lives and the lives of those around us. The truth is most people just accept jobs. They just do what is necessary to get a job, any job, and they do not do one thing more.

Don't Accommodate Poverty

Accepting anything that comes is what John Galbraith calls "*accommodating poverty.*" You have a choice to make right now. That choice is to accommodate poverty and accept the position in life that you are currently in, or make a difference in your life and the lives of those around you. You do this by choosing to build a burning desire that will better your life no matter how long it will take, because you realize you will be older with or without your dream job. If you choose to build a better life, write it out. Then put in it action.

Here is an outline you can use to put what you want to accomplish in writing. Use this outline by replacing the underlined text with your own words. Remember you do not have to follow this outline exactly; just remember to make it specific, with a time frame, while listing the things you need to do to be what you want to be.

How to Write out What You Want

I *state your name* hereby commit myself to building a better future for my life by becoming a *state the job you want*, no matter the obstacles that are before me. I understand that it will not always be easy, but it will be rewarding. I plan to accomplish this by *insert the year, month, and day*. I am willing to commit myself to achieving this goal and I will practice persistence in the achievement of this goal.

I will do this by admitting that I am no longer willing to accept my current position in life. I know I am endowed with the understanding that success is never given to people without effort. With that understanding I am committed to learning all I can about my chosen profession. I promise I will take time to invest in myself, as I am my greatest asset.

I know this vocation will be the right vocation for me because it will make use of the following natural talents and abilities.

1. List a natural talent and ability

2. List a natural talent and ability
3. List a natural talent and ability
4. List a natural talent and ability

I have examined myself and the job I desire, and I know that in order to get that job I need to develop the following skills, acquire the following knowledge, and gain the following experiences:

1. List the skill, experience, certificate, degree, or specialized knowledge that needs to be acquired.
2. List the skill, experience, certificate, degree, or specialized knowledge that needs to be acquired.
3. List the skill, experience, certificate, degree, or specialized knowledge that needs to be acquired.

I will be excited about having this job because having this job will *state a reason that will excite you and motivate you*. I would be proud of this vocation, because if I had this vocation I would be able to *state the reason you would be proud if you had this job*.

As a result, I will expect the following compensation *write your expected yearly income* in exchange for my services rendered to my employer, vocation, industry, and society. I will not expect more compensation than work I am willing to supply. I will also seek the following benefits, *make a list of benefits such as 401k, number of vacation days, personal holidays, etc.* This compensation is reasonable, because I will bring this to my vocation, *state what you will and can to make your vocation better*.

From this day forward I am committed to being, *state the job title or vocation you will enter*, and I will do at least one thing everyday to accomplish this. I will no longer accept positions in life that will hinder my growth personally and professionally. I will work in my self-interest, but I will not be selfish. I will do what I can to promote a positive, winning attitude in myself and others. I know that if I do this I will be able to turn my acorn size ideas into oak tree size realties. I know I can expect to have my dream job by *state the date you can fulfill the requirements*. I know that I will not be able to see all the obstacles in my path, so I will not ever give up, even it means taking longer than originally planned.

_____

Sign your name on the line and date it

Once you do this, put this written statement in a place where you can see and read it everyday.

In this chapter, I have discussed the importance of putting what you want to accomplish in writing. When you write out what you want to accomplish it helps you to make it a commitment. When you write out what you want to accomplish it makes a contract with yourself. It also turns dreams into goals, and goals into accomplishments. I hope that you will take the advice I have given you and take the time to put what you want into writing.

KAPS

➢ Writing out what you want helps you to make it a commitment.
➢ When you write out your goals you need to specific, have a time line, and list the obstacles that may be in your way.
➢ You need to understand what is in it for you, because you can only accomplish your goals and not someone else's.
➢ You need to be able to identify the skills, knowledge, and experiences necessary to accomplish your goal.
➢ When you put your goals in writing you need to refer to your written statement often.

Chapter 8

Creating the Greatest Brand Ever: YOU

Who Are You?

Harvey Mackay makes the following statement in his book Sharkproof, *"They can't hire you unless they know who you are."* He is right. You can never get a job if your prospective employer does not know you. If you are currently employed, you will not get a promotion until the boss knows who you are. Some misguided people seem to believe that it is possible to get a position or promotion without anyone knowing who they are. The fact is it just does not work that way. You have to do things to market yourself, and when I say market yourself, I mean you need to be doing things that will get you recognition.

The Branding of America

Most people just do not understand the impact marketing has on us. For example, before 1900, people in America did not know that body odor was a bad thing. The soap manufactures thought being dirty and smelling was bad. They at least thought if they could get the consumer to think that it would be great for business. That is when they set out the change the mindset of the American population. Through effective marketing they convinced the American population that it was unsociable to smell bad. This led to the development of deodorant and body lotion, along with other toiletries and it helped launch a multi billion-dollar industry called personal hygiene.

I believe that marketing touches every aspect of our lives. When we wake up in the morning we turn off our GE alarm clock. We drink Starbucks coffee, Coca Cola and Pepsi. We turn on our Sony TV and see commercials for products that will make us sexier, richer, and wiser and products that we just could not live without, although we have done without them all of our lives.

It is the jobs of marketers to convince us that buying and using their products will help us attain a desirable level of social status. It is their goal, in fact, to convince us that we cannot be desirable in any way without these products. These people have convinced us that in order to be what we want to be we have to buy what they are selling. This is called branding and its effects are overwhelming.

Why is branding so effective? I will tell you what the marketing experts say. Marketing professors tell us that branding is effective because brands offer instant recognition and identification. This adds a perceived value to the mind of the customer. The product may not be better; it may only appear better. For you, the job hunter, this is what you want to do. You should brand yourself as the best choice for the position even if you are not the most qualified for the position, because remember **the best job candidate dose not get the job -- the best job seeker gets the job**. For brand marketing to be effective, the customer needs reliable references that prove the quality of the product.

What do I mean by references? A reference simply means reasons why the product is better. People do not always operate logically. People typically operate emotionally. We all make emotional decisions and then we look for logical reasons to support that decision. This is why in the beginning of the decision making process people typically do not have to have logical reasons to assume a choice is good; emotional reasons suffice. They will come up with the logical reasons later. Think about it for a minute; have you ever bought anything for no apparent reason? Later, have you justified that purchase? Of course you have. We all have, and I want you to know that it is okay.

The Goal of Branding

The goal of brand marketing is to differentiate products in the marketplace and at the same time build an emotional connection with the product. Without branding, customers would not be able to tell one product from another. What does this have to do with you finding your dream job and making it a reality? It has a lot to do with the job-hunting process because you have to be able to brand yourself as the best job candidate if you want a job, because the best job candidate doses not get the job, but the best job seeker gets the job. You can do it with the information in this book. This book is your manual to get the job and life you desire. You can have the job you want, where you want it, at the rate of pay you deserve if you brand yourself correctly.

If you do not actively brand yourself then your competition will brand you and this will give them a competitive edge especially if they are more experienced and more educated. Proper branding can give you the edge in the job market, and that is what you want. You and I both know that you can do a better job than the other person applying for the position can do.

I believe in selling potential instead of experiences, because the past is behind us, and the future is waiting for us to make it. Unlike the other person, you are the one taking the steps necessary to get what you want out of life. Understanding the power of branding will give you the competitive advantage, while underestimating it will not. When you brand yourself, you start saying, "I'm a salesperson, I'm a consultant, and I'm a doctor" or whatever you want your job title to be.

Personal Benefits of Branding

There is also a personal benefit to branding yourself. It creates an expectation of yourself that you will fulfill. This works in a two ways. First, it creates an image of you in the minds of other people. Since they expect you to fulfill this image, you will be more likely to fulfill this image. Secondly, it helps you create a self-fulfilling prophecy about the job you are looking for.

When you first attempt to brand yourself as whatever you want to do, you should expect people around to resist this. This is because they have already formulated their opinions of you and they do not want to change their label of you. It means they have to change something about themselves and people resist change. In addition, they have already labeled you as your previous occupation or perceived role in life whether it was a student, airline pilot, actress, alcoholic, waiter, taxi driver, manager, or stay at home mom to name a few.

It would be easy if you were dealing with people's intellect, but the fact is you are dealing with people's emotions. A psychologist by the name of Dr. Frijda claims that emotions are caused by specific events that occur throughout our lives. More importantly he says that our responses to events in our life are appraised as real and help determine the choices we make, but according to Carl Jung this process is symbolic, and the only meaning events have in our lives are the meanings that we assign to them. The key action point for us is to consciously assign proper meanings to things that happen to us.

Reinventing Yourself

This is important to know and do because we are creating a new image of you in your mind and in the minds of the people around you. In essence, we are reinventing you. This is where this book differs from many other books on the market. Many novice authors will say, "Ask your friends and families if they can see you in a particular job. If they can, then that job is for you." What a bunch of bunk, and what a great way for you to remain in your current circumstances.

I agree that this statement may sound intelligent on the surface because if those people can see you in a particular job it helps reinforce it emotionally, but what if they can't see you in that job? Does it mean that you should not pursue that job? I do not believe so. I believe that it means you need to start working to reinvent yourself into a person other people can see in that position, and more importantly, you need to reinvent yourself into a person who you can see in that position.

During this process you will find that the people you are just meeting are more accepting of the new you, and the people that have known you for all of your life are less accepting of the new you. To effectively reinvent yourself I believe it is important to surround yourself with people that will reinforce the self-concept you want to develop. This may mean that you will have to create a new network of supportive individuals.

On the other hand, you do not want to burn any bridges. It is important to find a balance when doing this. If you burn bridges, it tells people that you cannot maintain relationships. I believe that maintaining relationships is important to succeed in any endeavor. Keeping this in mind there may be relationships that you may need to terminate. I hope this is not the case, but if you find yourself in this situation, you should be willing to do it.

The Real Purpose

I believe that we should always be reinventing ourselves. Some people believe the purpose of life is to be happy. They are mistaken; the purpose of life is improvement and accomplishment while making a positive impact on the world. All improvement begins with the individual. You change the world by changing you. In addition, the world in which we live is constantly changing and if we are going to keep up with the world, we need to be constantly reinventing ourselves. If we are not keeping up, we are in the process of becoming obsolete. If we are obsolete, our skills, talents, and expertise will not be worth much in the market place. If our skills, talents, and expertise are not worth much we cannot expect much compensation. This is why if we are going to be successful and make a good income we need to be in a constant process of reinvention.

Here are some tips that will help you reinvent yourself
- Take charge of your thoughts.
- Understand that no one is going to do anything for you in the effort, and the results are going to be a result of your own efforts.

- ➤ Constantly ask yourself these questions: What do I really want to do? Why do I want to do it? What is holding me back from doing it? What am I doing about the perceived obstacles in my way?
- ➤ When you lapse into your old ways do not worry and remember the process takes time.
- ➤ Do something everyday that will help you become what you want to be.
- ➤ Make positive, reaffirming claims about your progress.
- ➤ Tell only supportive people about what you are doing.

The Role of Self-Confidence

Not only will you have to reinvent yourself you will need self-confidence if you want to be successful at creating the greatest brand ever. For whatever reason many people never develop the self-confidence needed to become the person that they can, should, and deserve to become. I believe you can become who you want to become. I believe you can achieve what you want to achieve. I believe that you can have any job or career you deserve. That is why in this section, I will give you some insights on how to improve your self-confidence.

I believe one key to increasing your self-confidence is the language you use to describe yourself. For many people this is implicit. In everyday conversation, people use words that unnecessarily limit their abilities and potential. If you find yourself using self-limiting language, stop, and I should warn you that this is harder than it sounds. To do this, make it a point to use self-empowering words. Quit using words or phrases that give you an easy out if you do not succeed. Start questioning your word choice. Analyze what you said and why you said it. Then start looking for empowering words to use.

Another key to increasing your self-confidence is to focus on what you do well. There are things we all do well and then there are things that we can improve. The problem is many people use the things they are not good at as a way to define who they are. This is not necessary. Instead of this, try using the things you are good at as a way to define who you are. Remember it is not what has happened to you but how you define those events. Make it a point to use the things you are good at as a way to define yourself.

The last element I will discuss that will help you increase your self-confidence is to start acting confident. Research shows that emotions follow actions. If you act confident, you will become confident. Here are some things you can do to act with more confidence:

- ➤ Make it a point to find and discuss other people's positive characteristics.
- ➤ Make it a point to speak with force, conviction, and with a lower pitch in both interpersonal and public settings (be sure not to overdo it).
- ➤ Make it a point to give a firm handshake.
- ➤ Make it a point to stand up straight.
- ➤ Make it a point to focus on the positive side of any situation.
- ➤ Make it a point to smile.
- ➤ Make it a point to practice tolerance.
- ➤ Make it a point to control your emotions, including your temper.
- ➤ Make it a point to take leadership while in group settings.
- ➤ Make it point to take the initiative and go the extra mile when possible.
- ➤ Dress in a manner that makes you feel more powerful.

➤ Become diverse in a wide range of subjects, interests, or topics.

Now that I have discussed how to brand yourself and the process of reinventing yourself, what do you do? You promote yourself using the information in the upcoming chapters. This is information that you can use not only to promote yourself, but you can use these steps to promote organizations you belong to, ideas you have, or anything else that you think needs promoting.

KAPS

➤ They can't hire you unless they know who you are.
➤ If you do not market yourself no one else will.
➤ Make sure your marketing efforts create yourself as the greatest brand ever.
➤ Make sure you consciously assign proper meanings to things that happen to you.
➤ When marketing yourself you may need to reinvent yourself.
➤ You need self-confidence to market yourself well.

Chapter 9

How to Effectively Market Yourself for Today's Job Market

Up to this point, this book has focused on how to determine what you want to do and why. Now the focus is going to shift. In the rest of this book, I will discuss the marketing aspect of finding your dream job and making it a reality. I believe it is extremely important to market yourself. The fact is if you do not market yourself no one else will. I believe that you have skills, talents, and knowledge that will be an asset to any organization.

The problem is at this point you may face two common problems. The first problem is the person doing the hiring at the organization you want to work for does not know you. The second problem is they may know you, but they do not realize that you are an expert. This next section will focus on both issues. If they do not know you they will, and if they do not perceive you as an expert they soon will. To do this I have identified ten easy steps that will help you market the greatest brand ever, which is yourself. While I may call this the 10 steps of Magic Marketing, the reality is there is nothing magical about it.

The 10 steps of Magic Marketing

1. Know your product (you).
2. Know your customer (the organization you want to work for).
3. Know how to answer this question: Why should I do business with you instead of your competition? For you the question is: Why should I hire you instead of the other people applying for the job?
4. Know how to target your market and message.
5. Know how to develop a compelling message.
6. Know how to be creative.
7. Know how to be persistent.
8. Know how to increase your visibility in order to increase your employability.
9. Know how to plan, organize, and take action.
10. Know how to sell yourself. For you this means getting a job, but not just any job . . . the job you want.

Marketing schools tell their students that there are four P's of Marketing. They are place, product, price, and position. Place is where you want to work. This could be the industry, company, or geographic location. Product is what you and you skills have to offer the market. Price is the salary that you deserve for your talents, skills and abilities. Position is the job or career you desire. I would like to add a 5th P: people. People are the heart of this process and it is important to remember the needs of all the people involved. When looking at the 10 steps of magic marketing you need to incorporate these five P's in every step in order for your marketing program to be effective. Now lets continue to create the greatest brand ever: YOU!

Chapter 10

Knowing Your Customer

Knowing your customer means different things to different people. We of course are talking about the organization you are going to sell your labor to. If your dream job is to be an entrepreneur, we are talking about the customers who will buy your product or service. If your dream job is to be a good husband, we are talking about your wife. If your dream job is to be a good wife, we are talking about your husband. The reason it is important to know your customer is because you have limited resources.

The first step in understanding your customer is to know your customer's decision-making process. When hiring, most employers go through a five step decision-making process, which includes receiving a stimulus, recognizing a problem, searching for information, evaluating alternatives, and then offering a job.

The second step is researching your customer. In this process, you search for all the information about the organization you are targeting. The three primary purposes of research are:

1. To determine if there are any job openings at the target organization.
2. To determine the culture of the organization.
3. To determine if you want to work in that organization.

Before the discussion of how to research organizations we should focus on the decision-making process that an organization goes through before they hire someone.

The Decision Making Process

The first step is receiving a stimulus. By definition a stimulus is anything that arouses activity. There are two types of stimuli, internal and external. The internal stimuli can come from the employer's recognition that the organization needs a person to fulfill a specific task or role in order to fulfill an organizational goal, objective, or some other outcome. The external stimuli can come from you sending a resume and cover letter explaining how you can increase the firm's profits, decrease expenses, or how you can solve an organizational problem.

The second step is for the employer to recognize the stimulus as a problem. In order for the stimulus to be perceived as a problem the organization is going to need to feel out of balance. This imbalance occurs when there is a difference between the actual state and desired state of the organization. Sometimes they may not notice the imbalance and it may need to be pointed out to them. If you can point out the imbalance and how you fix it better than anyone else, you should get the job. I would like to say that job seekers are not determining the needs of employers, but the best job seeker is discovering the needs of the employer and working to fulfill those needs.

What do employers want? Unless we sit down and talk about the specific field you want to go into I can only give you some generalizations. According to a recent report by CNBC, businesses are looking for people with computer skills and communication skills. According to Dr. Kathy Rice-Clayborn, the director of career services at the University of Central Arkansas, employers are looking for people that are committed, for people who have maturity and confidence, and who are professional, adaptable, and punctual. It is up to you to recognize unfulfilled wants and needs. The two most common wants and needs occur when someone in the company is not performing and when the company is growing and new positions are being created.

The third step is the search for information. After the problem has been exposed, it is only natural to look for a solution. People want to be in balance, or at least what they perceive as balance. If a person or business is in a state of imbalance, they will look for balance and will not stop looking until they are balanced again or at least what they perceive as balance. For example, when you are thirsty you are in a state of imbalance. You are going to think about being thirsty and wanting a drink until your thirst is quenched.

There are two basic ways for an organization to search for information. There is the internal information search and the external information search. In the internal information search, they will ask employees in the business if they want the new position or if they know someone who can do the job. They may also go through their files and look at applications and resumes that have already been sent in. This information is a collection of past information stored somewhere in the business or it is relying on the people in the business for information. Depending on what statistics you use, as many as 70 to 80% of all jobs are filled using internal information.

The second way to gather information is using external information. Businesses are using this more because of the shortage of qualified people for high paying jobs. They seek information about possible job candidates from outside sources. The Internet is making this more economically feasible, but at the same time it is creating an information overload. Currently there are hundreds of career and job-hunting related sites that you can post resumes on and search for jobs. Many universities have web sites that students and alumni can post their resumes on. Be sure you check with your school and see if they offer on-line resume posting.

Another place firms go for external information is job placement agencies and headhunters. Some businesses use these services instead of using in house human resources. I would use a little caution when approaching these places. Some of the places charges fees so when you register, ask if there is a fee, how much it is and who pays for it. Sometimes the employer will pay the fee. I would use caution and recommend that the job seeker does not pay the fee.

Remember when dealing with employment agencies that they make money by getting you a job. Most of these agencies will have a wide variety of positions and they may try to put you into a job that does not fit your mission in life. If the agency is giving you the hard sell to take a job that you don't want, consider switching agencies. When this is the case think of the agency as the uncontrollable river of life. Then ask yourself "Am I willing to turn over my success to someone like this? Am I willing to give my career to this person who does not know me or who does not care about me, just so they can make another dollar?" I wouldn't. I do believe that there are many more people out there that are genuinely concerned about your success. I am one of them because I truly want you to get the job you desire.

I am not saying not to use employment agencies; there are many out there that provide a valuable service. I have used them in the past and I have had both good and bad experiences with them. They are useful especially if you are still in school, if you are working, or both. When you go to the agency, ask questions to make sure the agency will work for you. Here are some general tips for dealing with agencies.

> Ask for references and the names of companies they work with.
> If they ask you to sign a contract, take it home and read it carefully, because it may be in their best interest and not yours.
> If they ask for money up front or boast high placement rates of 90% or more, run away.
> Is this employment agency one that specializes in placing people who work in your particular field?
> Be suspicious of an agency that promises to rewrite your resume and find a position for you at a charge. The fact is you don't have to be brilliant to write a resume.
> **RUN**; do not walk from agencies or individuals that insist that their offer is a once in a lifetime offer and that you must sign on NOW.
> If you ever find yourself being pressured to sign a document immediately, you are most likely dealing with a shady character.
> **DO NOT** let the agency persuade you to go for an interview that you are not qualified for "for experience;" this is not a good idea because it could keep you from a future position that you may be suitable for, unless your goal with this agency is getting more experience at interviewing.

Do Your Homework

Up until now, this chapter has focused on your customer's decision-making process, where they go for information and what they want. Now I will shift the focus to how to research a company. Effective research will help reinforce your job search because it increases your ability to see job choices that you may not have known existed. The unfortunate thing about researching organizations is too many people believe they do not have to do their homework.

You should do your homework. If nothing else this lets you know if you want to work for the organization. When researching an organization you should think of yourself as a detective. Just like a detective, you are searching for clues, but the clues you find will help you get your dream job and make it a reality. Like a detective trying to solve a difficult case, you should not stop with a few names, articles, or addresses. When you effectively do your homework and research an organization, you can expect the following benefits:

> You will be able to talk intelligently about the organization during the interview.
> You will uncover new job opportunities that you did not know existed.
> You will gain insights into the organizational culture.
> You will be able to tell how financially sound the organization is.
> You will be able to determine if the organization will match your career objectives.
> You will be able to effectively negotiate the job offer.

➢ You will be able to write a better resume or cover letter.
➢ You will be able to determine the organizations that have the best opportunities for you.

The purpose of researching is to gain an understanding of the organization. After researching an organization, you should be able to answer the following questions:

1. How old is the organization?
2. What are its products and services?
3. Where are its plants, offices, or stores located?
4. What is the price of its stock?
5. Is the company privately or publicly held?
6. What are the organization's plans for the future?
7. What is the organization's mission statement?
8. What are the organization's core values or beliefs?
9. What is the organization's business philosophy?
10. When and where was the company founded?
11. Who are the officers of the company and what are their functions?
12. What are some popular corporate stories at the organization?
13. How large is the organization? What is its industry rank?
14. What were the company's sales last year? What are the sales this year?
15. What is the turnover rate for the organization and for the position for which you are applying?
16. What problems has the organization faced in the past?
17. What problems does the organization currently face?
18. What problems will the organization face in the future?
19. How do they compare to the competition?
20. What makes this organization different from other potential employers?
21. Who are there customers?
22. Are they profitable?
23. What are their training programs like?
24. What is there approach towards technology?
25. Is the company expanding?
26. Is the company downsizing?

You can answer these questions by going to the library, company websites, public relations departments, friends and acquaintances, and news sources. Between these sources, you should be able to find everything you need to know to help make your job search more effective. However, when doing your research there are five rules you need to follow.

5 Rules of Research

1. **Know what you want.** Before you start your research, take time to identify the type of information that you need to gather in order to make an intelligent decision about the organization. If you are researching the company culture, look for the words and phrases they use to describe the organization. If you are looking for career advancement, you should find out if they hire from within. In the beginning, you may not know what kind of information you need and that's

okay. Just be prepared to spend hours digging through mountains of information that may be interesting, but in the end has no real value for your job search.

2. **Don't reinvent the wheel.** Look to see what other people have done at the start of your research. Find people who have interviewed with the organization or who work for the organization and talk to them or find out what they have done. You may find this very helpful.

3. **Look for leads**. During your research look for potential sources such as publications, websites, contacts, etc. If you find a contact ask them for an "information gathering" interview. When looking at websites follow all links from useful websites. Do not forget to look through bibliographies and reference lists in publications about the organization. Look at the source of all your information and follow it. For example, if the source was a newspaper or magazine article, talk to the journalists and find out where they got their information.

4. **Keep references.** This is for your benefit, because if you found that something you thought was true is false you will want to protect yourself by keeping track of who said what. This will take effort, but it can save you from an embarrassing situation. This will also help you in the future because throughout this process you will learn how to distinguish good resources from bad resources.

5. **Separate "the sell" from "the tell."** Much of the information you receive from an organization about itself, including news articles, press releases, and information on their website, will try to create a positive impression of the organization. This is because most organizations focus on selling their products or services rather than telling about the issues or problems in the organization. When you are researching the organization try to distinguish the sell from the tell.

Sources for Research

The primary key in effective researching is knowing what sources are useful in your gathering of information. In this section, I will give you some ideas and places that will help you to research most organizations. I should note now that not all organizations are required to make financial or other information easily available to the public. If you are researching a small organization or a privately held organization you may find it more difficult to gather useful information about the organization, but not impossible.

Since finding information about small organizations is more difficult than well-known organizations, I will give you some ideas that will help you find information about most small organizations. The first place I would start is the Internet. I would see if that organization has a web-presence. Even if they do not have a web-presence, you can search for news articles about the organization. This may mean that you may need to go the local newspaper website and search the archives.

The second place I would go is the chamber of commerce in the area of that organization. If that organization is a member, they will be able to tell you something about the business. Hopefully someone from that organization is an active member in the chamber. If this is the case, you could ask to talk to that person.

The third thing I would do is find out who that organization's customers/clients are, and then go talk to them. This will be a great source of valuable information about how the organization is run and whether or not you should seek employment with that organization.

The fourth thing I would do is talk to someone from that organization. If you know someone associated with the organization ask them to lunch or dinner and ask them about their job and what the organization is like. If you do not know someone from the organization, you may need to do some careful networking in order to get to know someone.

The fifth thing I would do is call the organization. If all else fails call and ask questions. Do not be afraid to tell them your purpose. If things go well you may even ask if you can set up an appointment to speak with someone from the organization, or you could ask to spend a day at the organization observing what goes on there.

If the organization you are researching is publicly held then you should not have any problem finding information about it. There will be websites, news articles, directories, and other sources. You will be able to gather more information than you can use.

The best and most obvious place to find most of these resources is the library, but I should warn you that not every library will have all of these resources. You may need to visit multiple libraries, or get an interlibrary loan.

16 Resources to Research any Organization

> **The Business Ranking Annual**. This offers selected lists of ranking of organizations, brands, and services by various traits. It is organized by name and gives a ranking of each organization.
> **Dun & Bradstreet's Million Dollar Directory**. This is a leading guide to both private and publicly held organizations. It also gives the names of the organization's executives, which may be very helpful when sending out resumes and cover letters.
> **Standard & Poor's Register of Corporations, Directors, and Executives**. This is another leading guide that targets the business community and the executives in the business community. It gives corporate listings with more than 55,000 names, addresses, phone numbers, and functions of 500,000 officers, directors, and principals.
> **Dun's Regional Business Directory**. This is a regional directory of businesses for various regions of the United States.
> **Directory of Corporate Affiliations**. This is a master index to organizational name's and their affiliations. This includes a brand name index to organizations, locations, and companies. It also includes a personnel index of many of the organizations listed.
> **Hoover's Handbook**. This profiles more than 500 corporations. This gives basic company data and lists various factors within their industries.
> **Hoover's Guide to Private Companies**. Are you looking for information on that elusive privately held company? This resource may help. It is a guide to information about the 500 largest privately owned companies in the U.S. ranked by sales. It contains an operations overview, lists of products, key competitors, key strategies, up to 10 years of financial and employment data, lists of products/services, and executive information.
> **Hoover's Handbook of Emerging Companies**. If you are looking for growth, this directory profiles about 250 of the fastest growing companies in the U.S. It

provides a history, financial information, competitors, products/services, and overview of these companies.

➤ **Hoover's Guide to Computer Companies**. You may be looking for a job in the high tech computer world. This directory will help you pinpoint job opportunities by providing you a perspective of the computer industry. It gives you industry leaders and players.

➤ **Hoover's Master-list of America's Top 2500 Employers**. This is a valuable resource because it provides you with the names of human resource managers of the 2,500 largest employers in the U.S.

➤ **Moody's Industrial Manual**. This list has over 3,000 companies that are listed on the stock exchanges.

➤ **Small Business Source Book**. This is a list of profiles of small businesses.

➤ **Thomas Register**. This a 12-volume directory of U.S. manufactures. It includes names, addresses, and phone numbers of company executives.

➤ **Value Line Investment Survey**. This gives overall economic prospects and historical averages of stocks, bonds, and etc.

➤ **Ward's Directory of 51,000 Largest U.S. Corporations.** This directory includes names, addresses, phone numbers, president's names, as well as sales and financial information.

➤ **Ward's Directory of 49,000 Private U.S. Companies.** This is another useful directory when trying to gather information about a privately held company. It includes the names, addresses, and phone numbers, of many private companies.

Along with these resources, be sure to read trade publications and visit their websites, because you may be able to look through back issues on-line. Every industry has some sort of publication whether it is a small newsletter, magazine, or large newspaper. While this may not help you with a specific organization it will get you up to date with what is happening in that industry.

Do not forget the most effective, but often overlooked method of research. This is working your network. Check with friends, family, or acquaintances to see what they know about a particular industry or organization. These people may have valuable knowledge, and they may be able to introduce you to someone who could help you even more.

In closing, knowing your target organization better than the other people applying for the same position can give you a competitive advantage. It also helps you to know if you want to work for that organization. The time spent researching, although it may be time consuming in the beginning, will be worth it in the end.

KAPS

➤ Researching helps you to determine three things: job openings, organizational culture, and if you want to work for that organization.

➤ Employers want someone who can solve a problem and not create a problem.

➤ When you start your research, know what you are looking for.

➤ When you are doing your research know how to separate "the tell" from "the sell."

➤ When you are doing your research, make use of the local library.

- When you are doing your research, make use of your network.
- When you are doing your research, make use of your local chamber of commerce.

Chapter 11

Know Your Product:
Gaining a Better Understanding of You

Would you buy a product from a salesperson that could not explain its benefits? Imagine going to a car dealership to purchase a new car. The salesperson greets you by shaking your hand and asks if you have any questions. "What model is this car?" you ask. "I'm not sure," the salesperson says, "either this year's or last year's." You ask how much gas mileage the car gets. The salesperson replies, "I don't really know, but instead of keeping track of how many miles you drive we have a nice digital gas gauge that will let you know when you are about to run out of gas."

Then you ask what kind of tires the car has. The salesperson says, "Round rubber tires that inflate with air." Then you ask if you can take the car for a test drive. You do and the salesperson does not know which key starts the car, how to adjust the seats, turn the lights on, set the clock or adjust the radio. After returning to the car lot after a test drive in which the salesperson got lost, they ask if you would be interested in buying the car, the product the salesperson knew nothing about.

That is what happens when most people go to a job interview; they do not know enough about the product they are selling. Just as you expect a car salesperson to know how many miles to the gallon a car gets, **the interviewer will expect you to be able to describe yourself.** In a job interview, you are a salesperson and it is your job to understand your product. You will be expected to be able to clearly explain the benefits of your product (what you will be doing for the organization). If you cannot explain the benefit of your product (you), you will not be able to get the sell (job offer) even if you have a superior product. This is another reason why the best job seeker gets the job and not the best job candidate. The best job seeker can clearly define their product or what she/he can do for the employer.

What Are You Selling?

If you want to successfully sell yourself, you have to know what you are selling. You need to be able to communicate what service you can provide for your future employer. To help you do this you need to perform a SWOT analysis of yourself, an idea introduced in chapter five, but expanded upon in this chapter. A SWOT analysis is a written report of your strengths, weaknesses, opportunities, and threats. Successful businesses use SWOT analyses and you should too.

For example, a degree or experience in your desired field would be a *S*trength. A *W*eakness would be a lack of skill or knowledge. When listing your weaknesses figure out ways to eliminate or at least minimize them as soon as possible. I had a friend once say, "My greatest weakness in finding the job I want is I never finished my degree, and as soon as I find an employer that will pay my tuition I will finish my degree and get the job I want."

What a ludicrous idea! You have to put into life before you can be rewarded by life. The sad thing about my friend is that he wants to be a computer programmer, and he of all people should understand that input precedes output. If you lack skills or knowledge and you are actively gaining the skill on your own, you are demonstrating your initiative and enthusiasm, which makes you an asset to any organization.

The *O*pportunity section of your SWOT analysis could be a list of careers or positions that you currently qualify for or are in the process of becoming qualified for. If you still have to acquire some specialized knowledge or experiences for your dream job you can list the position(s) that will become stepping-stones to your final destination. In your opportunity section, you can map out a career path and share this with perspective employers and other people that can help you achieve your goals.

Be careful with whom you share this with because there are people who will try to steal your dreams from you. These people do not want you to live your dreams, because they would have to admit that they could live their dreams only if they were doing what you are doing right now. I know this is true because I have many ideas and goals, and I used to share them with anyone who would ask.

I mistakenly thought they were interested and wanted to see someone succeed. A lot of times they would be semi-supportive and say things like I should wait until I could afford to be an entrepreneur, which is another way of saying, you should not live your dreams because I am not living mine. They would give me reasons why I could not do something and never any reasons on why I should do something. If I had listened to those people, I would not be here helping you right now.

The opportunity section should be fun because it is your chance to dream, and it will not cost you anymore to dream big than to dream small. Do you want to know a secret? Most people do not dream big because they are afraid of the risk. What if they do not achieve their dreams? They worry they will be perceived as a failure.

The Cost Big Dreams

The truth is people are naturally attracted to people who dream big. The truth is if you dream big you will get big results even without completing 100% of your goals. In fact, the bigger your dreams, the smaller percentage you have to attain to get amazing results. For example, let's say in ten years time you want to have $1,000, and at the end of ten years you have $1,000. You have successfully reached 100% of your goals.

Let's say at the end of ten years you want a million dollars, and you work for that million dollars diligently but you only accomplish 10% of your goal, how much money will you have? You will have $100,000. Let's say you want ten million dollars at the end of ten years and you work for it with a workable and realistic plan. If you only achieve 5% of your goal, you will have half a million dollars.

Let me ask you a question, which person has benefited more, the person who wanted a $1,000 and accomplished 100% of their goal, the person who wanted a million dollars and accomplished 10% of their goal, or the person who wanted ten million dollars and accomplished 5% of their goal? The answer is the person with the ten million dollar goal.

Let me ask you another question, how much more did it cost to plan to have ten million dollars than one thousand dollars? It cost nothing more. I said this to illustrate that it is not only okay, but it is better if you make your opportunity page as big as possible. When you do your worst-case scenario will be better than your original best-case scenario.

Do I believe this? I believe it without a doubt. I can prove it, because on my wall I have a check made out to me for the sum of ten million dollars along with the work I need to do to be able to cash that check on May 8, 2010. What if I cannot cash the check and I reach only 10% of that goal, will I be a failure? I don't think so, and if someone says I am a failure then I must be a million dollar failure.

Since we are talking about me, I would rather be a million dollar failure then a thousand dollar winner. The question for you is do you want to dream so big that even if you reach a small percentage of your goal you will have accomplished more than the millions who set small but easily attainable goals?

The next thing in understanding your product is knowing your *T*hreats. What are threats? If you think about your life as a boat, threats are anything that will cause your boat to sink. For example, if you share your goals with the wrong person and they believe it is impossible for you to have your dream job, that is a threat.

If the job market is not promising, that is a threat. That is like boating during a storm and it is up to you to find a port. I would like to say this about the job market. I have noticed that no matter how good the job market is there are certain people who can never find a job. I have also noticed that no matter how bad the job market is there are still people who get new high paying jobs and are successful at them. The difference is one person makes excuses while the other person makes opportunities.

Self-Sabotaging Behaviors

The greatest threat comes from within in the form of self-sabotaging behavior. Self-sabotaging behaviors come in many forms. If you suffer from a poor self-image and you do not believe you can get the job you want, this is a self-sabotaging behavior, and this is a major threat to your success. If this is you then you need to build your self-image. A poor self-image is not the only self-sabotaging behavior, and a poor self-image manifests itself in many ways. To illustrate this, here is a list of 27 self-sabotaging behaviors, some of which come from having a poor self-image.

27 Self-Sabotaging Behaviors
1. Constantly changing goals for no apparent reason.
2. Constantly changing goals because the goal is harder to achieve, is taking longer to achieve, or is requiring more energy than originally planned for.
3. Constantly working in the wrong direction.
4. Refusing to change or adopt new goals when previous goals have become obsolete, ineffective, or outdated.
5. Not setting goals.
6. Not developing a major purpose in life.
7. Not returning phone calls, emails, letters, or other forms communication.
8. Not showing respect for other people.
9. All or nothing thinking.
10. Unrealistic expectations about results.
11. Procrastination or waiting for your "ship" to come in.
12. Excessive drug or alcohol use. This will interfere with self-promotion and/or self-improvement.
13. Excessive spending and not sticking to a budget.
14. Intentional or unintentional dishonesty in your words and actions.
15. Letting superstition and/or fear be your chief advisor when making career and life decisions.

16. Lack of planning.
17. Lack of initiative.
18. Lack of discipline.
19. Lack of effective networking.
20. Having and maintaining an egotistic and arrogant attitude.
21. Associating with the wrong people.
22. Making false connections about the cause and effect of things.
23. Negative thinking.
24. Negative self-talk.
25. Waiting until the time is right.
26. Being unwilling to help other people.
27. Starting projects and not finishing them.

To deal with self-sabotaging behavior you first need to identify the behavior. Then you need to think of a positive behavior to replace it with. One way to do this is to write out the negative behavior and then decide on an appropriate positive behavior to replace it with. Write out the new behavior, keep this piece of paper of with you, and refer to it often. When you realize that the old behavior is sneaking up on you, take out the piece of paper and read it again. Albert Einstein says that it takes 11 positive inputs to replace one negative input. Remember this when replacing self-sabotaging behaviors.

In this part of the SWOT analysis you should know it is important to identify all the obstacles (internal and external) that stand between you and your job. It can be anything that will keep you from succeeding. Things that could be a potential threat are shifts in the economy or increased technology that can make your job or career obsolete. The government may have a policy or pass a new law that may limit or eliminate your chosen profession.

A lack of experience can threaten your ability to get your dream job. Industry regulations may require you to have certain permits or certifications in order to work in the profession. In some cases, you may need to join a union or other association to get work. If relocation is involved, you might not be able to afford it. A real and common threat to your job search is not having a clear direction for your career path. Of course, this is just a partial list of threats, but *the biggest threat preventing you from getting the job you want is a lack belief that you can have the job you want*.

The purpose of writing down the threats is to identify obstacles so that you may overcome them. When writing down your obstacles, you should also write down what you need to do to overcome that obstacle. Most people never identify what is keeping them from achieving their goals, and when they do, they never create a plan to overcome the obstacle. They just accept defeat as a way of life.

You do not have to accept defeat as a way of life. When you identify what is keeping you from your dream job and find a way to overcome the obstacle, you are proving the only obstacle between you and your dream is a lack of belief. It is true that the only real threat is a lack of belief and the only real obstacles are the obstacles you set up in your mind. Like Chuck Yeager said in his autobiography, "Breaking the sound barrier was a real let down, but looking back it had to be, because the real obstacle was not an invisible barrier in the sky but our lack of knowledge of super-sonic speed."

Remember, preparing a SWOT analysis will help you in your understanding of the product you are selling. Remember when an interview begins with the question, "tell me a little about yourself," they are not asking about your childhood, where you were born, or what type of movies you like. They want to know about the product you are selling in relation to their needs. They want to hear what you can do for the organization and why you are the best job candidate.

This is why you need to share with your interviewer your accomplishments, skills, and abilities. Highlight all the best attributes of your product and do not be afraid to share your weaknesses with them. A key point to remember is when you share a weakness make sure that you explain what you are doing to turn that weakness into a strength. We all have weaknesses so it isn't necessary to pretend you are perfect. Be honest, and at the same time let the interviewer know that you are taking the initiative to improve yourself.

KAPS

➢ If you are going to successfully sell yourself, you need to know yourself. A SWOT analysis can help.

➢ When an employer asks about you, what they want to know is how you can solve their problems and contribute to their business.

➢ It is important to replace self-sabotaging behavior with self-enhancing behavior.

Chapter 12

Why Should I Hire You Instead of The Other Qualified Applicants?

The third step in magic marketing is answering the following question, **"Why should I do business with you instead of your competitor?"** For you this question is a job-hunting question and it should say, ***"Why should I hire you instead of the other qualified applicants?"*** This is a hard question, but once you are able to answer it your chances for job offers will dramatically increase.

This is not a mud-slinging competition like the one politicians use to get the jobs they want. *Trying to destroy someone's reputation only results in the destruction of your own reputation.* Would you want someone who is going to talk badly about other people working for you? In grade school, did you like the kid who told on you every chance they got? Most adults have even less patience for other adults who operate that way.

The best thing to do is talk of others only in a positive way. This will show that you are mature and relate well with other people. If the job choice is between someone who slanders the other job candidates and someone who is mature enough to give praise to people, who do you think will get the job? On a practical note, if the tattletale gets the job you might be better off without that organization.

What do you say in answer to the question, "Why should I hire you?" There are two answers. The first answer is the answer you give to yourself. The second answer is the answer you give the interviewer. Both answers can be the same, but they do not have to be the same. The fact is in most cases they are not the same. The reason you go to work is often different than the reason you are offered the job. In order to get the job you want you need to know to how to answer this question for yourself, and how to answer this question for the interviewer.

When you can answer this question for yourself, you may say that you deserve the job. You may say you deserve the job because your feet stink. You may say you deserve the job because you want to make a difference. You may say you deserve the job because you have been paying your dues. You may say you deserve the job because you had a poor upbringing. When answering this question for you there are no right or wrong answers. However, the answer you give to the job interviewer may and in most cases should be quite different. I understand that people have this idea they deserve a "break" because they have met with misfortune. I believe that this answer is okay when answering the question for yourself, but it is not okay when giving an answer to an interviewer.

Like many people, I could write a book about my misfortunes. I was born into poverty, and I grew up in a variety of dysfunctional families. For example, I lived in eight different households including both sets of grandparents, mom, dad, aunts, and uncles. I finished high school with a 2.0 at best, and it took me 10 years to get my first degree. During this period I lost jobs, almost went hungry on occasions, lost everything I had and lived on the edge of homelessness. Do I deserve a break for all of this? No, I do not and neither does any one else. What I do deserve is reasonable wages for work performed and the right to pursue success and happiness for my family and myself.

Breaks Come From Overcoming

You do not deserve a break for having misfortunes; you deserve a break for overcoming them. My grades in high school were bad, because I was labeled as "non-college" material. When I took the ACT, I only made a 16, and when I applied to college, many people said I would never get in. I was admitted conditionally to college and I had to take several remedial classes. It took me two years to get off academic probation and as a result, many of my professors thought I would never finish college.

It was not until my sixth year in college that professors realized I was not quitting. I never made above a C in any English class, but here I am writing a book. The fact is, we all have hardships, and the people that get ahead are the ones who keep moving forward. While overcoming my particular hardships, I discovered that I already had a PhD ... I was poor, hungry, and driven. I believe this helped propel my desire to be successful.

I guess that is why, like many people, I enjoy the movie Rocky. The main character has these traits. Sylvester Stallone says the movie is a metaphor for life. If you look around, you will realize this. It gives inspiration to accomplishing personal goals. In short, Rocky confirms the American dream that you can make something out of yourself if you just have enough devotion to your goal.

I hear stories on a daily basis of people who are every day Rockies. They have overcome great obstacles to become extraordinary people. Countless sports figures, politicians, movie stars, millionaires, philanthropist, and intellectuals all fit into this category. Along the way, I have found the PhD attitude develops a warrior/survivor sprit that inspires people.

I do not deserve a job because my life started out bad. I had no control over that. I deserve success because I have mastered the skills needed for success. I have met obstacles and found ways over, through, around, or under them. I have done what I have needed to do to be successful, and I believe you should too.

I mentioned Rocky because this is the type of person that employers are looking for. They want to know you can meet with a problem and solve it. They want to know that you are adept at finding solutions. Employers have problems and it is up to you to show them a better solution to the problems than your competitor.

You deserve the job because you have taken the time to get the necessary skills and knowledge for your career path. You deserve the job because of your previous work experience. You deserve a job because of your new degree or certificate. You deserve a job because of the internship you did and not only did, but you did to the best of your ability even though you may not have been paid for it.

Why You Deserve a Job...

You deserve the job because you have learned everything you can about the job. You deserve the job because you are still learning about your job. You deserve the job because you are constantly bettering yourself by reading more about the job, going to seminars, and joining trade organizations. I know you are improving yourself because you are reading this book and when you finish this book, you will be a better person for reading it. You deserve the job because you are becoming both the best job seeker and the best job candidate. You deserve the job because you are making it your life's mission.

What I would like you to do now is to make a list of reasons why you think you deserve a particular job. This list should be a functional list; it will list the skills you have that will enable you to perform the job. In previous lists, you were asked reasons for why you want the job. Those reasons could have been anything from making more money to having better hours or wanting more responsibility. All of which are fine and all of which apply to you. The reasons you are putting on this new list should apply to the organization you are interviewing with.

This list will list the reasons you deserve the job. This list will include times you have gone the extra mile, or times you took extra classes or read books on your chosen career. This list will not have things like I deserve this job because I was treated badly and I need a break. It will say I deserve this job because I have worked hard and here is a list of my accomplishments. These reasons can include technical skills you have acquired like computer or accounting skills, or non-technical ones like good people skills etc. Doing this will help you to answer the important question, "**Why should I hire you instead of the other applicants?"**

I have a reason for this. I do not want you to list the bad things that happened to you as reasons you deserve your dream job. My primary reason for this is ***you get what you focus on***. I used to work with a manager who had to work every Saturday, and every Saturday he would lose his temper. He would yell and scream at his workers to the point where his face would turn bright red. He would spend all week telling everybody he dreads Saturdays because he loses his cool and acts like a "real ass."

What happened? He spent all week focusing on losing his temper, and when Saturday came around, that is exactly what he would do. The words he would yell out on Saturday in a fit of rage damaged his relationships with his employees and it set the climate in his business's environment. His attitude and temper also affected the performance of his employees, often not intentionally.

Since the workers were not performing the manager would lose his temper again. I believe his customers could sense when something was not right and then they felt uncomfortable, so they did not want to come to spend the Saturday in an uncomfortable environment. Then the customers would complain, which would make the manager mad, and he would go and yell at the employee again. Then the employee would get mad and treat the customer with less than good service and then another customer would complain and that brings us back to where we started. What does this have to with your list? It has to do with ***focus***. The manager always got what he focused on. Just like you will get what you focus on.

What does all this have to do with why someone should hire you instead of your competition? Let me see if I can pull it together and make sense of it for you. Being prepared gives you an edge over your competition. It also gives you an edge over your own perception of yourself. Being able to clearly define things is an asset. You no longer need to say I deserve this job because I deserve "a break." You know to say I deserve this job because I have done this, this, and that. I deserve this job because I have learned how to turn problems into solutions. I deserve this job because even though I may lack actual job experience, I do have the specialized knowledge, and I have learned the value of persistence. I deserve this job because it is my mission in life to function in this position and I have committed myself to learning all I can about the profession.

I deserve this job because unlike the other job candidates who may appear to be more qualified, they lack the creativity, motivation, and energy I possess. I deserve this job because I am committed to becoming the best in the industry by focusing my dominant thoughts on how to improve my vocation, my company, and myself.

In this chapter, I have discussed why an organization should hire you instead of the other qualified applicants. When answering this question, remember not put down other people. This question should be answered in a way that shows your dedication, experience, knowledge, and willingness to not only do the job, but to do the job well.

KAPS

➢ When answering this question you should not put other people down.
➢ When answering this question you should be able to clearly articulate your abilities, experiences, and knowledge related to a given position.

Exercise: Write out your own answer to this question: "Why should I hire you?" Do this several times until you have the perfect answer and then commit it to memory.

Chapter 13

How to Target Your Job Search

The ability to effectively target your market is necessary if you are committed to finding your dream job and making it reality. Depending on your dream job, you may need to focus on an industry, vocation, company, position, or a combination of these elements. Not everyone reading this book will have the same dream job; we are all different, and we all want different jobs for different reasons, which I believe is wonderful.

It takes all types of jobs for our society to operate properly and we need all of them. I would say as long as your dream job is honest, moral, and legal it is a worthwhile profession and a noble pursuit. Since we all have different dream jobs, I will give you the principles that will help you target your market no matter what your dream job is.

You may be thinking that you could work for just about anyone and this is not important. I believe it is important. For example, could you imagine a dress shop trying to sell dresses to lumber jacks? Could you imagine a meat company having a display at a vegetarian conference? Do you think these people would be successful selling their product? Successful businesses know the value of targeting their markets, and since you are a successful job-candidate, you need to know that you should target your market and you need to know how to target your market.

Target marketing involves two things: First you need to clearly define your target market(s); there may be more than one customer that you can sell your product to or more than one employer you can go to work for. Secondly, you must set clear goals. Setting clear goals is absolutely necessary.

An understanding of how to segment a market is vital to your success in this area. How do you segment a market? The first thing you need to do is understand your product. In this case, the product is you, and by now you should have a better understanding of your product. The second you thing you need is to know what your dream job is. I will remind you that until you make a definite commitment and decide what you want out of life, life will never give you what you want or deserve. Remember the world will make a path for the person who knows what they want.

Defining Your Target Market

Step one of defining your target market is you must know what your customers look like. I am not talking about physical traits. It does not matter if the interviewer is 5'10", 165 lbs, with brown hair, blue eyes, and a big noise. What matters is the type of organization you find attractive and how you want to invest your time, energy, and effort with that organization. Do you want to work in a large multinational firm, a smaller local startup, or somewhere in between? Where is the company's headquarters and do you want to work there? Most importantly, does the company have the position, one similar, or are they willing to create the position for you?

How To Start

You are probably wondering how to start this step. The first step is to make a list of organizations you would like to work for. If you need help in compiling this list go to the yellow pages, look at industry directories, talk to friends, look on the internet, go to job-fairs, or read newspapers and magazines. Try to incorporate as many sources as you can to aid in your brainstorming. Many people worry about whether there are job openings, but at this point, it doses not matter if they have advertised openings for the position you want. As a matter of fact, much of the research on the subject claims that the majority of all jobs are filled without any advertisement about the position.

At this point, you should be concerned with locating potential customers to sell your labor to. Even though you only need one job, the list you create should not reflect that. The list you create in this step should include as many organizations as you can think of because you want to create possibilities. Possibilities are the foundation of choices, and success is directly related to the number of choices you see. This is why you want to create choices and not limit your choices. After you have done this, you will need to profile the organization you are considering for employment. To do this profiling ask questions like the following about the organization:

- ➤ Is this organization publicly or privately held?
- ➤ Does this organization have a long-term competitive advantage?
- ➤ How many people are employed by the organization?
- ➤ What product or services do they offer?
- ➤ What is the organizational hierarchy like?
- ➤ What is the organizational culture like?
- ➤ What are the annual sales of the organization?
- ➤ What room is there for advancement?
- ➤ What do I have to offer this organization?
- ➤ What does this organization have to offer me?
- ➤ Do I believe in the value of those products or services?
- ➤ What originally attracted you to this type of firm?

This information will be useful in the interview, because it will show the interviewer that you are willing to take initiative. This also indicates that you take great care when making decisions. It shows that you look for solid reasons when making decisions. The last question is especially important because it will help you determine if you want to work for that organization.

If your dream job involves a geographic location you will need to look for areas that will support your occupation. If you wanted to be the captain of a yacht, you probably could not find a job in Phoenix, no matter how hard you tried. There just are not enough oceans in Arizona to support the industry. Some people dream of living on a farm, and those people would have a hard time finding work on Wall Street. I'm sure there are people living on a farm that would love to work on the floor of the New York Stock Exchange, but the commute from central Kansas is just too long. The geographic region has to be able to support your occupation. If it does not, you have three choices: move and live your dream, change your dreams, or remain a "wandering generality".

It is important to use the five P's of magic marketing when defining your target market. I know this may be redundant, but when it comes to getting your dream job, I want you to have all of the advantages. The first P is place. This is where you want to work, geographically and industrially. The second P is product, and in this context it is a person and that person is YOU. The third P is price, or how much you can reasonably sell your labor for. The fourth P is position, which is the vocation, job, or career you are seeking, and for the purpose of this book, it is the most important because it is a major component of you living your dreams. The fifth P is People, and you should always remember that people are the heart of the job-hunting process.

Goal Setting

Step two in defining your target market is setting goals. Some people say that the number one reason people do not have their dream jobs is because they have not made a definite decision. If that were true then not setting effective goals would be a very close second. I think they are related because when you make a definite decision to pursue a career path then you have set a goal. However, you may have never been taught how to effectively set goals. In essence, you are being expected to go somewhere you never have been without a map, a compass, a vehicle, or any other support.

When I am talking about setting effective goals, what I am talking about is clear, well defined goals, with clear objectives, clear measurements, and clear expectations that can be reasonably met. Successful businesses set a target, which is a goal, and to be a successful individual you need to set a target and then work towards accomplishing that target (goal). Why do people not set goals? According to the nation's leader of motivation, Zig Ziglar, there are four primary obstacles. They are fear, a poor self-image, underestimating the importance of goals, and not knowing how. Reading this book and other books like it will help you overcome these obstacles. Reading books like this will reinforce the importance of setting goals. I will help you overcome these obstacles in this next section by explaining what I call the 7 elements of effective goal setting.

The 7 Elements of Effective Goal Setting

Desire

This is the starting point for all great adventures. Columbus had a desire to find a new route to India. It is the same desire that will turn your acorn sized ideas into oak tree sized realties. It is desire that creates power and it is this desire that will push you to victory.

Belief

If you think can, you might be able to, but if you believe you can, nothing will stop you. I believe that a **lack of belief in yourself is the only obstacle between you and what you want to accomplish**. When you believe in yourself and what you want to accomplish, you will wake up one day and find that the world is making a way for you.

Belief is more than just saying, "I believe." A belief is marked by action, like the story about Zumbrati, a great tightrope walker who walked a tightrope across Niagara Falls. It was a cold windy day and he was worried that he might not make it across. As he made it across there was a man on the other side who meet Zumbrati with a wheelbarrow and said, "Zumbrati, I believe you could have walked that tightrope pushing a wheelbarrow."

Zumbrati thanked the man for his confidence and assured him that he could not walk across the tightrope pushing a wheelbarrow. The man was persistent and finally

Zumbrati said, "You really believe I can?" The man said, "I sure do." Then Zumbrati said, "Do you *really* believe I can?" The man said, "I believe you can without a doubt." Then Zumbrati agreed and said, "Since you believe I can let's make this a really great stunt. Why don't you get in the wheelbarrow and I will push you across the falls." The man did not get in.

He didn't get in because he did not really believe. When you believe you can do something you are getting in the wheelbarrow. A belief is a belief when you whole-heartedly know what you believe is the truth and then you do what is necessary to make that belief a reality.

Write it Down

This part makes your goals concrete. By writing your goals down, setting a deadline, and signing your name, you have made it a commitment. Jim Carrey had a goal to make 20 million dollars. He wrote a check to himself, signed it, and postdated it. Guess what? He cashed that check. How is that for specific?

Push the Limits

Often people set their goals way too low. There is no challenge in that. Make your goals something challenging. Set the bar where you can barely touch it with your fingertips. When you set your goals too low, you are stealing from yourself. You are not ever going to get what you could have had if you had tried just a little harder.

I have read crime stories about computer hackers who have used their abilities and talents to steal millions of dollars from banks just to be caught and sent to jail. I read in the newspaper about con artists that sell bogus investment plans. I hear about counterfeiters that get caught printing money and then have to spend the rest of their of lives in jail. I have even heard about a counterfeiter who painted one hundred bills by hand. The irony is he would spend as much as a day or two on just one bill.

These people not only stole from society, but they stole from themselves. They all had talent they could have used in a legal business. I believe these people could have been great entrepreneurs, but like many people, they wanted the easy way out, and what they got was hard time. The truth is you can steal from yourself and never get caught. No one will ever know that you did not live your goals. Actually, you may be the only person who knows that you cheated yourself by not living up to your fullest potential.

I believe to prevent this you should want to push the limits of what have been accomplished before. I believe you can accomplish more than what you are currently demonstrating. When we are talking about pushing the limits, remember the words of Lou Holtz when he said, "*if what you did yesterday seems big, you have not done anything today.*"

Break it Down.

Have landmarks on the way to your ultimate destination and reward yourself for little accomplishments. This does two things. The first thing it does is it helps you to measure your progress. The second thing it does is motivate you to continue. *Remember, the only way you can climb Mount Everest is one step at a time.* You accomplish goals the same way.

The reason you break it down is because it is not what you do every now and then that makes you successful; it is what you do regularly that makes you a success. You do not lose fifty pounds by occasionally skipping dessert, and you do not put on fifty pounds by occasionally having dessert.

People who run marathons didn't start running on a whim. They didn't decide to train a month before race day. Dedicated runners not only run every day, but they keep running logs and they log their daily distance and time. They note the weather conditions and the way they felt that particular day. In order to win a marathon, you not only need to become an elite runner, but you must become a goal setter who believes they can make the goal and are willing to push the limits in order to do so. Marathon runners aren't weekend warriors. They are an elite class of goal setting athletes.

I told you about running because it relates to breaking your goals down. You have hurdles to overcome when you are training for a race. When you are in the process of finding your dream job and making it a reality, you will have hurdles. You may not be able to go out right after you finish this book and get your dream job, but you will be able to get your dream job if you start working and accomplishing the little goals that will make up the big goal.

Believe me when I say that there will be hurdles that you will have to overcome, but it is overcoming those hurdles that will separate you from the millions of people who do not dare to live their dream. The fact is those hurdles will be there, and goal setting is your way over, under, and around them. So, break your goals downs one hurdle at a time, and determine the best way to attack that hurdle and success will be much easier and much more attainable.

Plan to Win.

In order for you to accomplish your goals, you must have a plan. This plan will enable you to overcome obstacles. If your plan doesn't work the first time that is okay; it just means you are one step closer to accomplishing your goal. A plan that doesn't work is not a sign of failure. A plan that doesn't work is a sign of progress because you are figuring out what does not work first. You may need to adjust your plan from time to time. That is okay; it means you are discovering new choices, possibilities, and most importantly new opportunities to explore.

Planning takes time. Not only does it take time, but it also requires knowledge and experience. In addition, planning should also take into account the obstacles that are in the way and changes that may occur in the environment. While you may not see all the obstacles in the road ahead, you should try to uncover as many as you can. Instead of thinking of them as obstacles, think of them as opportunities or challenges. Personally, I do not believe in obstacles; I believe in opportunity. Where most people see an obstacle, I see an opportunity to overcome and a greater level of success to be gained. You see, the greater the difficulty the greater the success. That is why when I meet an obstacle, I am thankful because I know I will receive a greater reward for overcoming it.

Be Persistent.

It is more than a cliché to say that *people do not fail, but they quit before they are successful.* Being persistent is rewarded by success. It took me ten years to get my marketing degree. People used to ask me, "Why don't you quit?" The fact is no one would have thought less of me for quitting, because I obviously just "couldn't grasp the material." I could have said, "At least I tried."

The real fact is at the time I just lacked direction. It would have been easy to quit, but where would I be now if I had quit? The answer is nowhere. This also means that I would not be here talking to you today. If I had quit, I would have never gone to graduate school, I would have never gained the benefits of having a graduate degree, and I would be living a mediocre life at best.

The truth is I may have finished sooner if I had had someone to pay my tuition, if I hadn't partied as much, or if I had come from a supportive family. I would agree these factors could and typically do play an important part in success. However, they are not as important as having direction and a definite purpose, mixed with effective goal setting.

When I started to develop these traits, finishing started to become easier. I remember one year during finals week I had to work the 4 p.m. to 4 a.m. shift in a warehouse. I had two finals that semester at 8:00 a.m. on two consecutive days, work was a 45-minute drive each way, and I still had to study. So what did I do? I stayed up for 48 hours studying and working.

After that week, I analyzed my job, and thought about what I really wanted to accomplish with my life. It was a hard decision because at the time I was making eleven dollars an hour, which was the most money I had ever made in my life up to that point. I had to recognize the fact that the job did not fit my long-term goals, and I decided I needed take a short-term cut in pay. I had to believe that a college degree would yield greater rewards later. As a result, I left that warehouse, took a pay cut, and worked at finishing my degree.

The point of this section is to develop persistence, and persistence is more than doing something for a long time. Persistence is doing something every day. Persistence is what it takes to get the things done now that you need to get done, so that one day you can do the things you want to do when you want to do them. When you finally develop the habit of persistence, you will find a way to overcome any obstacle even if it means not doing the things you normally enjoy doing or deem necessary.

This could mean not sleeping when you would like to sleep, going out with friends, having the nicest clothes, or driving the newest car. It also means developing new and improved priorities that reflect what you want to accomplish, and developing a vision of what and who you want to become and then not straying from that vision. Most importantly, it is recognizing that the only real obstacle between you and your dream job is a lack of a belief, and the only reason you will not succeed is if you quit too soon.

Now you should have a better idea of how to use this information to get started, but remember to stay committed to learning more about the goal setting process. Lets review this chapter. In this chapter we learned how to target certain areas of the job market. This involves two things. The first is to define your product, which is defining who you are and what you can do for an organization. The second thing is setting goals and we just finished talking about goals along with why they are important and how to effectively set goals. To close out this chapter I will offer some thoughts on targeting your market.

One Last Thought About Targeting Your Market

Keep in mind that there is an unlimited number of ways to market yourself in today's job market. When targeting your market you should think about what marketing strategies you wish to use. Some of these strategies may have financial or time constraints.

That is why you should be careful when you are in the process of analyzing your options and deciding which ones fit your situation best.

This process also includes deciding how long you plan to run your marketing campaign and how you plan to evaluate your marketing campaign. To put it another way, how long do you think it will take you to find your dream and make a reality? This may include developing alternative and creative ways of marketing yourself if you are not getting the results you desire. The truth is you do not know how well a marketing tactic will work until you try it.

Regardless of the strategy you develop and implement, remember that all great marketing starts with what you are trying to sell. Use what I call the **PAM technique.** This technique is made up of Product, Advantages, and Marketing (PAM). The way this works is you define your product, which in this case is you, and then you highlight your advantages, and then you market those advantages. This strategy focuses on you as a valuable product, and the success of this technique is dependent on how well you develop and define your product (yourself).

It could be that you have a lot of education and experience in your dream job. If this is the case it will be easy to use the PAM technique. It could be that you are entering an industry or starting a new career path. If this is the case you will need to clearly define your potential and you will need to focus on selling your potential rather than trying to cover up your lack of experience or education. No matter your situation, it is important to target your market. The narrower the focus the better chance you have of being successful. At the same time, constantly look for new and better ways to market yourself, and remember that you can combine, take away, or do what you need to do to get a marketing strategy to work for your own unique situation.

KAPS

- ➤ To effectively market yourself you need to define your target market. This may mean a specific industry, organization, or geographic location depending on what your dream job is.
- ➤ To effectively market yourself you need to set specific, clear, and written goals that are measurable, attainable, realistic, and include a deadline for accomplishment.
- ➤ To effectively market yourself you should remember the PAM technique, which is product, advantages, and marketing. You define your product, determine its advantages, and market those advantages.
- ➤ To effectively market yourself you should realize that there is no one best way to do it. Your market strategy is dependent upon your unique situation.

Chapter 14

How to Develop a
Compelling Message

What is a compelling message? A compelling message is a four-part message that gets people interested in what you are marketing. Part 1 arouses the attention of the reader so that the reader becomes interested in what you have to say. Part 2 establishes a connection with the person. Part 3 establishes credibility. Part 4 generates a desire that should lead to the phone call or email for the interview.

The goal of this chapter is to teach you how to grab someone's attention and keep it. While much of this chapter will be directly related to what you put into your cover letters and resumes, the same concepts can and should be applied to your other forms of communication including interpersonal, written, phone, and email messages.

How to Develop a Headline

The purpose of your headline or attention getter is to attract someone's attention. The headline should clearly introduce the message, be easily understood, and it should relate to the reader's problem. In your case it should show how you are the best candidate for position because of your ability to solve the reader's problem.

The headline for your job-hunting message will most likely include your name, address, phone number, and career objective. This will be placed in the objective part of your resume, cover letter, business cards, follow up letters, and all other personal marketing materials. The headline should be short and to the point. Your headline could be **bold face**, or *italicized* or ***both.***

> Your headline should stand out and focus your reader's attention on the message you are sending.

You should try to get your headline to be spine tingling. You should create a headline that conjures mental pictures, arouses emotions, and most importantly it should be easy to read. Most people, when trying to develop a compelling message, especially when they are preparing their job-hunting materials, try to impress the reader with jargon. Do not do this because at best it makes your marketing material hard to read, and at worse it makes you sound arrogant and possibly difficult to work with.

I believe one reason we do this is in school we are taught to use logic, reason, and our intellect. The truth is people make decisions based on emotions. It is a rare occasion that someone buys a product or hires a person because of logic alone. It is because of emotions that we build what are called neuro-associations. These are emotional states that we associate with certain words, pictures, actions, or settings. This is also why recovering alcoholics drink a lot of coffee, soft drinks, or something else. They do this because they are used to drinking and having something in their hand. Smokers do the same thing when trying to quit by chewing gum or eating more. These are all neuro-associations, and to be an effective marketer you want to have positive neuro-associations associated with yourself.

If you don't believe me, start looking at ads and see how many ads try to associate their product with emotions. The most popular is sex, because sex is one of the strongest emotions. Since sex is the most pleasurable of all emotional states it is no accident that sex sells. Now I am not saying to put a sexy picture of yourself on your resume. You need to be tactful, but if you can find a way to associate pleasure with hiring you, the avoidance of pain by not hiring you, or a combination of both you stand a better chance of getting the job. The headline you use in your personal marketing materials needs to be short and simple while gaining the reader's attention. You must gain the reader's attention; if you do not, there is a good chance that your cover letter and resume will be headed to the trash.

Roles of Headlines in Marketing Yourself

What roles can headlines play in your personal marketing material? There are four primary types of headlines. They are the advantage, knowledge, provocative, and reference headlines. These are classified by the message they are delivering.

The **advantage headline** assures the reader that you have something valuable to offer them, whether it is a unique ability or characteristic, or certain ideas or knowledge that will make you profitable to the organization. The message assists the reader's understanding of you. An example would be: "**Ten years experience in turning sales leads into sales results**."

The **knowledge headline** announces your specialized knowledge about a particular field of interest to the employer you are contacting. An example of this would be "**An exciting and motivated problem solver with proficiency in Microsoft office, HTML, and all other windows-based software.**"

The **provocative headline** arouses the reader's curiosity. The reader will want to learn more so they will keep reading. This is typically accomplished by asking a question. An example of this would be: "**Can I keep deadlines and work well with others? Yes I can! Can I find ways to improve efficiency in my job? You bet I can!** This is most effective when you are asking questions that will be the solution to a known problem that the prospective employer wants you to solve.

The **reference headline** gives your reader some sort of shared knowledge. This is a great headline because it will act as the first step in developing rapport with the person reading your personal marketing materials. An example of this would be "**My professor Dr. Markham has informed me of the position at your firm, and he feels that my education, experience, and talents would be a perfect match with your organization.**" In fact, this very headline got me a job with a nationally recognized ad agency working on their account with a fast food chain you may have heard of . . . Taco Bell.

These four headlines can be used in a number of ways. They are most effective when you combine them and add your own personal touch to them. Creativity in the job search is a great asset. While creativity is important, remember that you do not have to reinvent the wheel. There are a number of books on the market that address the topic of writing resumes and cover letters if you get stuck. I recommend checking one out from your local library or buying one.

Arousing Interest

Now that you have the reader's attention it is time for you to arouse their interest. The job-hunting experience is a marketing experience and just as effective marketing is well planned, your job hunting needs to be well planned, and that is why your ad needs to arouse your audience's interest. To keep a person's interest you can try asking questions, quoting statistics, using a quotation, or sharing personal experiences that relate to the position you are applying for. To make sure it relates to the position remember that responding to the requirements of the job posting will go a long way in keeping your reader's interest.

Now that you caught your reader's interest, they will want to hear what you have to say. This is what people in advertising call the body copy. This is where the selling starts. For your body copy to be compelling you need to speak to the reader's self interest, and explain how you can solve their problem and make their life better.

Experts cite the following 9 techniques for writing compelling advertising copy:

1. Stress one major theme.
2. Clearly state what position(s) you are applying for.
3. Call attention to your strengths and how you can benefit the organization.
4. Use your name. This will help the reader to remember you by name and this will make you a person and not just a piece of paper.
5. Keep your writing lean and mean. Tell the whole story and nothing more. When you are finished saying what you have to say-- stop.
6. Use bullet points if possible.
7. Follow this public speaking pattern: tell them what you are going to tell them, tell them, and then tell them what you told them.
8. Make sure your grammar is perfect. Do not give them a reason to put you in the TBNT (Thanks But No Thanks) pile.
9. Put the most important information first. You only have a few seconds to catch the reader's attention.

The Three Body Styles

Just as there are different headline types, there are different body styles. They are straight-sell, philosophy, and story line body. In the **straight sell** you immediately explain the headline by listing what the employer desires and what you can do to fulfill that desire. It is a factual presentation with the emphasis on problem solving. It is particularly useful when the employer has a list of qualifications and you meet all of the qualifications. An example of this would look be:

You seek:	I Have:
A Bachelor's Degree	BBA: Business Administration
3 years experience	I have four years retail experience
Computer Skills	Microsoft training, A+ certification

The **philosophy copy** promotes you as being able to fit into the corporate climate or culture. It can also paint a broad overview of your personal goals and how this job will lend itself to accomplishing your personal goals. Employers like this because you can make company goals personal goals and successful employers understand that we all work harder when are trying to reach our goals. An example of this would be "**Because of my childhood experiences, I understand the importance of guiding our youth. I** understand the need young people have for mentors and guidance. That is why I am applying for your parent support position."

The last example we will discuss is the **story line**. This narrative style is ideal for the creative person. It gives you a chance to be creative and explores the boundaries of what has been done before. It will set up a situation and then resolve the situation. An example of this would be "**Are you tired of searching for the one employee who can consistently get the job done? Are you to the point where you believe that self-motivated people are outdated? If you are to that point then I can help! I am consistently getting the job done on time. I am self-motivated and I am ready to work. Call me today!**

The last element to a compelling message is developing your own personal catch phrase. This is often referred to as a slogan or tag line. No matter what you call it, it should be used so that when someone hears the line they think of you. Some slogans I have used are:

> Helping turn acorn-sized ideals into oak tree sized realties.
> The difference that makes a difference.
> Closing training and communication gaps.

Notice that some of them are not that original. While originality is great, selling yourself is more important, and if that means using something a little more generic, that is okay. I like to use slogans that have visual appeal. People respond better to visual stimulation and if they can make a visual connection to what you are saying then they are going to be able to remember it better.

In addition, you should make your slogans short, easy to read, easy to remember, and they should make a clear point. Catch phrases or slogans will make your marketing memorable. Remember they are short, simple, easy to repeat, and they conjure mental pictures in the minds of the listeners.

If you want to know what compelling ads (resumes and cover letters) look like for a job hunter I have a few listed in the appendix of this book. Look through them and see what you can use for your own job-hunting materials. I also have included a list of action words that will make your message come alive. Remember not to limit yourself because the only limits on people are the ones they place on themselves.

To close this chapter I will remind you that it is important to develop a compelling message. This message needs to be used in all of your communication. While creativity is good, getting the job you want is great. So, do not spend all of your energy trying to be too creative. Focus more on the job you want and how you should go about getting that job.

KAPS

> A compelling message is a four-part message.
> A compelling message gets the reader's attention.
> A compelling message effectively markets you to the person hiring you.
> A compelling message makes use of slogans or catch phrases.

Chapter 15

How to Be Creative
In Your Job Search

Creativity lights the world. Thomas Edison was one of the most creative men who ever lived, and he used his creativity to find his dream job and make it a reality. Mr. Edison, with only three months of formal schooling, found the creativity he needed to be a great scientist/inventor. Thomas Edison is famous for his development of the first electric light bulb. He is also given credit for creating the world's first "invention factory" where he and his partners would work day and night inventing things like the movie projector, phonograph, and the Universal Stock Printer.

Many people think that stories about people like Edison are rare. I am not sure if I believe that. I believe the world is full of success stories and the good news is you can become a success story if you want to. When you look around you, you will see the result of the work of creative people. The clothes you are wearing, the TV shows you watch, the radio you listen to, the car you drive, and the food you eat are all the result of someone's creative effort.

You Really Are Creative

If you look in the mirror, you will see another creative person. That's right; you are creative. The problem is you may not know it because people are not born creative. People become creative. If you do not believe me, stop reading and look in today's newspaper. Go to the birth announcement section and see if any creative people were born today. It would be my guess that only girls and boys were born today.

I believe people are taught to believe they are either creative or not creative. It is sad that some people go through life believing they are not creative. Someone else placed this negative and self-limiting label on them, and the result is they spend the rest of their life proving that person right. You may have had a teacher, parent, boss, or some other person tell you that you are just not creative. If this has happened or is happening to you stop believing the lies. I believe if you believe in yourself and in your ability to develop your own unique form of creativity, then you will become a creative person who can accomplish anything you put your mind to. If you are not as creative as you would like to be I will give you some insights on how to become more creative.

Can being creative help you in finding your dream job and making it a reality? Have you ever heard of someone being famous for his or her lack of creativity? You might be thinking I do not want to be famous, so what does being creative have to do with me? It has a lot to do with you. If you are applying for a job and you are more creative in developing solutions than the other people applying for the same job, you should get the job. However, the prospective employer needs to be made aware of your creativity and how you can use that creativity on the job.

Creativity is not reserved for individuals who want to be rich and famous. Creativity is for anyone who wants to live his or her dreams. What matters right now is that you have made the decision to pursue your dream job and to live the life you deserve to live. Once you have made this decision you should no longer settle for the results you have been getting. If you want different results you need to do something different, and doing something different will require creativity.

Creativity Defined

The question at hand is what is creativity. According to the dictionary, creativity is having the ability or power to create things. It is something that is characterized by originality, expressiveness, and imagination. **Notice the definition does not say creativity it is reinventing the wheel.** So, in your endeavor to be creative, do not waste your time trying to reinvent the wheel.

Look to see what organizations are currently doing to market their services or products, and then ask yourself how you can apply this to finding a job. Life is too short to engineer all new ways of doing things. I'm not saying to copy other people's ideas, but I am suggesting that you look at what has been done before and see what you can do to improve it and make it your own. If someone said something or did something that you cannot do better, use it, give them proper credit, and move on. What is the creative process? The creative process is a series of key ideas that will help you become creative. I have put these ideas into five concepts that should help you build creativity into your life. If you are going to live your dreams, you will need to build your creativity.

Building Your Creative Muscles

Build your creative muscles. In the chapter about decisions, I mentioned that you might need to build your decision-making muscles. In a way, being creative is like making decisions. They are similar because the number one reason people do not make decisions is because their decision-making muscles are weak. The same is true with most people's creative muscles. They are flabby and weak, and in some cases, people have not used their creative muscles since childhood.

Don't Be a Know it All

Do not be a know it all. If there is one thing that stifles creativity, it is knowing everything there is to know about a subject. If you know everything there is to know, what else is there to be discovered? The truth is you will never know everything about any subject you study because it is virtually impossible to know everything about any subject. I believe you can study in order to now more than most people about a subject. While I believe you can become an expert I do not believe that you will know everything. So let go of your ego.

Nurture Your Creativity

Nurture your creativity. This means you should create an environment that is supportive of your creativity. This thought recognizes the importance of both nurture and nature. For years, there have been debates on the subject. One person says it is natural ability, the next person says it is because of nurturing. I believe they are both right and have solid arguments. I personally believe that creativity is a combination of both. If you create an environment that will nurture your ideas, you will become more creative.

Start the Creativity Habit

Make it a habit to be creative. **Myth**: creativity just comes and goes and there is nothing that can be done about it. **Fact**: creativity is a habit, and when you get in the habit of being creative it will be easier to be creative when you want to be.

Our lives are controlled by the habits we develop. You may have a bad habit that you would like to quit. It could be smoking, drinking, drugs, or overeating. No matter what it is, the reason you have not stopped is because it is a habit. It is part of your daily routine. You do it without thinking about it. The good news is you can change habits. Here is your chance replace the old habit of non-creativity with the new habit of creativity.

Make it a habit to do something creative everyday. Make a habit of doing something creative at the same time of the day. For example, when writing this book I would write at least one hour five days a week. I would do it at the same time on the same days every week. The end result was a completed manuscript. The habit of writing enabled me to finish a book that is impacting the lives of individuals across the country.

What can you do to be creative? Learn to like new foods or try a new hobby. Take up cooking, dancing, or reading. Trying new things will help you become creative. I should warn you that doing drugs or drinking is not a way to get in the habit of being creative. It is getting in the habit of being destructive. I know because I used to drink and like a lot of people I thought it was helping me be more creative, but the only thing it created for me was problems. Looking back, most of my major mistakes and some of the biggest failures in my life came from drinking and the lifestyle associated with it. Remember no one ever said, "Things were going really bad, then I started drinking and my life turned around for the best." Therefore, don't kid yourself and think that drugs or drinking will increase your creativity.

The Two Types of Creativity

There are two basic types of creativity. The first is spontaneous creativity, which is coming up with a completely new idea, or concept. This is the least common form of creativity, however, it can be the most exciting. With this form of creativity comes an infusion of emotions and ideas, with a stimulus that can move mountains. This elusive form of creativity is without a doubt hard to manifest. The second form of creativity is derived creativity, which is rearranging old concepts, ideas, or plans into new ones. Let's talk about spontaneous creativity first.

You can tap into spontaneous creativity only if you know what you want out of life. The key to spontaneous creativity is focus. Once you can focus in on what you want out of life then you can begin creating a vision for how to get what you want out of life. This will create the forces necessary to put spontaneous creativity into action. Remember life is energy, and whether we know it or not our thought impulses are energy. The same energy makes up the universe.

You are probably asking, "Jason, what are you talking about?" Let me explain, all forms of matter and energy are made up of atoms, and all atoms have particles that move around the nucleus. These particles can be spilt and the energy that is released can destroy a city, like what happened twice in Japan during WWII, or it can create electricity like the nuclear power plants. An atom has three potential states. In the first state, it can remain an atom, and nothing will happen to it. In the second state it can be destructive, and in the third state it can be constructive. In the same way, you have three potential states:

you can do nothing with your life, you can be destructive with your life, or you can be constructive with your life. The choice is yours.

This concept is extremely important. I know it may be hard to understand such an abstract concept, but you have to be able to understand it if you are to begin the process of spontaneous creativity. Remember that your thoughts are energy. The only difference between your thoughts and the material world around you is the way you organize that energy. I do not believe you can think a material object into existence, but I do believe that your thoughts are made up of the cosmic material that has fashioned the universe, our world, and everything in it together. I also believe that you can channel that energy to get the life, job, and results you deserve.

Derived Creativity

The second form of creativity is derived creativity. How do you use derived creativity? First, you develop a keen sense of understanding of many different subjects. Learn all you can and then cross apply the knowledge you gain from one field to the next. Marketers use this form of creativity quite often. They sell the products to different demographics at different prices. To do this they look outside their industries and research what people are doing to sell products and services in an unrelated industry, and then they use those same strategies in their industries.

What does this mean to you as a job hunter? It means that you should look to see how people in other industries look for new and rewarding careers. Then see if it would be appropriate for someone in your industry to do the same. Look not only at job hunters, but also look to see what grassroots or personal marketing businesses are doing. Then analyze your job hunting and see what you can do to apply those techniques. The more you see what creativity looks like, the easier it will be for you to develop your creative talents.

Whether you use spontaneous creativity or derived creativity, it is important to be creative. Your creative job-hunting efforts should be an indication of what you can do on the job. Your creativity can and should give you an edge in the job market. On the other hand, your lack of creativity can handicap you. I believe that the job you want awaits you. It is out there and all you need to do is to develop your creativity and discover a way to go out and get it.

KAPS

➤ You are a creative person; you may just need to develop your creative muscles.
➤ Creativity is a habit.
➤ Drugs and alcohol do not make you more creative.
➤ There are two kinds of creativity: spontaneous creativity and derived creativity.
➤ Creativity is a powerful force that provides you with the energy, drive, and motivation to get things done.

Chapter 16

Creating Resumes and Cover Letters That Give You The Edge

Creating A Resume That Will Give You the Edge

Many people think of resumes as an obstacle between them and their dream job, but you do not have to think of them that way. Think of a resume as your opportunity for a first impression. I believe that resumes are not ways to keep you from a job; they are ways for you to show an organization what you know, what you can do, and most importantly how you can solve the their problems.

I believe that it is safe to say that organizations want to employ individuals who can do the job. While this is obvious, less obvious is the fact that organizational decision makers want to hire people who fit in. The fact is they are looking for individuals who can fit into and compliment the organization's culture, environment, or climate. In some cases fitting in with the culture or having the right attitude can be more important than experience or knowledge.

When applying for a job you need to remember that the organization has a problem, and by showing that you can solve that problem better than the competition, you have an increased chance of getting the job. If you can do this while also showing that you fit into their culture, you will increase your chances even more. Traditionally employers use resumes as a way to learn that people can solve more problems than they create. Knowing this piece of information puts you miles ahead of the competition who look at the organization hoping the organization can solve their problem of being unemployed.

For your resume to give you an edge it must achieve the following goal: give the organization written evidence of your qualifications, expertise, education and skills, while at the same time indicating that you know how to use those qualifications to help solve the problem at hand. When creating a resume or completing an application form, you need two different kinds of information: facts about yourself and facts about the job you want. With this information in hand, you can present the facts about yourself in terms of the position you are applying for.

Before you can prepare a resume, you need to know yourself. Before you start writing your resume, prepare a SWOT analysis of yourself. If you have not done a SWOT analysis, you may need to take a moment to refer to the chapter that discusses knowing your product. Remember a SWOT is a written assessment of your strengths, weaknesses, opportunities, and threats. Along with a SWOT, you need the following information on virtually every resume or application form:

> ➤ **Current address and phone number.** If you are rarely at home during business hours, put your cell phone number or the number of a friend or relative that will take messages for you. It is best to list only one number, remembering that you are trying to solve a problem, not create one.
> ➤ **The Job sought or career goal**. This is often in the objective or summary of the resume. If you know the job title you are seeking, use it, but if not

make sure it is a problem solving statement. It should establish rapport with the reader and make them want to read the resume. This is what marketers call an attention getter. Please avoid the number one mistake when writing resumes, which is talking about your problem. Remember you are trying to get the interviewer to talk to you about how you can solve *their* problem.

➤ **Your career experiences, paid and volunteer.** This includes dates of employment, name and address of the employer, and your job title. Remember volunteer experience is work experience. On my resume, I list my tenure as Vice-President of Education for Toastmasters International Club 4901, an elected position that required work and effort.

➤ **Education.** Include the school's name, the city in which it is located, the year you graduated, or the years attended along with the diploma or certificate you earned, and the related courses of studies you pursued.

➤ **Other qualifications.** This could include a hobby, organizations you belong to, honors you have received, seminars/workshops or other education, articles published or leadership positions you have held.

➤ **Computer skills, office machines, tools, and equipment you have used and special or technical skills that you possess.** Be specific. If you are skilled with Microsoft Office, Adobe PageMaker, or other specific programs, list them. The fact is the prospective employer is not going to know your skills unless you tell them.

Other information, such as your Social Security number, is often asked for on application forms but is rarely presented on resumes. Application forms might also ask for a record of past addresses and for information that you would rather not reveal, such as a record of convictions. If asked for such information, you should be honest. Honesty does not require that you reveal information not asked for, disabilities or other circumstances that do not affect your qualifications for a job.

Know the Position/Job You Want

Do some research and gather specific information about the position, industry, or organization you are entering. You should know the pay range for the position (this is helpful in the negotiation process so you can make their top your bottom), education, experience required, hours, and shifts usually worked. Most importantly, you need to know the job duties (so that you can describe your experience and education in terms of those duties).

Study the job description. Some job announcements, especially those issued by a government, have a checklist that assigns a numerical weight to different qualifications so that you can be certain as to which is the most important; looking at such announcements will give you an idea of what employers look for even if you do not wish to apply for a government job. If the announcement or ad is vague, do not be afraid to call the organization to learn what they want. Once you have the information you need, you can prepare a resume. Depending on your situation, you may need to prepare more than one master resume. This is especially true if you are searching and willing to accept a variety of positions. If you are preparing a resume for the first time, or later in your career, beginning one can be intimidating. What do you put? What do you not put? Is there a form to follow?

Two Basic Types of Resumes

There are two basic types of resumes; the way you arrange your resume depends upon how well your experience seems to prepare you for the position you want. You can either describe your most recent job first and work backwards (chronological) or group similar skills together (functional).

When laying out your resume, reverse chronology is the easiest method to use. It is also the least effective because it makes when you did something more important than what you can do. It is an especially poor format if you have gaps in your work history, if the job you seek is very different from the job you currently hold, or if you are just entering the job market. About the only time you would want to use this type of resume is if you have progressed up a clearly defined career ladder and want to move up to the next level.

Resumes that are not chronological are typically called functional, analytical, skill oriented, or creative. The differences are less important than the similarities, which is what can you do for the organization. These resumes have an advantage to the potential employer and, therefore, to your job campaign. The organization can see immediately how you will solve their problem. This format also has advantages for many job hunters because it camouflages gaps in employment and avoids giving prominence to irrelevant positions.

You begin writing a functional resume by determining the skills the organization is seeking. Remember the organization is trying to solve a problem. Again, study the job description for this information. Next, review your experience and education to see when you demonstrated the skills sought. Then prepare the resume itself, putting first the information that relates most obviously to the job. The result will be a resume with headings such as "Engineering," "Computer Languages," "Communications Skills," or "Design Experience." The heading will be dependent upon the industry and job sought. I believe that these headings will have much more of an impact than the dates that are found on a chronological resume. A functional resume makes what you did more important than when you did it. No matter which format you use, the following advice applies.

- ➢ **Use specifics**. A vague description of your duties will only make a vague impression.
- ➢ **Identify accomplishments**. If you headed a project, improved productivity, reduced costs, increased membership, or achieved some other goal, say so.
- ➢ **Type your resume**. It is best to use a standard typeface. If your field is creative and lends to a creative type, it is okay to be bold. Just be sure it will be seen as appealing and not unprofessional.
- ➢ **Keep it short and simple**. Keep the length down to two pages at most. The ideal resume is one page, but do not limit yourself. Often, the higher up in the organization the job you are seeking is, the longer your resume is permitted to be.
- ➢ **Be positive**. Remember your mother's advice not to say anything if you cannot say something nice. Leave all embarrassing or negative information off the resume, but be ready to deal with it in a positive fashion at the interview.

➤ **Proofread.** Read the master copy carefully, and have someone else proofread the master copy carefully. Proofread not only for grammar but for flow as well. A good way to proofread for grammar and punctuation is to read what you wrote from the bottom up. This prevents your brain from automatically inserting what should be there. You cannot proofread your resume too much, and if grammar is a problem, get help!

➤ **Appearance.** Use the best quality photocopying machine or printer to which you have access. If possible, use laser or laser quality printing equipment and good quality white or off-white paper.

➤ **References.** Often just a statement that references are available will suffice. If your references are familiar to the person who will read the resume, their names may be worth listing depending on the relationships and organizational cultures involved.

It is important to include all of the basic information on your resume. However, what is also important is the way you say it. Do not use dull, lifeless statements. Instead, use action words.

Useful Action Words:

Accelerated	Engineered
Achieved	Edited
Advised	Generated
Approved	Implemented
Assisted	Managed
Calculated	Operated
Completed	Organized
Conceived	Planned
Controlled	Revised
Coordinated	Scheduled
Designed	Tested
Developed	Trained
Directed	Verified
Earned	Wrote

These words and the ones listed in the appendix can help you create an impression that will make a positive impact on the person reading your resume or application. They also show how you have been responsible to do various types of jobs and tasks. In other words, these words can show that you are not just a follower, but that you are a leader in the industry. Of course, you should always be truthful. Do not try to oversell yourself by claiming you did things that you did not do.

Applications for Employment

Many organizations will require applications along with resumes. If this is the case you can use your resume as a guide when completing an application. It is also okay to submit a resume even if they just ask for an application. By doing this you can promote your qualifications. Submitting a resume with an application is a good idea because your resume is considered a marketing document. Until you have your dream job you should be constantly marketing yourself. You also want to submit a resume because many people mistakenly think that application forms are just resumes in disguise. They are not the same because applications are considered legal documents.

At first glance, application forms seem to give a job hunter no leeway. The forms certainly do not have the flexibility that a resume does, but you can use them to your advantage. Remember that the attitude of the person reading the form is not, "Let's find out why this person is unqualified," but "Maybe this is the person we want." Use all the parts of the form, the experience blocks, the education blocks, and others to show that the best individual for the position is you.

General advice on completing application forms

➢ Request two copies of the form. If only one is provided, photocopy it before you make a mark on it. You want the application you hand in to be perfect and this is why you will need more than one copy to serve as rough drafts.

➢ Use your best handwriting.

➢ Read the whole form before you start completing it. If you do not know what something means, ask.

➢ Prepare a master copy if several divisions within the same company or organization use the same form. Do not put the specific job applied for, date, and signature on the master copy. Fill in that information on the copies as you submit them. Since applications are legal documents you may have to hand copy each application. The organization has the right to refuse to accept and/or may not accept a photocopied application. However, they may accept a photocopied application if the signature is an original.

➢ Leave no blanks; enter N/A (for "not applicable") when the information requested does not apply to you; this tells people checking the form that you did not simply skip the question. It also shows that you pay attention to detail.

➢ Carry a resume and other frequently asked information (such as previous addresses) with you when visiting potential organizations in case you must fill out an application on the spot.

Creating a Cover Letter that Will Give You the Edge

Along with a resume, you will need a cover letter every time you send a resume or application to a potential employer. The letter should capture the reader's attention, show why you are writing, indicate why your employment will benefit the organization, and it should ask for an interview. Let them know you are serious about joining the organization, you can do the job, and you can fit in with the culture.

Cover letters are more organization-specific than a resume, which means that each cover letter should be written individually. Not only are cover letters designed and created for specific organizations and jobs, you should also take the time and effort to make sure that each letter is typed perfectly, which may present a problem for some people. Again, if grammar is a problem, get help! Libraries have books on grammar and punctuation, and investing even a little time will help you later. Spell-check and Grammar-check are helpful, but they cannot be the only resource you depend on.

To help with the proofreading, have a basic outline you follow and change the organization's address, first paragraph, and specifics concerning qualifications or interview requests. The other items are easily adapted. If you do not have access to computer equipment, you might be able to borrow a friend's, rent one, or go to a library. If you are willing to invest a little money, you might be able to have your letters prepared by a resume or employment services company listed in the yellow pages. My recommendation would be not to depend on such services. While helpful, they may become a handicap later on because knowing how to develop resumes and cover letters is essential to your success. Let's go through a letter point by point.

> **Salutation-** Each letter should be addressed by name to the individual you want to talk with. That individual is the one who can hire you. This is almost certainly not someone in the personnel department, and it is probably not a department head either. It is most likely to be the individual who will actually supervise you once you start work. Call the company to make sure you have the right name, and be sure you spell it correctly.

> **Opening-** The opening should appeal to the reader. In reality, cover letters are sales letters. Sales are made after you capture a person's attention. You capture the reader's attention most easily by talking about the company rather than yourself. Mention projects under development, recent awards, or favorable comments recently published about the company. You can find such information in the business press, including the business section of local newspapers and the many magazines that are devoted to particular industries. If you are answering an ad, you may mention it. If someone suggested that you write, use his or her name (with permission, of course). My wife once applied to work at the Heifer Project International. She made a connection by mentioning field trips she used to take as a child to the Heifer Ranch and by mentioning how much she believed in the work of HPI. This personal connection got her the interview she was after.

> **Body-** The body of the letter gives a brief description of your qualifications and refers to the resume, where your sales campaign can continue. In this section be sure to use specifics and remember what was discussed in chapter 14.

> **Closing-** You cannot have what you do not ask for. At the end of the letter, request an interview. Use a standard complimentary close, such as "Sincerely yours," leave four lines for your signature, and type your name. I would be sure to type my phone number under my name because this makes it easy for the person reading your letter to call you.

> **Remember that attention spans are short**. You have just a few short moments to make an impact with your cover letter and resume. Since the cover letter is what most hiring managers and HR people read first, yours should make the most impact in the shortest time. I believe that you have less than 10 seconds in which to make your reader want to put down your cover letter, pick up the phone and call you for a job interview.

Now that you have read this section you can create a cover letter and resume that will give you edge. Remember that resumes and cover letters are not obstacles, but they are your tools to gain the edge in the job hunt. Resumes and cover letters will be your primary marketing tools in your job search. This is why they need to be flawless and this is why they should be of the highest possible quality.

KAPS

➤ You cannot get the job unless they know who you are.

➤ A resume is a tool used to get the job you want, not an obstacle between you and the job you want.

➤ A cover letter should be organization specific.

➤ Include action verbs in your resume and cover letter

Chapter 17

In order to find your dream job you will need some help along the way. According to the Missouri Work Connections/Career Information Hotline, 48% of all jobs are filled because of friends and family, 24% are filled because of direct contact with employers, and 80% of all job openings never reach the public. This is why to be successful, it is important to network.

You need the right connections if you are going to succeed. Even if you think you know many people, you can always know more. Even if you know many people, it does not mean you know the right people. The truth is you should dedicate a significant amount of time to networking. I promise that there will be a time when getting a job is a matter of knowing the right person and being at the right place at the right time.

Networking is a powerful job search technique; it will make use of your talents and the talents of those around you. It helps you establish relationships so that you don't just take a job . . . you accept a job. Here are 11 networking fundamentals that will help you become a better net-worker.

11 Networking Fundamentals

Start Where You Are

Take some time and make a list of everyone you know. Make it a brainstorming list--do not judge the names you put on it, just list every name that comes to mind. In this list strive for quantity and not quality because you never know who can help you. This is why you should include the names of everyone you know. To do this effectively you should spend at least a few days up to a week engaged in this process. After you have compiled your list, start looking at it and trying to figure out what each person on this list can do for you. Also, make a note if you can or cannot get in touch with them. If you cannot get in touch with them, but they are useful for your cause, try to find a way to get in touch with them; use the Internet; contact a mutual friend, or any other means if necessary. Do not be afraid to tell people why you need to get in touch with that person. Anyone you meet could potentially help you so do not put boundaries on your networking.

Make a List of People Who You Would Like to Know

This list is different from the previous list. This list of people is people that you would like to meet. They are the ones you know that would be able to help, if they just knew who you are. After all, you are a great person who is on the road to success, and you make a great friend. This list can include more than job contacts; it can include people who you would like to mentor you.

Let People on Your Lists Know Your Purpose

Once again, do not be afraid to let people know you are looking for a job. Be careful, you want to treat people with respect and build friendships above all. Nobody likes to be used, but people love to help. Give people an opportunity to help you, and at the same time you should be offering to help them with something. When letting people know your purpose they should be able to sense the passion you have for your chosen career. This is why your job-hunting purpose should relate back to your personal mission statement. The reason for this is the fact that most individuals are eager to assist others who have passion mixed with a definite purpose or mission in life.

Send Handwritten Notes

President George Bush Sr. sends handwritten notes to people thanking them for efforts. You should do this as well. This is a personal approach and people will like the fact that you took time to handwrite something. Think about the last time you received a handwritten note; how did it make you feel? It obviously works, and if it worked for a former President and his dream job, it may help you get yours as well.

Develop a Plan of Action

Do not just expect networking to happen, make it happen. Remember the list of people you would like to meet. Plan to meet them, know what you want to ask, know why they are valuable, and pursue professional relationships with them. To do this you must believe that you can meet them, and that you have something of value to offer to them. Imagine yourself meeting these people so that when you do, you will have an intelligent conversation already mapped out.

Rework Your Plan

You may have made plans and still didn't get the results you expected. That's okay; it only means that you are finding out what doesn't work first. Whatever you do, do not keep working the same plan and expecting different results. This is NOT planning! At best it is called insanity.

Get Involved

The Great Gold Rush would not have been great if people were not involved in it. The fact is those people wanted gold, so they went to where there was gold. If you want your networking to be golden, go to where there is gold. Look in your community and see where things are happening, and go there. Any chance you get to get involved, take it, especially if it is a chance to showcase your talents.

Follow Through

This is critical if you want the continued support of your network. When you ask for advice, take it, and if it does not work it is not your fault. It will show that you listen, and chances are if you follow through you will have the opportunity to get more and better information from that source or a new source. This really communicates that you are willing to listen and learn from, and this is a compliment everyone likes to receive.

Learn How to Listen

Keeping your mouth shut and your ears open will give you many opportunities to uncover job leads or job ideas. Listening to people is a great way to get someone to like you, and remember that people do things for those they like. Here are a few techniques to help you to become a better listener.

To effectively listen to other people you need to give your full attention to what is being said. You should stop what you are doing and make that individual the center of your attention. To indicate that you are doing this maintain eye contact with the speaker, use appropriate non-verbal cues such as head nods, and if you do not understand what the speaker is saying try paraphrasing what they have said and/or ask questions such as, "I am not sure I understand what you mean could you explain it another way?" or "I think you said…am I understanding you correctly?"

There will be a time when you will be involved in a conversation with an individual who has a hard to handle accent or tone of voice, but do not let that stand in the way of listening to the person. Remember this person is a unique individual who is willing to help you if you just listen. Remember the message is more important than the delivery. So do not judge the speaker based on quality of voice, but judge the speaker on the quality of the advice rendered.

You should also prepare beforehand for the conversation. To do this take a few minutes and think about your purpose while meeting or talking with this person. This will help make the interaction much more meaningful for you and the speaker. Also this will help you to mentally collect the main points of the conversation. This is important because in order to get all you can from the conversation, from time to time you will need to ask the speaker for clarification about what is being discussed.

Develop a Winning Personality

Become the type of person people want to claim as a friend. If you need some help with this, read Dale Carnegie's *How to Win Friends and Influence People*, *The Art & Skill of Dealing with People* by Brandon Toropov, or *21Days To Unlimited Power With People* by James K. Van Fleet. If you do not want to read these books try talking to other people about what they find interesting. In addition, try to be responsive when you are talking to other individuals and give comments such as "very impressive!" or "I have never thought of it that way!" or "could you tell me more about…"

Here are some other tips on developing a winning personality. When you meet someone new, pay close attention to that person's name. You should always repeat the name immediately and use it at least two to three times during the conversation as a way to help you remember it. If they have a difficult name to pronounce ask the individual for assistance on saying it correctly. This can also give you something to talk about because you can ask about the origin of the name. When talking with others try to look directly at them while leaning slightly towards the person.

Remember that people always want to talk about themselves or what they find interesting, so once you get them started do not interrupt them. Remember you have an interest in keeping the conversation going. Don't be so self centered or short sighted that you think you have to be the center of attention. This will do two things. First, it will give the speaker a positive image of you. Secondly, when they run out of things to say they will be glad to listen to what you have to say.

Manage Your Networking

To help manage your networking program you should invest in a three-ring binder with loose-leaf paper. In this binder you should have the following:
- An address book.
- Business card file.
- Professional directories and membership rosters to the clubs you belong to or clubs you would like to join.
- A page for new contacts and ideas on where to meet people.

- ➢ News articles about people you need to meet. You can send these articles to the person and ask for a meeting. Mention what a positive impression they have made on you and ask them if you could meet with them.
- ➢ Special interest groups you should join.
- ➢ Anything else you can think of that will make your networking more efficient.

The Most Important Networking Step

All of these steps are important, but I would like to focus on developing a wining personality since this is the most important networking step. Without developing a winning personality, you will find yourself fighting an uphill battle trying to get the other steps to fall into place. Before we go any further, let's define what a winning personality is. A person with a winning personality is a person who can inspire other people. They are a person who other people trust. A person with a winning personality is someone who can get things done. People do things for the person with the winning personality because they like them and they want to help that person. That is why I am going to take a moment to discuss some of the elements of a winning personality.

The foundation of a winning personality is character. Developing and maintaining character makes you a person of value. When you have character you will be able to look at your life and say, "What I do really does make a positive difference." I believe this is something we all want. When you build your life on a foundation of character you will begin to seize opportunities for service, ways to make contributions, and ways to do things for other people without any expectations of reward . . . at this point you have become successful.

When you live your life according to character, what you use to measure success changes. You no longer use money or position as a measuring tool, but you use your actions, thoughts, and deeds to gage success. When living with character it becomes okay to lose, because you will no longer allow yourself to "win at all cost." The sad thing for many people is when they win at all cost, they have lost what is most important. Lily Tomlin said it best when she said, *"The problem with the rat race is even if you win you're still a rat."* If you want to develop character, think what you want people to say about you after you die and then live your life in light of that.

Remember networking is just not for executives who have made it big; it is for people like you who want to make it big. It will help avoid or lessen career crisis, and it can help you get a better position inside or outside the company. You will find as you network that people face many of the same issues you face, and it gives you and them an opportunity to share solutions. Networking only works if you work at using it. That is why you should use your network so your network can use you.

KAPS

- ➢ 80% of all jobs are never advertised.
- ➢ Networking should be planned.
- ➢ You should constantly network at all levels.

Chapter 18

19 Great Personal Marketing Ideas

Wouldn't it be great if job offers just fell out of the sky? They don't. Job offers come as the result of well planned and well executed marketing plans. The ability to market yourself is essential for success in today's job market. I wish that I could say that in order to find your dream job and make it a reality all you need to do is to read the classifieds and send in your resumes. The fact is it just does not work that way.

The information in this chapter is the result of many years of experience working with many different people from all walks of life. The following information, when used effectively, will help you market yourself. I should state that the purpose of this chapter is not to help you develop a creative message since that is discussed elsewhere in this book. The purpose of this chapter is to expose you to practical marketing tactics and strategies that have brought thousands of job seekers and employer's together.

1. **Business cards**. The fact is all professionals have business cards and you should too. They are great for networking. The other day I saw an old friend that I have lost contact with, and he gave me a business card he had printed on his own computer. It contained his name, address, phone number, email, a personal slogan, and a clever graphic. You can do the same thing by making cards with your personal information and objective on them. This will give you a professional appearance and an added networking tool.

2. **Brochures.** Most computers come with some sort of publishing software with a brochure template, making it easy for everyone. You could even do a mass mailing with either your services listed on the brochure or sections of your resume that highlight your talents and abilities in a fast, easy to read format. It even shows some creativity on your part, and perhaps this could get you the job you are seeking.

3. **Follow up letter**. You should follow every interview or networking event/meeting with a follow up letter. Thank the person for their time, give new information, or anything that may be appropriate. This shows social and communication skills, both of which are needed for success in today's world. If you express this during the meeting it will also show initiative and follow up, both rare traits in today's business world.

4. **Promotional products**. Businesses use these to keep their names in front of you. Why can't you use these to keep your name in front of your potential customer? (The person you are thinking about selling your labor to.) Depending on what you purchase and where you purchase your products from, this can be expensive. I would surf the net and look for things like pens, magnets, and other cheap items. This is a creative way to make yourself visible.

5. **Volunteer for high profile events**. This will definitely get your name mentioned where it needs to be mentioned. It will also create a favorable

impression of you, and it could even give you some valuable work experience to put on your resume or in your brochure.

6. **Write articles**. This will make you an expert in your field. Study a specific problem or new technique being used in your industry and write about it. Then send it to magazines, newspapers, or company newsletters for publishing.

7. **Create a newsletter**. If you take the time to research and write an article and no one publishes it, what good did it do? If you said it did no good, you were right. What should you do? Publish your own newsletter on your own computer. Fill it with your articles and information, and make it creative, not flashy. This will show a great deal of initiative.

8. **Join a trade association**. This will not only help you in your networking, but it will create a professional image for yourself. When you do this individuals will look at you as a professional. Once you are involved, run for an office or join a committee and become an active member.

9. **Attend conferences and seminars.** This will give you the opportunity to meet other people outside of your current sphere of influence. When you meet people at these events, let them know you are looking for a job, but do not be too pushy. By attending these events, you are communicating two things. The first thing you are communicating is that you are serious enough about your career to invest in yourself. The second thing you are communicating to people is that you are a professional.

10. **Educate yourself.** If you start reading books and listing to tapes about the job or industry you wish to enter, you will be able to talk intelligently to people in the industry. You will be updated on changes in the industry. Most importantly you will learn how to do the job you want to do to the best of your abilities.

11. **Write a speech.** Develop a speech about the job and talk to anyone who will listen. Go to schools, churches, or civic club meetings and tell them about the industry and the job you want to have. Talk as if you already possess the job. If you talk to enough people, you will eventually talk to the right person, and you will talk yourself into a job.

12. **Take it to the Media.** Get on a radio or TV show and talk about the profession you wish to enter. Since you already have the speech prepared this should not be too hard and by being seen or heard, people will look at you like you are an expert.

13. **Formal education.** Seek an advanced degree or another certification. If you never finished college, finish. If you never started college, start and then finish. If you never finished high school, get your GED. Seek to attain the highest level of education needed for your chosen profession.

14. **Learn a new language.** With the global economy, it will not hurt to learn another language. While learning the new language, take time to learn the culture and gain an understanding about their beliefs and rituals.

15. **Website.** Register your name as a domain name if you can. My web address is www.jasonmcclure.com. Another advantage in networking is you can tell people your email is yourname@yourdomain.com. This makes it easy for

people to remember your domain name and to visit your site. It also keeps you on top of today's technology.

16. **Use email.** This may be the best way to get a hold of some individuals. A few individuals do not check their email, but most business people check their emails several times a day. While you may not want to come out and ask for a job in an email, you can use this as a way to introduce yourself and ask for a meeting with the person so you can find out more about them and their organization.

17. **Join Toastmasters International.** The communication skills you learn will help you in all areas of your life. I am a member and I love it. Toastmaster's International is unique because it is dedicated to the growth of the individual. I would not expect any direct job leads from Toastmaster's, but you will increase your communication skills.

18. **Make Phone Calls.** Pick up the phone and call the organization you want to work for. Call them and ask them if they have any job openings. By the way, when you use this tactic you should have a purpose for your phone call and you should develop a script that relates to that purpose. Then be prepared to rewrite and revise your script until you start to get the results you desire.

19. **Show Up.** Visit the organization. This works better in smaller organizations, but do not discount its effectiveness in larger organizations. This includes showing up for interviews. I am amazed at the number of individuals who do not show up. Do not become one of them.

Whether you use all 19 tips or a combination of these tips, you can expect to get more job offers. These tips are designed to help you increase your visibility, which will in turn increase your employability. These tips work best when you know what you want to accomplish. Earlier in this book, I discussed how to determine what you wanted to accomplish most in life. Determining this is crucial to your success because focus is crucial to your success.

KAPS

> ➤ Job offers are the results of careful planning.
> ➤ If your original plans are not working, change them and keep changing them until you start to get the results you want.
> ➤ Using these marketing tips will make you appear professional because you are professional.

Chapter 19

The Planning Process for
Your Job Search

The purpose of this chapter is to introduce you to key principles that will help you plan and organize your job search while helping you achieve balance in your life. At the end of this chapter, you will be able to do more of the things you want to do now. Notice I did not say you would be able to all the things you want to do now. *However, I firmly believe that if you do the things you need to do now and make that a daily habit, then one day you will be able to do the things you want to do when you want to do them.*

Planning Starts With Your Mission

The key to planning and organizing your job search starts with having a mission. The majority of people in life are drifting aimlessly. They often go from job to job and they do this at someone else's suggestion. They are drifting through life just going with the flow, without the slightest idea of what their ideal job is. In my opinion, this is one of life's greatest tragedies. It is a tragedy because without a mission, life is lived without purpose, and without purpose, there can be no passion.

Having a mission in life and having that mission firmly fixed in your mind influences your actions. The stronger your mission, the stronger your passion, and the stronger your passion the more determination you have to fulfill your mission. People with a mission do not change jobs at someone else's suggestion. People with a mission know what they want to accomplish and since they know what they want to accomplish in life, they develop plans to fulfill that mission. People with a mission become what Brian Tracy calls a meaningful specific instead of a wandering generality.

I believe that your mission in life needs to be chosen with great care. When defining your mission you need to assess two things. The first thing that needs to be assessed is who you are now. The second thing that needs to be assessed is who or what you want to become. When analyzing these two things, remember to be honest with yourself. Your success is dependent upon your ability to accurately and honestly to do this.

I know I keep talking about having a mission. I keep repeating this point for two reasons. The first reason is repetition is the key to learning. I want you to learn the importance of developing a mission. The second reason is developing a mission is really crucial to your success. If this book prompts you to do at least one thing, I hope that it will prompt you to develop your own unique mission in life.

I want your life to have the direction that only a clear, well-defined mission can provide. I want you to have a positive mental attitude and having a mission helps you develop this. I also want your dream job to become a reality. Now let's examine the process of planning and organizing your job search. I have broken this down into three sections or steps. The first step is planning to plan. The second step is planning the game, and the last step is working the plan. All three of these work together, and sometimes they need to be repeated, but with each step you are closer to accomplishing your mission in life.

Planning to Plan

I understand that this section sounds redundant, but the old cliché is true, "You don't plan to fail, you just fail to plan." It is no surprise that having a clear mission guides the process of planning. By now, you should have a clear idea of the occupation you are going to make your life's calling. If you have not already written out your job description or mission statement, take a moment and do it now.

When you have your dream job written as a mission statement, you should refer to it often and read it aloud saying something like, "I am committed to becoming _____, no matter the obstacle." I recommend that you do this several times a day, and be sure to do it before you go to bed and first thing in the morning. This will help you to develop the laser like focus for your career that is a prerequisite for success.

The second step in planning to plan is determining your current time budget. Why did I say budget? I said budget because time is a valuable resource. I believe that time is even more important than money. Let's talk about time and money. Which one of these is replaceable? Once a day is spent, it is spent. When you spend money, you can always make more.

We all know this, but we continue to make financial budgets and treat money as if it was more important than time. It is not more important than time, because what you do with your time is what you do with your life. I do think it is important to budget your money and to be a good steward of your resources. I just think it is more important to be a good steward of your time.

Think about it like this. We all have a deposit in the bank of life, and we spend it 24 hours at a time. The difference is we cannot save our time for future use. This means that the real value of time is the present. If you waste all of your time today, you cannot make it up in the future. The good news is if you use your time wisely today, you will be rewarded in the future. Here are four ideas that will help you to budget your time.

Time Budget Tips

Take time to list all the things you do. Include everything you do, and remember this list will require some revisions. The purpose of this is to compare what you do with what you need to do. Just remember when making your list put your daily activities, weekly activities, monthly activities, and so on. Do not put what you wish you did, plan to do, know you should do, or want to do.

When you are finished with the list of things you do, look at it, study it and think about it for a few minutes. Rate the activities on your list on a scale from 0 to 10, with 0 being not important at all and 10 being extremely important for you to fulfill your mission. For example if you watch too much TV, you may give TV a 0. If you work or go to school, you may put those activities as a 7 or 8 because they are helping you get the job you want. If you have a job interview with a company you have always wanted to work for, this may be a 9 or 10 on your scale. Also, think about the actions that you need to take to fulfill your mission, and make a note of these activities and give them a rating compared to the activities on your list.

Start eliminating or shortening time wasting activities. I am not going to tell you to quit watching TV, but I will say that you may need to cut back on watching TV. In addition, look for procrastination activities and think of ways you can substitute those activities with achievement related activities.

When you do these three things, you should have a better understanding of how you are spending your time. Finally, ask yourself if you are overdrawing your account of time. Most people never do this, because they may have to say "Ouch" or make changes in their use of time. They also fool themselves by thinking they can do it all. The fact is no one can do it all, and the key to controlling your time is developing the ability to say no. People will use as much of your time as you are willing to give them in order for them to accomplish their goals without any regard for the accomplishment of your goals.

As you probably know there are 24 hours in a day, which means that in a week, we have 168 hours to accomplish our goals. If you are working full time that means you are already using 50 hours, and if you sleep 8 hours a day you are using another 56 hours which means you have 63 hours left. That is 9 hours a day. Various research shows people watch an average of 4 to 6 hours of TV per day. This means you may have as little as 3 to 5 hours to devote to achieving your goals. My advice is not to waste your time watching other people live their dreams . . . which is what you are doing when you watch television.

Planning the Game: Making the Most Your Time

This is going to build on the inventory you have taken of how you spend your time. Now you will learn how to structure your time so you can make the most efficient use of it. This is going to be a six-step process. If you use it, it will greatly help you get more out of your day, week, month, and life.

Conduct a Self-Audit

Using the information you gathered in the previous section, use your time budget to perform a self-audit. Here are some basic questions to ask yourself:

1. When was the last time I used short-term goals to accomplish long-range objectives?
2. Are my daily activities supporting my mission in life?
3. Do I judge accomplishment in terms of activity or process?
4. Do I look for ways to turn downtime into uptime?
5. Do I have a priority list and do I stick to it?
6. Do I say no to activities that are distracting me from my mission?
7. Do I allow flexibility in my schedule?
8. Do I have clear stopping and starting times?
9. Do I have a plan for the unexpected?
10. What things can I do that will make my time reflect my values and help me accomplish my mission in a timely manner?

Get a Planner

A planner will help you plan your day, week, month, quarter, and year at one a time. Some planners will break your day into 15-minute sections. A planner will be your monitor and it will help keep you accountable, but the key to having a planner is using it. To help you with your planner here are some easy steps.

Get to Know Your Planner

Different planners have different sections. Before you buy a planner, take the time to see if that particular planner will fit your needs. Do not buy a planner at someone else's recommendation. They have different needs than you do. Invest your time in checking out various planners because there are a number of planners on the market.

Keep Your Planner With You

If your planner is not with you, you are not using it. You have to use the planner in order for the planner to be effective.

Update your Planner Daily, if not more often

As you get new appointments, write them in immediately, especially re-occurring appointments because these can be the easiest to forget. I used to have a monthly appointment, and after a while I started thinking, "I have this appointment every month; I can remember it." Guess what? I forgot it two months in a row and suffered a significant loss. Since then, I write down every appointment as soon as I make it.

Review and Preview Your Planner

Every night before you go to bed look at tomorrow's activities. This will help you prepare mentally for the day ahead. Look at your planner before you start your day, this will also help you get mentally ready and it will prevent you from overlooking something. This would be a good place to put your personal mission statement or goals because the more you read these things the more you will be able to focus on your definite purpose.

Use Only One Planner

Some people think that they are so busy or important that they need two or more planners, or they may think they are being more organized. Neither is true. If you think you need two or more planners, you are probably confusing accomplishment with being busy. They are not the same. It is not organization because true organizing is eliminating unnecessary tasks, not creating them. Having more than one planner increases your chances for error because you are actually less organized.

Be Aware

Be aware of how you are spending you day. This is where having a planner will help. In the beginning, you should break your day into 15-minute sections, allowing time to move from one activity or appointment to the next. Allow time for the unexpected such as traffic delays, getting gas, or missing your exit. This also means knowing when to stop one activity and move on to the next. When you have flexibility built into your schedule, if an appointment runs over, you will still have time to make it to the next appointment. Doing this will greatly reduce your stress level, and it will increase your performance because you can focus your attention on the present instead of the future.

Where Are You Going?

Know where you are going. I know I have been talking a lot about having a mission, but what I mean in this section is you should know where your appointment is. Even if it is in your home city, get a map, get directions, or find road marks that will help you get where you need to go.

Depending on the importance of the appointment you may want to drive by your destination a day or two in advance. Even the less important appointments you want to leave early enough so that you can arrive 15-20 minutes early. If you are going out of town, you should add at least 30 to 45 minutes to your travel time depending on your familiarity with the city you are visiting and the distance you are traveling.

What's Important?

Know what is important. What I am talking about is setting priorities. You should set your own priorities and this is easy to do when you have a mission in life. When you are in the process of turning your dream job into reality, it is crucial. Unfortunately, most people are never instructed on how to set priorities. Then there are the people who know how but do not do it. Here is a three-step process to setting priorities.

1. **Have a mission**. This makes setting priorities easy.
2. **Ask the question, "How does this help me with my mission in life?"** Rank the activity on a scale of 0 to 10. Zero being this does not help me at all, and ten being it is actively fulfilling your mission
3. **What part of my life am I willing to sacrifice or exchange for this activity?** If the activity does not score a 7 or 8 and you still want to do it, ask yourself this question while remembering how you spend your time is how you spend your life.

Working the Plan

Nothing works if you don't work. Most people have no problem with planning to plan, or planning the game. They even have no problem talking about working the plan. They just have a problem taking action and working the plan. They come up with excuses but they never follow Nike's advice to *Just Do It*.

There are several reasons one might not work the plan. It could be laziness, lack of self-esteem, thinking success is owed to you or maybe just not knowing how to work a plan. If you are lazy, I cannot do it for you. If you think it is owed to you, you are wrong. If you lack self-esteem, keep reading books to help you and practicing positive self-talk. Another reason an individual may not work their plan is their plan may not be workable.

Is Your Plan Workable?

The reason your plan may not be working is your plan may be flawed. Notice I didn't say the process of planning was flawed. Many people make the mistake of assuming the planning process was flawed. The fact is the decision to plan and to work that plan was a great decision. If you are not successful at the first attempt perhaps you are just finding out what will not work first. The good news is if you keep doing this, you will eventually find out all of the ways that will not work, and when this happens you are bound to succeed.

This is where many individuals fail to succeed. They mistake the temporary defeat of a flawed plan with permanent failure. It is not permanent failure and this is why to succeed in your career you will need to continually develop new and improved plans. To do this you must have persistence, dedication, and resolve to your mission in life.

I personally believe that your success is directly related to the quality of your planning. To make sure you have a quality plan you will need to examine your plan and ask other people to review it, but be careful who you ask. The people that you seek to review and examine your plans should be wise and trusted counselors. The people you need to avoid are the dream stealers; these are often the people closest to us. Depending on your family and sphere of influence, you will know who will encourage you and who will do everything but. Why avoid the people closest to you? You would think those people would want you to succeed. If they are successful, chances are they will, but if they are unsuccessful don't expect them to be excited about your success.

If you think of your family as a tree, you would be a branch. A speaker I once heard said "If your branch or limb of the tree grows, don't expect the rest of the tree to like it." What does this mean? It means you are upsetting your family system. By changing yourself, you are changing the system, and systems resist change. The family you come from and friends you have are a system, just as a tree is a system of roots, trunk, bark, and limbs. When you start living your dreams you are changing the system. Therefore, these people will try to keep you from living your dreams. In most cases, they may not even realize what they are doing.

Just Say No

One thing that keeps people from working their plan is interruptions. Saying no will keep your interruptions to a minimum. This is hard to do, because if you are like me you are given offers that are more appealing than the present task. The key to this is discipline. It may help to remember that you are doing the things you need to do now so that one day you will be able to do what you want to do when you want to do it. Saying no is hard for two reasons. The first reason is we may actually want to do what was offered. The second reason is we do not want to reject the person. Remember you are not rejecting the person; you are just rejecting the current activity or offer at a point in time. It does not mean that you cannot make time for it later, you do not want to do it, or you are rejecting the person. If you have a hard time saying no, here are six steps that will help you say no to the offer without saying no to the person.

- ➤ *First,* review the facts and reasons for saying no. This will help you build an argument in a step by step, easy to understand process with supportive evidence.
- ➤ *Second,* give this information to the person asking. Communicate clearly with them why you cannot do what they are asking you to do at the current point in time.
- ➤ *Third,* remind the person you are not saying no to them, but to the current offer only. Make a distinction between the person and the offer.
- ➤ *Fourth,* offer to do something in the future when your schedule permits. If it is something that you can do later, offer to do it later. If it is not, offer a replacement activity.
- ➤ *Fifth,* say something good about the offer like, I really enjoy mountain climbing, but this is not a good time for me to take off and climb Mount Everest because I have to find my dream job and make it a reality.
- ➤ *Sixth,* if necessary use the broken record technique. If they keep asking you to do something, be assertive and repeat to them over and over why you are rejecting the offer, and keep reminding them that you are not rejecting the person

but the offer at the current time. Do this until they accept your rejection of the offer.

Following these six steps will make saying no much easier. We are usually asked to do much more than we can accept. You will find when you say no people will respect you for your ability to do so. If they do not, then you might want to reconsider your relationship with that person. Remember *Just Say No* to anything that will take away from your dream.

Avoiding Procrastination

Take a moment and think of a time you have procrastinated. What happened? If you had to do it over again would you have procrastinated? Chances are good that you wish you had not procrastinated. What is procrastination? Procrastination is putting off tomorrow what could and typically should be done today. Procrastination is also laziness and no one ever became a success because of laziness. In addition, procrastination is a disease that leads to lowered self-esteem. It also creates a damaging comfort zone that is disabling to your success because it promotes passivity.

Curing Procrastination

The good news is there is a cure for this deadly disease. Just like any disease, the key to the cure is catching it as early as you can. However, it is curable without early detection. To cure this disease you need to look at the source of the procrastination.

Ask yourself the following questions when faced with procrastination.

1. What will this cost me if I act now?
2. What will this cost me if I do not act now?
3. Will it be easier to do it now or later?
4. What will happen if I do not do it at all?
5. How will doing this help me achieve my long-term goals?
6. How will doing this later keep me from achieving my long-term goals?
7. Would my spouse, children, friends, family, or anyone else be proud of me if I put this off?
8. Would I be more proud of myself if I did this right now or if I chose to put off living my dreams until later?
9. What is the real obstacle to the task?
10. Do I believe if I do the things I need to do now I will one day be able to do the things I want to do when I want to do them?

When it comes to procrastination, remember that *nothing* was ever accomplished by procrastinating.

Don't Take Life Casually and Become a Causality of Life.

My friend and motivational speaker Norith Ellison tells his audiences that if you take a casual approach to life you will become a causality of life. He's right, but what does this have to do with working your plan? Do not be so casual about life that you allow opportunities to drift away. Life is fun and you should enjoy it, but it should also be treated with a high level of respect and seriousness.

Constantly Rework Your Plan.

Chance are good that your first time at planning you may find some things you have overlooked. This means you are moving in the right direction! Remember the only person who does not make a mistake is the person who is not doing anything. It's okay to rework your plan, and it is even desirable. When you rework your plan you can take advantage of new opportunities that were not available when you first developed your plan. Reworking your plan is a wonderful and positive learning experience. Remember, *People learn something every day and a lot of the time it's that what they learned the day before was wrong.* --**Bill Vaughn.**

In this chapter, we have covered the importance of organizing and planning your job search. I hope that you can use this information in order to take one more step towards turning your dream job into a reality. Being organized is essential in becoming successful, and developing and working workable plans is equally important.

KAPS

➢ In order to organize your job search you need to have a clear mission.
➢ Planning involves making a time budget.
➢ For your plans to be workable, you have to be able to say no.
➢ It is important to plan to plan, plan the game, and work the plan.
➢ It is important to revise your plans as needed.

Chapter 20

Selling Yourself:
The Key to Winning the Interview

Here is an interesting fact. Did you know that most people are nervous when they go to a job interview? Some people are so nervous about the interview that they do not even show up. It's true; I have known people that are so afraid of interviewing they actually did not show up for the interview. This self-sabotaging behavior comes from what I call interview anxiety.

Reducing Interview Anxiety

To reduce this anxiety you should take time to prepare for the interview. The number one reason people are nervous or anxious about the interview is they do not know what to expect. They do not know what kind of person the interviewer is. They do not know what questions the interviewer will ask them or how they will respond to those questions.

Another interesting interview fact is the person conducting the interview is nervous too! That's right. The person interviewing you is nervous because they are interviewing people they do not know. They do not how you are going to respond to their questions. They do not know if you are going to accept the job offer. They do not know what questions you are going to ask them. They do not know how they are going to respond to the question you are going to ask them. Finally, they do not know if they are going to find a qualified candidate for the position they are trying to fill.

You Only Have 10-Minutes

The last interviewing fact that you need to know is that most interviewers make a decision about you within the first 5 to 10 minutes of the interview. The good news is there are some steps that you can take that will greatly improve your chances of getting your dream job. To help you sell yourself during the interview process, I will discuss your appearance, interview do's and don'ts, commonly asked interview questions, and questions to ask the interviewer.

I will start with appearance because this is the first thing the interviewer notices when you arrive for the interview. It should be no surprise that you should always dress appropriately for the job you are applying for, but depending on the job this does not mean you should dress like you are ready to go to work. I personally believe that a nice suit is always your best bet. For men I typically recommend a black, dark blue, or a gray pinstripe, with a solid color tie. I recommend that men avoid loud ties and other flamboyant accessories. Make sure all of your clothes are wrinkle free and that your shoes are polished. I believe that women should wear a conservative suit or dress, and you should avoid excessive jewelry, make-up, perfume, and bright nail polish. Now that we have covered the basics, let's look at the seven keys of dressing for success.

Seven Keys of Dressing for Success

Dress in a manner similar to the interviewer

Do some homework and find out how people in the organization dress. You should know beforehand if they are conservative. You should know if they are not. You should have an idea of what the organization's culture says about what is appropriate dress. Here are five things you can do to find out what is appropriate dress, and by the way, this will help you to gather valuable information about the organization.

Five ways to determine appropriate dress

- Find out if you know someone – however distant- who works for the target organization and ask him or her what the dress code is. Be sure to get specific with this question. Ask this person what the interviewer wore when they were interviewed. Also, if the boss does not do the interviewing ask your contact person what the boss wears. In most cases, you can never go wrong if you look like the boss. Do not forget to ask who the key people are in the organization and what they wear to work and then wear it to the interview.

- If you do not know anyone there, call and ask the receptionist your questions. You can be truthful and tell them you feel awkward about asking what to wear, and you would rather not give your name and chances are they will understand. If you want them to know that you are interested enough in the job to take a risk to find out a small but important detail, go ahead and give them your name and then tell them you look forward to meeting them in person.

- If you want to find out what people are wearing in the organization, attend business meetings, luncheons, seminars, or networking events. Just go to one of these things and observe what the people are wearing. If you notice a person with an outfit or accessory that you admire, do not hesitate to go up and introduce yourself, compliment the garment and ask them where they got it. If you let them know why you are asking, this may even open the possibility for another interview with an organization that you never considered, or it could be another important networking contact for your records.

- Read trade magazines and look at the pictures of the people in the industry you want to enter. Look to see what clothes are they wearing. Chances are good they will be trying to look their best for the magazine pictures much like you would want to look your best in the interview.

- The Internet is a great resource. Most organizations have web sites. Look and see if you see people on their site. Do they have pictures of their employees? Do they have a picture of the person interviewing you? If not, do not be discouraged. Many search engines have places to search for fashion. So, look for web sites that are dedicated to dressing for success. Another good option is to ask a friend, particularly one you have noticed is a good dresser.

Match your accessories with your skin, hair, and eye color.

I once heard a speaker say "This morning before you got out of the shower you already had your best colors on." This person was referring to your natural skin tone, hair and eye color. For example I have a tie that has the following three colors: brown, the same shade as my hair, blue that matches my eyes, and then a flesh tone that matches my skin. Every time I wear this tie, I am always complimented on how good I look. This advice is the same for women-- do not change makeup to go with your clothes. According to my friends in the field, when you choose make up it should be chosen • according to your skin tone. This tone changes, as you get tanner in the summer and paler in the winter. I would recommend visiting a professional because these people have the formalized training to help you look your best.

If it does not fit or if it is not clean do not wear it.

This communicates to the interviewer that you are careless. It screams out "Don't hire me because I do not pay attention to detail." If a suit has out grown you, you may be able to alter it for less than the price of a new suit. If you have out grown a suit, you only have two choices. One is to take off the weight (assuming you put on unnecessary weight) or buy another outfit. Wearing clothes that are too small or too large can indicate an image problem. The bottom line is to take extreme personal care in your appearance, from head to toe.

Invest in everyday accessories such as a nice pen or briefcase.

By spending a few dollars and purchasing a few nice accessories, it tells your prospective employer that you are a professional. People will notice these things and they may even compliment one of these items. Nice accessories could be a great way to break the ice with a little small talk. Other common everyday accessories you can invest in are a nice planner, leather bound pad holder to hold a legal pad (this will serve nicely to take notes during the interview), and a nice watch.

With accessories, remember too much is worse than not enough. Big gold chains, bracelets, and earrings, along with other loud accessories, may drown you out. This will cause the interviewer not to hear what a great asset you would be to the company. When in doubt always stay conservative. Also do not be afraid to ask a reliable source such as a college professor, counselor, good friend, parent, or some other person whom you can count on to give good advice.

Casual dress means professional dress.

What is casual dress? When a prospective employer says to dress casually, they do not mean jeans and a T-shirt. They are not talking about wearing workout clothes, or your lounging around outfit. As matter of fact, they are not even talking about what you wear to class. Lastly, they are not talking about wearing the latest fashion or what you would to wear to a party or a club.

If they are not talking about those things, what do they mean? When you are told to dress casually for an interview, what they mean is business casual. Business casual is still professional. The fact is you will not be penalized for dressing too nice. Typically, business casual dress is a khaki type of pants (Dockers or a comparable brand) with a turtleneck, mock turtleneck, or solid color polo shirt.

You could even wear a button down shirt. (Remember no loud colors with any shirt or pants, and if you are not sure about a particular pattern stick with a solid pattern). With a matching solid color sports coat, this would be casual. For women this type of dress might include khakis and a dress shirt, turtleneck, or sweater. Many people consider this to be dressed up, and it may be for many social settings, but this is a business setting. Things to avoid when dressing casual are sandals, tennis shoes, shorts, short-skirts, jeans, and club clothes. Once again, dress conservatively and in a manner suitable to the interviewer and the people you are going to be working with.

Five steps to dressing casually

> **Wear a solid-color.** Avoid loud patterns that are too elaborate and flamboyant. Remember the most important rule here is when in doubt throw it out.

> **Press your outfit.** Casual dress is not a ticket not to iron. Remember that if you do not press your clothes and they are wrinkled it will show a lack of attention to detail. Depending on the culture it may even be seen as a sign of disrespect.

> **Match your clothes.** Some general rules of thumb. White shirts go with everything. With a solid button down, or polo style shirt, you can wear any color pants. If you want to be a little more daring go with a solid navy blue, or red polo style shirt with khaki pants. I would caution against a button shirt of this color, because it may be considered flashy. If you keep it simple with a solid white shirt, and solid color pants you will be safe.

> **Ties and scarves are optional.** Be conservative. I would recommend waiting until you get the job before wearing your favorite loony tunes tie.

> **Wear a sports coat.** A navy blue coat with khaki pants and white shirt will be appropriate for most situations. Above all, make sure your jacket and pants match if they are the same color. I find it easier to use contrasting colors such as khaki pants and a navy blue jacket instead of trying to match pants and coats of the same color unless they were purchased at the same time.

Wear clean, polished shoes.

Many people make the mistake of thinking that what is on their feet is not that important. It is important. When wearing shoes that can be polished they should be polished. Polishing only takes a few minutes. That few minutes can mean the difference between a good or bad first impression. Do not underestimate the influence of polished shoes, because this communicates to the interviewer that you pay attention to detail.

Having the right shoes begins with buying the right shoe. There is a myth that claims that shoes have to be broken in. Shoes should feel good the moment you put them on. In addition, when buying shoes you need to wear the pants that you plan to wear with the shoes. This will enable you to see if the shoes match the pants. If you are not sure ask the salesperson or take a friend who is a shoe expert. Remember if your feet hurt your whole body will hurt, so buy shoes that fit.

If you are a woman and you are planning on wearing a high-heeled shoe, try for a heel that is 1 1/2 to 2 inches high according to research by John F. Waller Jr., MD, chief of the foot and ankle center of the Lenox Hill Hospital in New York. His research has indicated that this heel height is more comfortable then the traditional 3/4-inch hill. I should offer a word of caution that most shoes with this heel size tend to be more of the "go-go boot" style or club shoes and you should make sure that the shoe is appropriate for business. Lastly, purchase shoes in the late afternoon when your feet have had a full day's work. The reason is by this time of the day your feet have swollen to be as big as they will normally get. If you do this, you will be able to put your best foot forward with confidence.

By the best fabric and tailoring you can afford.

I understand that money may be tight, which is why I am not saying that you should to go out and buy a two thousand-dollar tailored suit. According to the book "The Millionaire Next Door," the typical millionaire has never paid more than $400.00 for a suit. Even more shocking is that fact that 30.4% of the responding millionaires owned JC Penny's credit cards and preferred Penny's private label brand because if its durability, cut, and fit. That is why it is not necessary to spend a million to look like a million.

To some people all of this may be new, to others it may not, but it is not designed to be comprehensive. It would be impossible to cover all the literature and material on this subject, just as it is with most subjects. There are books, magazines and whole industries dedicated to the subject and I encourage you to look at all the information you need. Now that you are looking your best, we will move on to things to do and not to do in an interview.

16 Interview Do's and Don'ts:

1. **Do arrive early**. If you arrive late, you will be rushed and the interviewer may consider you unreliable. It is optimal to arrive 10 to 15 minutes early.
2. **Do walk briskly**, with purpose, and stand up straight.
3. **Don't** smoke, chew gum, or slouch.
4. **Do** read some of the company's literature, if it is available, while you are waiting.
5. **Do give the interviewer a firm handshake**, and do not be afraid to look him or her in the eye.
6. **Do carry an extra copy** of your resume, references, academic record, and other related materials.
7. **Don't talk too much or too little**. However, during an interview you should be expected to do the majority of talking.
8. **Do bring samples** of your writing, speeches, and examples of your work.
9. **Do have a clear idea of exactly how long it will take** to get to where you are going, and if possible the name of the interviewer. Drive by the location a day in advance so you will know how long it will take to get there.
10. **Do your homework** and research every aspect of the company.
11. **Do be positive,** natural and relaxed.
12. **Do ask questions** when you do not understand a question.
13. **Do control** your temper, even if you feel like you have a good excuse for getting angry.
14. **Do paraphrase** what the interviewer is saying and asking you. You want to make sure you are answering or responding to what the interviewer is really saying.

15. **Do show** a desire to learn more about the company and the position.
16. **Don't** take a cell phone or beeper into the interview.

Now that you have some Do's and Don'ts, you are probably wondering about the questions the interviewer is going to ask you. Do not be afraid of the interview questions. They are not going to bite you. If you are prepared they will actually help you get your dream job. When it comes to interviewing, remember that questions are opportunities to sell yourself to the organization. Before I give you some interview questions, here are some things to remember when answering interview questions. Remember to keep it positive and honest. Always remember that people want to hire people that are like them and who will fit into the organization. This is why you need to make sure you have done your homework. At this point, you should have an understanding of the organization's culture.

Have an Open Mind

When answering questions you need to remember the importance of having a pleasing personality. To demonstrate a pleasing personality you need to have an open mind. I am not saying you cannot hold a firm opinion on a subject, but when you close your mind you close off new information that might help you make a more informed decision in the future. Having a closed mind also prevents you from growing. The interviewer may not want to hire someone who has made the decision not to grow anymore.

Have a Sense of Humor

Along with an open mind you will need a sense a humor. A sense of humor does not mean you should use "wise cracks" or other remarks that can be misinterpreted as disrespectful towards your previous employer, friends, family, or any group. A sense of humor does not mean you should walk into the interview telling jokes. A sense of humor means that you can see a lighter side to your circumstances. A sense of humor means you can look at yourself and laugh. A sense of humor means that you can look for the seed of opportunity in the middle of adversity.

Be Clear and Specific

You should also speak frankly, clearly, and use specific examples to support your statements. If you avoid a question the interviewer will notice, after all they are taking notes on what you are saying and they will know if you do not answer a question. Be sure to use words that are appropriate for the interviewer and the industry. Avoid using jargon and slang during the interview. When speaking, monitor your pitch and rate of speech. Simon and Schuster audio produces a product called *Speaking Effective English*. I would recommend investing in that product if you need help in this area.

The Role of Nov-Verbal Communication

Most importantly, watch your non-verbal signals. Non-verbal signals include your facial expressions, body movements and gestures. Make sure you maintain eye contact without staring. Make sure you smile at the interviewer. Make sure you give the interviewer a good strong handshake. Make sure you move with purpose. Avoid tapping your fingers and feet. Avoid playing with the rings on your fingers. Avoid playing with your hair. Avoid looking down when you are asked a question. Avoid bouncing around in your chair. Avoid shifting too much.

When interviewing, use movement and gestures to indicate that you are aware of the interviewer's questions and messages. Gestures may include nodding your head, and/or leaning forward towards the interviewer. When you lean forward, you are showing the interviewer that you are interested in them as a person and in the current position. This could also be vocal utterances which are sounds like "Mmm," "mmm-hmm," "I see," "You don't say," "I never thought of it that way," "I don't believe it," "really," and "uh-huh." Make sure you use what is appropriate for the interview situation.

Here is what one interviewer said about nonverbal communication. "I recently interviewed a young lady who was recommend by a mutual acquaintance. They told me this girl could ace the interview if she could just get an interview. The position was for a customer service position and I believe that good customer service people should be the best interviewees because the uncertainty of an interview situation is much like the uncertainty of dealing with our customers."

"When this young lady came in I thought she was obviously on drugs. This girl could not stop twitching and looking around. She never looked me in the eye. I did not feel I could trust her on a basic level. When I asked why she quit her last job, she said it was because she couldn't get along with her previous manager." I thought to myself how can you get along with a person you cannot trust? Needless to say she didn't get the job.

We only hear the interviewer's point of view in this story, and I am sure if I talked to the young lady, she would tell a different story. I do not know which story would be the most accurate. Really, it does not matter who would tell the most accurate story. What matters most is she did not get the job offer. Chances are good that this young lady may not have been on drugs, and she may have been trustworthy. She may have been a wonderful worker. She may have been the best customer service person this organization could ever employ. But because of her nonverbal communication, she did not get the job. When you get an interview, you want to monitor your nonverbal communication because it is a very important part of selling yourself to the interviewer.

When answering the interviewer's questions you need to be mindful of your posture because this communicates so much to the interviewer. Do not be tense or overly proper, but do not slouch in the chair and prop your feet up. The best way not to look tense is not to be tense. The best way not to be tense is to enjoy the interview process. If you cannot enjoy the process then the next best thing you can do is to be prepared for the process.

Other non-verbal elements that I will discuss are space and posture. In regards to space, do not invade the interviewer's personal space because this will make them feel uncomfortable. Let them determine the appropriate distance and maintain what makes them feel comfortable. At the same time you want to be close to the speaker. This is because you want to be able to hear the interviewer, and secondly you want to communicate positive feelings towards the interviewer. Lastly, remember your posture and sit up straight.

Remember that you are selling yourself to the interviewer. When you answer questions, you want to relate your answers to how you can solve their problem and not cause them more problems. To help you get ready here is a non-comprehensive list that you need to be able to answer:

- What are your career goals?
- How many sick days have you taken in the past two years?
- Why did you pick your major?
- What are your strengths?
- What are your weaknesses?
- Do you have any hobbies?
- Why do you want this job?
- Tell me about yourself.
- What did you like most or like least about your last job?
- Do you have any questions? *You should always have at least one question prepared to ask.*

The interviewer may also ask you some specific questions that relate to equipment or procedures you will need to use on the job. This is a way of determining your overall knowledge and skills. If you lack these skills and knowledge, the interview is your opportunity to indicate to the interviewer that even though you are not the most skilled candidate you are still the right choice. You indicate you are the right choice by letting the interviewer know that you are a perfect fit into the organization's culture.

Remember you are selling yourself to the interviewer. You need to relate all of the questions to the job you want to get. You need to indicate that you are the most creative, dedicated, and hardest working candidate applying for the position. The interviewer is not your friend or co-worker. The interviewer wants to hear about what you can do for them. In the appendix, I have added a larger list of questions to help you practice interviewing. Remember that before, during, and after the interview...

1. Be positive and enthusiastic.
2. Try to focus on your accomplishments and achievements in past jobs.
3. Find out as much as possible about the job duties and requirements of the position for which you are applying. This will help you to be able to ask further questions.
4. Find out as much as possible about the organization.
5. If you are really interested in the job, let the interviewer know about it.
6. Questions you need to ask include: When will the job start? To whom do I report? What would a typical day be like? (Look for more questions in the appendix.)
7. Do not be too concerned about salary and benefits at first. If you are selected, they will make you a salary offer.
8. Always ask the interviewer questions. "How did you get started in this company?" is always a good one.

Remember your answers to questions before, during, or after the interview will reflect how the interviewer will perceive you.

After the Interview

The selling process does not stop after the interview unless you get the job offer. If you have not yet received a job offer, there are still some things you can do that can show you have more drive, determination, and social skills than your competition. Doing what I am about to instruct you to do should indicate that you are the best job candidate.

1. Write a follow up letter. If you really want the job, say so in the letter. This will also keep the channels of communication open.
2. If you have not heard anything within 8 to 10 days, you may want to call. Assure them that you are not trying to be pushy but that you are just interested.
3. If you are not hired, you can still send a follow up letter to the company and ask them to keep you in mind for any other similar job openings. In addition, you may want to ask the interviewer for a specific reason as to why you were not hired. This information will help you as you search for other jobs.
4. Contact the interviewer about another position in the organization.
5. Evaluate your interview performance. Reflect upon what you did well, what you could have done better, and most importantly, what you wish you had done.
6. Ask the interviewer for an honest evaluation of your performance during the interview.

Four tricks to getting more job leads

Contact the person who got the job

That's right; contact the person who got the job you interviewed for, and ask that person for their job leads. The fact is they do not need these leads anymore, and it will not cost you anything to ask. If you use these leads, send a thank you note. This is an opportunity to expand your networking circle.

Contact the interviewer

The interviewer may know of similar positions in other organizations. Many of these people belong to industry organizations or know people in other organizations. Once again, it will not hurt to ask, and if they don't you are no worse off, but if they say, "Yes," you have a great job lead.

Interview people in the industry or position.

Talk to these people to find out how they got where they are and do what they did. If it worked for them, it may work for you, and if these people really worked to get to where they are do not be so arrogant as to think you are exempt from this hard work. It is hard work to get to the top, and in many cases the work to get to the top involves jobs no one else wanted to do for whatever reason. The truth is if you are willing to do what it takes to go where you want to go, you can go anywhere you want in life.

Form alliances with fellow job seekers.

Most people only will need to accept one job but will have multiple job leads. The odds of you and another job seeker wanting to accept the same job at the same place are pretty high. This will help you network; for every job seeker you can potentially double the job leads, and they can too.

Getting an interview for your dream job is not always easy. However, if you use the strategies described in this chapter, you will stand a much better chance of success. Be persistent and when it comes to selling yourself, and don't sell yourself short! You deserve the best, and I believe that each job interview gets you one step closer to your dream job. When you stay in the game you may find yourself a much better job in a very short period.

For the average job seeker interviews are the most fearsome part of finding a job. While this may be so, interviewing is your best chance to show an employer your qualifications. The advantage of interviewing is it is more flexible than resumes, application forms, or tests. Use that flexibility to your advantage. Just like taking a test, you can reduce your interview anxiety and improve your interview performance by preparing for your interviews ahead of time.

Begin by considering what interviewers want to know. You represent a risk to the employer. A hiring mistake is expensive in terms of lost productivity, wasted training money, and the cost of finding a replacement. To lessen the risk, interviewers try to select people who are highly motivated, understand what the job demands, and demonstrate that their background and education has prepared them for it.

You indicate your motivation by learning about the company before the interview, by dressing appropriately, and by having a pleasing personality. You maintain that motivation by reading books like this one. You should show respect to the interviewer by putting your best foot forward and listening attentively during the interview. You also show respect and interest in the job by letting the interviewer know you are interested in the position, thanking the interviewer at the end of the interview, and by sending a follow up letter.

In Closing

One of the best ways to prepare for an interview is to have some practice sessions with a friend or two. For questions go to the appendix and practice with the most common interview questions. Remember your answers should reflect what employers want.

KAPS

- ➢ To reduce interview anxiety you need to be prepared.
- ➢ The interview process is a selling process.
- ➢ You are trying to solve a problem for the interviewer, not create a problem.
- ➢ When interviewing you should always look professional.
- ➢ The process does not end until you get a job offer.
- ➢ What you do before, during, and after the interview will be used to judge you.
- ➢ The interviewer is not your friend until you become their co-worker.
- ➢ Always ask the interviewer questions.
- ➢ If you are interested in the position, tell the interviewer and ask what the next step of the process is.

Chapter 21

The Power of Persistence

"The expectations of life depend upon diligence; the mechanic that would perfect his work must first sharpen his tools." -Confucius.

The one element of success that will always get results when applied is the concept of persistence. If you look around you will see that the world rewards persistent people. I believe if you prove that you are a person who perseveres, you will find yourself with more job opportunities then you can accept. **Success is a natural byproduct for people who develop this trait**. The world is full of stories of people who persevered until life gave them what they wanted. Let me give you an example of how persistence paid off for a man trying to live his dreams.

In 1934 during the Great Depression, an inventor from Germantown, Pennsylvania invented a new board game. He presented his idea to one of the largest manufactures of games and they rejected the game due to "52 design errors!" Nevertheless, this man was more of a seller of his idea than a buyer of the manufacturer's rejection. He did not buy the idea that his game had that many errors. He did not buy the idea that people would reject his game. He was sold on the idea that people would enjoy the game. However, like millions of other Americans, he was unemployed and nearly broke at the time.

With a little help from a friend who was a printer, Charles Darrow made and sold 5,000 handmade sets of the game to a Philadelphia department store. People loved the game some much that his production could not keep up with demand for his game. Since he couldn't keep up with all the orders, he took the game back to Parker Brothers, and this time they thought the game would sell. So they bought the game with 52 design errors, and in its first year the game Monopoly became the number one selling game, and since then, Monopoly has continued to be the best-selling game in America.

Because of the persistence of Charles Darrow:

➤ Over 200 million games of Monopoly have been sold worldwide.
➤ Over 500 million people have played Monopoly.
➤ He became a millionaire.
➤ Monopoly has become part of the American pop culture.

I believe that Persistence has made more successes than any other element of success. In the chapter about decisions, I gave you an 8-step outline for success.

1. Define your mission, purpose, or chief aim in life.
2. Decide what you will do and how you will fulfill that mission.
3. Decide to acquire all the knowledge about what you want to accomplish.

4. Decide to take that knowledge and put it into action.
5. Decide to take personal responsibility for the outcome of your actions.
6. Decide to take notice of what is working and what is not working.
7. Decide to constantly change your approach, not your mission, until you achieve your goals
8. Decide to be persistent.

In that chapter, I mentioned that some of these steps would be repeated throughout this text. To make sure I keep my promise, and to use repetition as a way to reinforce important concepts, I will dedicate this chapter to step number eight: decide to be persistent.

Persistence Moves Mountains

Persistence is the one part of the formula that you must possess. This will determine how you will deal with life's challenges. In his book <u>Awaken The Giant Within</u>, Anthony Robbins says, ***"Determination means the difference between being stuck and being stuck with the lightning power of commitment."*** In their search for dream jobs, this is what many people lack. They do not have the determination to push forward. They may say they want to push forward, but when push comes to shove, they decide to be shoved, instead of pushing back.

When you develop perseverance you will be able move to mountains, much like the man who had a mountain and wanted a field. Once there was a man who owned a mountain, but he wanted field so he could be a farmer. To live his dream of being a farmer, he set out to turn his mountain into a field. After investing a great deal of time, money and effort his mountain remained a mountain and thus prevented him from having the field he wanted so that he could become a farmer.

However, he never gave up on his dream of being a farmer. One day he found another man who wanted to buy a mountain, so the two made a deal, but they still had no way of exchanging their goods. They tried pushing and pulling the mountain, but of course, neither man had the strength. One day they were in town, and a fool overheard the two men talking about their dilemma. He offered the suggestion to move the mountain one stone at a time. The two old men initially thought the fool's idea was crazy, but after thinking about it, they decided to try the fool's suggestion. So, they started moving the mountain one stone at a time and after only ten years, they moved that mountain. The point is the man who moves a mountain begins by carrying one stone. The same thing goes for getting your dream job and making it a reality.

Notice in this story that neither man ever changed the vision of what they wanted. However, they did try different approaches. Please do not get persistence confused with doing the same thing over and over and expecting different results. That is not persistence. According to a Chinese proverb, doing the same thing over and over and expecting different results is insanity. It is okay to try different approaches because each new approach brings you one step closer to the plan that is going to work for you.

What do Thomas Edison, Orville Redenbacher, and Colonel Sanders have in common? These men each made up to 10,000 attempts before they succeeded. Thomas Edison sat through 10,000 experiments before he make a workable light bulb. Orville Redenbacher tried 10,000 corn hybrids before he developed his gourmet popcorn. Colonel Sanders spent three years going from restaurant to restaurant trying to sell his fried chicken recipe. You too can find your dream job and make it a reality or accomplish anything else you want to accomplish if you just use persistence to your benefit, just as these men did.

Persistence Creates a Lasting Impression

It is crucial to possess persistence if you plan to effectively market yourself. In marketing, we call this creating an impression. An impression is an external message that we send to create an image in the mind of another person. However, impressions only work if they are repeated several times over a period of time. I know people who claim to have tried marketing. They would say I ran one ad in the local paper or one commercial on the radio and did not get any response. Therefore, they decided that marketing doesn't work. It did not work for them because they did not work marketing. In reality, they quit before they got started.

If you question the effectiveness of creating impressions look at the Coca Cola Company; they are masters of creating impressions. They even have people buying their advertising. (Have you or do you know someone who has bought a Coca Cola shirt, hat, or anything else?) The story of Coke began in 1886 when Dr. John Pemberton invented Coca Cola in Atlanta, Georgia. For just a nickel, customers could enjoy a glass of Coke at the soda fountain. In first year, Coke averaged nine drinks per day.

How did this organization go from nine drinks a day to over three hundred and fifty billion a year? It took years and millions of impressions but the end result was success. Coke's success started when Robert W. Woodruff, son of Ernest Woodruff, became president of the Coca Cola Company. His insistence on quality and decades of leadership took the Coca Cola Company to unparalleled heights of commercial success, making the Coca Cola name known to the world. He did this by creating impressions and never quitting.

What are some of the impressions of the Coca Cola Company? Over the years, the Coca Cola Company has had only one basic message which is "It's the Real Thing." For decades they have used the same basic message. While they have had variations of this message, the fundamental message has remained the same. Some of the variations were:

"Things Go Better with Coke"
"Coke Adds Life"
"Have a Coke and a Smile"
"Coke is it!"

All of these messages go back to the point they want to make about Coca Cola, which is "Coke is the real thing." That is what they want you to think when you think about Coke. Coke is the best known, most admired trademark in the world, and today, sales of Coca Cola and other Company products exceed one billion servings per day.

Why are these impressions so effective? They are effective because the Coca Cola Company has been persistent with their message. Even when the company faced hard times, introducing New Coke for example, they held true to their basic message. The message was and still is Coke is great and Coke is part of America. This illustrates two points of being persistent. The first thing is to be aware that you are constantly creating an impression. Every cover letter, resume, or business card you use creates an impression. Every time you talk to somebody, you are creating an impression.

Because of this you need to be aware of what kind of impression you are making. The Coca Cola Company knew what kind of impression they were trying to make. You should be aware of what kind of impression you want to make in the market place. Just as Coke's impressions come from the company's mission statement, your impressions should reflect your mission in life.

11 Laws or Habits of Persistence

The Right Mindset

The first habit of persistence is having the right mindset. You should acquire a way of thinking that causes you to eliminate any thought that could cause you to quit before you reach your ultimate goal. This mindset has to be cultivated and it is cultivated the same way you cultivate a field. When you plant positive thoughts about success in your mind and you nurture those thoughts you will reap success.

The same law of nature holds true for your mind. Right now, you are in a state of mind or a state of consciousness. You may not realize what kind of consciousness you have. Think for a moment about what kind of consciousness you have. Is it a self-defeating consciousness? Is it a poverty consciousness? On the other hand, is it a success or persistence consciousness? The consciousness you hold is a decision. It is up to you to develop your own consciousnesses. If you fail to develop the right mindset you could fail to be persistent.

Results Equal Desire

The second habit or law of persistence is your results are equal to your desires. This law builds upon the first law, because if you plant seeds of weak desire you will get weak results. At this point, it will not cost you anymore to raise your expectations. If you do this, you will lose nothing. If you do this, you will gain greater success. Remember the words of Napoleon Hill: "*__The starting point of all achievement is desire.__*" Create for yourself a strong desire for the job and life you want. If you create a strong enough desire for what you want, your subconscious will go to work and help you achieve it.

Direct Your Subconscious

The third habit of persistence is to develop and direct your subconscious. Start visualizing yourself in the job or life you want. If you do not have a definite plan, start anyway. When you start seeing yourself the way you want to see yourself, two things will happen. Other people will start to see you that way, and your subconscious mind will take over and help fill in the gaps.

You will soon find yourself dreaming at night about solutions to your problems. When this happens you are on your way to success. To help direct your subconscious, read your personal mission statement when you wake in the morning, several times during the day, and before you go to bed at night. Read it aloud as many times as possible. If you do this everyday for a year, I promise you that you will get the results you want.

Have a Plan

The forth habit of persistence is having a plan. It may not be a fully developed plan. It just needs to be an outline at this point, but the more developed and the more organized your plan the better. A plan will help you be more persistent, especially if you continually update it and reorganize it. Do not be afraid to take out something that does not work, and be sure to use tactics that worked in the past or for other people.

Overcome the Only Obstacle

The fifth habit of persistence is belief. I believe the only obstacle between you and the life you want is a lack of belief. You have to believe that the payoff is worth the effort. If it takes twenty years, you have to believe it will be worth it. I heard Zig Ziglar say in an interview that he prayed and worked for over twenty years to become a fulltime speaker and a writer of a daily newspaper article, and he eventually got both.

He credits his success to the fact that he kept on pursuing his dreams long after many other speakers quit. Norman Vincent Peale said this about belief ***"People become really quite remarkable when they start thinking that they can do things. When they believe in themselves they have the first secret of success."***

How Long Should You Try?

The sixth habit of persistence is to know how long to try. How long should you try? According to Jim Rohn, you should try until you succeed. Henry Ford said it this way, "You can't build a reputation on what you're going to do." He is right. You build a reputation by what you actually do. Do you want to be known as someone who *tried*, or someone who *did*? It is more than a cliché to say the only difference between ordinary and **extra**ordinary is that little EXTRA.

Intrapersonal Communication

The seventh habit of persistence is communication. I am talking about **intrapersonal communication,** sometimes referred to as self-talk. How you communicate to yourself will directly affect your life. Do you say, "I will give it my best shot," "I will try," "I know I can't do it," or "This is just too hard"? If you say any of these phrases or any similar phrases, you need to change what you are saying to something like "I will achieve." "I will not be denied success."

Because how you communicate with yourself and others directly affects what you do and who you become, every time you talk to yourself you develop or destroy a belief you hold. When you talk to yourself, find ways and beliefs that will support you and who you want to become. Get away from negative self-talk and put-downs. Every time you communicate with another person, you affect the relationship with that person and yourself. Make sure it is positive.

Think about the effects of saying, "I will try." This type of talk is your opportunity for an easy way out. You cannot be successful with easy outs. This sets the stage for you to fail and for you to save face by responding with, "I gave it my best shot," when in reality you may not have. When you say, "I will do something" it cuts off all other possibilities.

Problems are Opportunities

The eighth habit of persistence knows the difference between problems and opportunities. I contend that most people's problems are not problems, but instead they are blessings in disguise. They are ways to test how thankful people are for what they have. I have an 80/20 test for problems. You may want to write this on a 3 X 5 card and keep it with you. When you are faced with a problem ask yourself this, "Would 80% of the world's population trade places with me right here, right now, if they could?" Then ask yourself, "Would I trade places with the 20% of the world who face starvation, murder, poverty, and tyranny as an everyday way of life?" I often find that this question gives me the proper perspective.

Permanent Failure Does Not Exist

The ninth habit of persistence is recognizing failure as a temporary event and not a permanent situation. There is nothing permanent about failure unless you want there to be. Failure is short lived and its effects are up to you. In a speech, I once heard George Foreman talk about getting started in his boxing career. One day he was sparing with a big guy that really laid some hard punches on George. George did not want to go back to the gym the next day because he did not want to lose to the same guy again.

Guess what? He went back to the gym to find out the other guy never showed back up because he took a beating from George Foreman. George Foreman went on to become a champion boxer and the oldest world champion; the other guy became an example of what happens when you recognize failure as a permanent situation.

Get Up and Go

The tenth habit of persistence is staying motivated even when you do not want to be motivated. This means developing the ability to get up and go when your get up and go got up and went. Have you ever noticed how easy it is to be persistent when you are motivated? The days you do not feel like accomplishing anything are the days when it is most important for you to get up and do something even if it is not your best work.

When you find yourself in some unwanted downtime, do something that will motivate you. Find some inspiration, motivation, or information that will give you the drive to get back to doing what you need to do now, so one day you will be able to do the things you want to do when you want to do them.

If you need help in getting motivated, re-read your goals, exercise, disassociate yourself from dream stealers, and avoid situations that drain you. If something tragic has happened and you need some time to adjust to a change in your environment, put a time limit on how long you will be down, and then create a get up and go holiday, and ritualize that day with some sort of symbolic and meaningful activity. Then just start working without worrying about results and you should be re-motivated.

Focus on What You Want

The eleventh habit of persistence is focus. Knowing what to focus on is a key element of persistence. If you focus on the negative, you will get negative results. If you focus on the positive, you will get positive results. If you focus on why your plans will not work, they will not work, and if you focus on why your plans will work, you will succeed.

If you think about your golf game on the way to a job interview, your interview will suffer. If you think about your job interview while you play golf, your golf game will suffer. If you focus on an unbreakable habit and why that habit is unbreakable, it will remain unbreakable. If you focus on how you will break those habits, why you should break those habits, and replace them with new productive habits, those bad habits will be broken. What and where you focus your passing thoughts on will determine how you will pass through life and what you will get from life. **Remember you get what you focus on.**

I would like to end this chapter with the words of Calvin Coolidge who said, "Nothing in the world can take the place of persistence. Talent will not. When you look around you will see that nothing is more common than unsuccessful men who possess talent. Genius will not; un-rewarded genius is almost a proverb. Education will not; the world is full of educated failures. Persistence and determination alone are omnipotent."

I believe that persistence makes us equal. It is a fact that there are people who have certain advantages because of circumstance or they may acquire advantages through various associations. These advantages do not do many of these people any good because they quit. As matter of fact, many people become lazy because of these advantages, which quickly turn them into disadvantages. I believe that over a lifetime persistence makes us equal. I believe that persistence is what separates the losers from the winners.

KAPS

➢ Persistence is a key element of success.
➢ If you try long enough, hard enough, and change your approach enough, you will become successful no matter what you want to do.
➢ Persistence is not doing the same thing over and over and expecting different results.
➢ Persistence takes time.
➢ Persistence means getting up and going even after your get up and go got up and went.
➢ Persistence requires focus.
➢ Persistence requires having a definite mission.
➢ Persistence means never quitting until you have reached your goal.

Chapter 22

The Power of Effective Negotiating:
It's Not What You are Worth
It is What You Can Negotiate

Congratulations, you got the job! Now what do you do? There are two things that you need to do. First, you need to negotiate the job offer, and then you need to evaluate the job offer. You need to make sure that you have a clear understanding of what your job duties will be. Having a good understanding of what your employer expects from you and what you expect from your job will prevent conflicts in the future, and it will help you see what comparable positions are paying. Make sure that you are very clear on both of them.

The Eleven Basic Steps of Negotiating

Get the job offer!

Do not talk about salary until you get the job offer. Some organizations will try to lock you into a salary below what you are worth. After all they are in business to make money and if they can get you to do quality work for less than what you are worth, they have made a good financial decision while you have made a poor financial decision. Wait until you are sure they want you before you talk money.

Never make an offer until you hear their offer.

Until now you have been selling yourself to the organization. When the organization offers you a position, they are now trying to sell you on the idea of coming to work for them. Typically, when someone is selling something it is his or her responsibility to set the price. The buyer is not responsible to set the price.

Think about buying a new car. When you buy a car you know what the sticker price is. You also know that cars have a negotiable price; the sticker does not ask what you paid for your last car. Why then should the employer be concerned with what you made on your last job? You and the organization should be more concerned about what you are going to do for them.

Know what you are negotiating.

Before you make an offer, know what people are making in similar positions. The government has statistics on what people make. The Internet has websites that will help you with this. You can also get this information from trade associations or trade magazines.

Be flexible.

Be ready to negotiate other terms such as days off, vacation time, work duties, a faster career track, stock options, insurance, car allowances, country club memberships, membership dues, tuition reimbursements, and other things you find important. Remember there is more to work than money. If you can find a benefit that is more substantial than financial, take it; you spend too much time on a job just to earn a paycheck.

Ask for more.

Tell the interviewer what salary you had in mind, but add 25% to it. There are three reasons for this. First, it will not cost you any more to ask for this and you may get it. Second, if your raises are based on percentages this will mean more money in the long run. The last reason is typically employers are willing to increase what they were originally offering. The exceptions to this are most entry-level positions or government positions. Regardless of the position, just ask.

Give details.

Give reasons why you deserve this salary. While it is okay to state what the market pays, it is better to give specific reasons for why you are this valuable. This should show that your demands are reasonable. They must believe you are valuable if they offered you the job.

Learn the power of the pause.

When the job interviewer gives you a range, repeat the top of range and pause. Make sure you repeat it so the interviewer knows you heard the offer. If this amount is more than you expected, do not say anything, just sit there and think about it. See how they respond and then you respond. See if they offer a higher range or additional benefits.

Do not act too soon.

Postpone the decision as long as you can, but not too long. If they really want you, they can wait a day or two. This waiting may encourage them to increase the package offered to you or it may not increase anything. You will not know until you try this. Tell the interviewer you want to think about the offer and the job. Let them know that you take great care in your decisions because you know the decisions you make today affect the results you get tomorrow.

Be rational.

Do not expect too much or too little. Do not miss a great opportunity because you are making a little less than you wanted. Do not take a poor offer because you feel you have too. If this is your first job out of college, it is okay to take an entry-level position. If you have a great deal of work experience, education, and results in a given, field do not think you have to start back at the beginning and rework your way up.

Be committed.

Be committed to what you want out of life. Don't sell your dreams for any amount of money. If the job is not your dream job, and you will not get up and look forward to going to work, say no. The only time you should say yes is if you really need the job. Otherwise say no and they will respect you for it, but more importantly, you will respect yourself. It is hard to say no at first, but believe me the more job offers you refuse the easier it gets. I find myself saying no to all sorts of jobs because they are not a part of my mission in life, and no position or amount of money can ever change that.

Don't negotiate against yourself.

You know what your minimum requirements are, but remember the person offering you job does not have access to this information. When you negotiate against yourself, you will always strike a great deal for the other person. You will give this person a reason to doubt your abilities and talents, and this may make them question their decision to hire you. The last reason you should not negotiate against yourself is this always takes away from the integrity of the negotiating process. You want to add to the integrity of the negotiating process and not take away from it.

Do you want them now that they want you?
How to assess the job offer

Now is time to find out if you really want the job offer. You have negotiated a compensation package, but is this really your dream job? If you are having doubts, that is okay and even positive. It shows that you are really thinking about what you want out of life. If you really need the job because you need to pay for the essentials of life, my advice would be to take it. But if you have the luxury of choosing your employment, I would look at all the options and weigh your choices.

Before you can make a good decision, you need to know what you have. So fill in the worksheet below, or make a copy so you can do this as many times as it takes to get the job you want.

25 questions to help evaluate your job offer.

1. Starting Salary:_____
2. Bonuses: _____
3. Company Car: _____
4. Travel? If so, how much? _____
5. Future potential at the organization: _____
6. Other compensation: _____
7. Benefits: _____
8. Educational opportunities: _____
9. Moving expenses: _____
10. Training: _____
11. Starting Date: _____
12. Vacation: _____
13. Management style: _____
14. Organizational reputation: _____
15. Commute: _____
16. Organizational culture: _____
17. Hours per week: _____
18. Sick Time: _____
19. Performance reviews: _____
20. Cost of living raises: _____
21. Profit Sharing: _____
22. Retirement or 401k plan: _____

23. Employee stock purchase plan: _____
24. Vesting requirement: _____
25. Holidays: _____

This is not an exhaustive list and you can add to it and take away as you need to. It is just a way to get started in evaluating your job offer. This list is primarily geared to the day-to-day job related issues, but some other things you need to consider are:

1. Will this job help me fulfill my mission in life?
2. How long do I plan to be in this position?
3. Is this just a stepping-stone to something bigger and better?
4. Will this job give me the opportunities necessary for success?
5. What will happen if I do not take this job?
6. What will happen if I do take this job?

If you are asked to relocate, that brings up a new set of questions that need to be answered. Relocating is part of today's business world, and chances are you will be asked to relocate sometime in your career. If you are, you will need to consider carefully the costs of relocation. When relocating, always be sure to check the cost of living index, which is a composite of groceries, housing, utilities, transportation, health care, clothing, and entertainment for geographical regions across the country, with 100.0 as the national average.

Here is an example of determining your purchasing power. I will pretend that I live in Fayetteville, Arkansas, and I plan to move to Minneapolis, Minnesota. I would find out the Cost of Living (COL) for Fayetteville, which is 90.8, and then I would find the COL for St. Paul, which is 101.5. I would then divide 90.8 by 101.5, and the answer is 0.89.

Let's pretend that the people in St. Paul offered me $35,000 to come work for them. I would take .89 and multiply that by the salary offered by the people in St. Paul to find what it is Fayetteville dollars. So $35,000 times 0.89 is $31,150 in Fayetteville dollars. This means if I were making $32,000 a year in Fayetteville, by moving to St. Paul I would have a decrease of purchasing power or real income by $850.00, even though by salary it would look like I was increasing by $3,000. Minnesota, however, might ultimately offer you greater opportunities than Arkansas. This why it is up to you to decided what is best for your career.

If this seems confusing, I would recommend that you use a Cost of Living Index Calculator that can be found on the Internet. You can go to any search engine and type in "Cost of Living Index Calculator" or "salary comparison" and you will get a number of sites that will help you. Other things you need to consider if you are relocating besides salary and COL are: relocation expenses, transportation, weather, environment, your family, your friends, social activities, places of worship for your religion, political atmosphere, schools, job market, and accessibility back home.

After you have answered all the questions about how to evaluate a job offer, take some time away and ask yourself all the pros and cons to the job offer and make your final decision from that list. Once you have done this, you should be able to find your dream job and make it a reality.

Once you have that dream job you need to make sure that you become successful. To help you with that success, I have added a bonus chapter on how to be successful at work. While getting your dream job was work, the real work begins when you show up for your first day. I want you to make sure that your time on the job is rewarding. This new job is a new starting point. When you had the idea to go into that position, it was the size of an acorn. Now is the time to turn that acorn-sized idea into an oak tree sized reality. That is why I would like to end here and start a new beginning to this book.

KAPS

- ➢ Before you accept the job offer, you should negotiate the job offer.
- ➢ Wait until you get the job offer before you talk about money.
- ➢ You can negotiate more than money.
- ➢ Do not negotiate against yourself.
- ➢ Always ask for more.

The End!

The Beginning

Bonus Chapter 1
Success on the Job and Beyond

This may be a strange place to begin a book, but the book is not beginning -- your dream job is beginning. In my opinion getting your dream is just the beginning. Success comes from what you do on and off the job. I know you have worked hard to acquire the skills needed to get your dream job, and I know you have worked just as hard to land your dream job. As with everything else in life, every ending has a new beginning and the ending of your job search is the beginning of a new career.

I do not believe that you changed jobs or entered the job market because you wanted to make less money. I do not believe that you changed or entered the job market because you wanted to work longer hours at a job you hate. I believe that you changed jobs or entered the job market because you wanted to make more money. I believe that you changed jobs or entered the job market because you wanted rewarding work. I believe that you changed jobs or entered the job market because you wanted to make a difference in your life and in the lives of those around you.

I call this a bonus chapter because unlike the rest of the book it is not about job-hunting strategies or tips. This chapter is about how to make your dream job a successful experience. The purpose of this chapter is to give you the motivation, the inspiration, and the information that will help you get ahead on and off the job. Remember as you read this chapter there is much more to a job than a paycheck.

Part of this chapter is about helping you earn more money. After all, I believe that we all would like to make a little more money. Do not listen to the people who say that wanting more is greed. It is not greed. Money provides choices and money provides you with the opportunity to help other people. When someone criticizes you for wanting more money I believe what they are really saying is they don't feel like they deserve more money.

Do not base your rewards on what other people think they deserve. Base your rewards on the work you are willing to do for those rewards. If you work hard and make a difference, I believe you deserve the rewards that are equal to the quality and quantity of service you are willing to render. Wanting more money does not mean that you are greedy, it just means that you want more of the choices that only money can bring. This chapter will help you get the most of life by helping you earn more money and by helping you get more free time.

Expect the Best But Prepare for Adversity

You should always expect success because you get what you expect. While planning for the best, you should prepare for the unexpected. Even the best plans do not cover every possibility. You should always have a plan B and sometimes a plan C in case plan A is not effective, but do not rush into your back up plans. I believe you should stick to plan A until you have exhausted all possibilities.

For example, I have a graduate degree. The reason I have a graduate degree is that the worst-case scenario is I will end up working for someone else in a human resources department. The best-case scenario is I will be a nationally known motivation expert lecturing and conducting seminars for thousands of people at a time, while selling millions of copies of this book and other books I plan to write.

Do I need a graduate degree to be a motivational speaker and trainer? Zig Ziglar, Brian Tracy, and Norith Ellison do not have graduate degrees. Tony Robbins and Tom Hopkins just have high school diplomas, and the list of successful people in my field and in other fields with less formal education than I have is endless. Notice I said formal education. I believe that there are two types of education: formal education and self-knowledge. Formal education is what you receive by going to school and earning degrees. I personally think that this is a great form of knowledge, and this type of knowledge opens many doors. However, it will not make you rich. What will make you a fortune is self-knowledge.

Self-knowledge is what you learn after you leave the formal education system. This means you will need to read, study, and search for information that will help you to become successful. Self-knowledge is developing the understanding behind the reasons for your actions. Self-knowledge is periodically assessing your progress and skills to determine what you need to know in order to become who you want to become.

I decided to get a graduate degree because I understand that things may happen on my road to success. I decided to engage in a life long quest for self-knowledge because I know that adversity happens to the best of us. I also know that with each obstacle comes an equal benefit. That is why adversity is a great teacher, if you are willing to learn the lessons it is trying to teach.

Have the Right Attitude

It has often been said that attitude determines your altitude, and I believe this to be true. When you have a positive mental attitude, you create a 3-W attitude to "win, win, and win." With this attitude, you will win. I believe that we all are born to win. I do not believe that when you were created the Creator said, "Look, here is another average person." I believe that he said, "Look here is a _____! This person is going to make a difference because they are going to do _____."

When you start to think positively, everything around you will be positive. Whatever you really expect to take place will take place. This is because you are a human magnet in the sense that you attract what you focus on and think about no matter what it is. It's true. Another way to say this is water seeks its own level. This is why no matter where you are you will always find yourself surrounded with people who have a similar attitude as yourself.

Have you ever noticed that the people who are afraid of elevators are the same people who get stuck in elevators? Have you ever noticed that the people who just know that their spouse is going to cheat on them have a spouse that cheats on them? Have you ever noticed that people who know that things are going to be okay find themselves in good situations? Have you ever noticed that when you go anywhere where there is a large group of people, smaller groups form and in those small groups, people look and act the same? You need to develop and cultivate the kind of attitude you find the most desirable in others and you will find yourself not only having that attitude but associating with others who have it as well.

Be Confident

You must have confidence in yourself. If you are not confident in yourself, people will not be confident in you. People admire and respect confident people. Confidence is a very important leadership quality. People will not follow a leader who does not have confidence in his or her ability. I understand that not everyone wants to be a leader. That is fine, but when you have confidence, you will admire and respect yourself more. The more respect you have for yourself the more you will do for yourself.

One key to developing confidence is positive self-talk. You may question this technique, but this esteem builder works. You may not be aware of it but you are in constant communication with yourself. As you read this book, I am sure that you have said one of two things. "This information will really work." If you say this you will find that the information will work because you believe it will work and this gives you the confidence that makes it work. On the other hand you may be saying, "This won't work for me because I could never do _____." If this is the case, it will never work because you do not have the confidence to make it work.

It is these messages that you constantly send to yourself that determine who you become. When you make it a point to make these messages positive, confidence will come. When you say, "This will work, because I can make it work," you are creating the confidence that is necessary to make the changes you want to make.

Einstein said that it takes 18 positive messages to replace one negative message. When something bad happens do not say, "This always happens to me." Instead, say something positive like, "I am going to look for the opportunity in this difficulty." Or, "At least I know what doesn't work, so now I can better figure out what will work."

When you say something is luck, you are discounting your ability to influence your situation. Luck is a lazy person's excuse for not being successful. Give yourself the credit you deserve. To make these messages really work, speak them out loud, write them out, and put them where you can see them several times a day.

The Real Cost

What is the cost of success? Some people claim you have to pay the price for success. I don't believe it. I believe that you pay the price for failure. You pay the price for mediocrity. You pay the price for neglecting self-improvement. You pay the price when you put off until tomorrow what you should do today. When you are afraid to answer the phone because it might be a creditor on the other end, you are paying the price for failure. When you hate going to work you are paying the price for not finding your dream job and making it a reality.

On the other hand, you enjoy the rewards of success. You enjoy the money you make, or at least you should. You enjoy going to work knowing what you are doing is making a difference. You enjoy knowing that you are living your dreams. You enjoy the rewards of life when you know that you are living life with purpose. That fact is you do not pay the price to become successful; you pay the price for not becoming successful. When you take the steps necessary to be successful you will say I'm glad I did instead of I wish I had.

It takes more than hard work to become successful. I know hard working people who never became successful. Hard work is an important element because nothing works unless you work. To become successful it takes the willingness to invest in a constant program of self-improvement. It takes getting away from negative people. It takes looking for the seed of opportunity in every negative circumstance. It takes a positive mental attitude to become successful.

I believe that you can become the person that you want and ought to become. I believe that you can go where you want to go, and I believe that you can do what you want to do. I believe you can do all of the things you want to do if you remember that success is the ability to take from life whatever it is you desire without violating the rights of other people. As long as what you want out of life is legal, moral, and does not harm the world, I personally believe that you can and should live your dreams.

At this point, make a list of everything you would like to have, do, or become in your lifetime. The fact is you can have everything on that list if you invest in yourself and develop the skills, knowledge, and drive to go out and get it. If you do not, how you are going to accomplish the things on that list? You should start working towards acquiring the things on your list and you should plan to go as far as you can see. When you get that far you will be able to see farther. We can only go as far as we can see. While this is true it is also true the farther you go the farther you can see. Remember, when you put into life what it takes to get those things out of life, you will get the rewards. If you give in to fear and do nothing it will actually cost you everything on that list.

If you want everything on your list, take a lesson from nature. Squirrels gather nuts all summer so they can eat all winter. They do not have to gather nuts; they could just play all summer without ever thinking about the long cold winter. If they do this, however, what price will they pay in the winter? Think about yourself for a minute. Suppose you decided not to work now. What results could you expect when your winter comes?

No One Does it on Their Own

I believe in order to be successful you will need the assistance of other people. People will help you get where you want to go. Many people want to help people who are trying to be successful. I should warn you that there are some misguided individuals who will try to sabotage you since they are not successful. Since they cannot envision success for themselves or they do not think they deserve success they will think you do not deserve to be successful. This is why it so vital to surround yourself with positive, motivated, and caring people. When you do this you will find it easier to be successful.

On the way to the top, you will need mentors. You will need to mentor people. You need to build relationships. I believe that people can teach you to become a better person. I believe if someone helps you, you should reward them, but if you do something for somebody else do not expect a reward. Zig Ziglar says it this way, "You can get anything you want if you just help enough other people get what they want."

Small Things Mean Big Rewards

Some things that seem small to you mean a great deal to others. Do not ignore small problems; help people solve them. Treating small problems with importance shows other people you care. It shows that you can be trusted. When you take the time to perform the small task with care people will know you can be counted on to handle the big tasks.

The best story I have ever heard about this principle comes from the Bible. In Matthew 25 Jesus tells a parable about a businessman. I am not sure what he owned other than some land, but that's not the point of the story. The point is this man was successful. He had many servants who all had different talents, abilities, and motivations.

According to the Bible, the businessman had to make a long journey and needed to leave his business in the hands of his employees. He also wanted them to make more money while he was gone. He called together his servants and said to one servant, "I am going to give you five talents. I want you to see what you can do with them. When I get back from my trip I want you to give me a report." This servant said he would do his best. This man told his next servant, "I am going to give you two talents. I want you to see what you can do with them. When I get back from my trip, I want you to give me a report." This servant said he would do his best. This man told his third and newest servant, "I am going to give you one talent. I want to see what you can do with it. I expect a report when I return." This servant said he would do his best.

This man went on his trip and he was gone a long time. When he came back, he called these three servants and asked for their reports. The first servant said, "Sir, I have doubled your money. Here are your ten talents." The man said, "Great, I'm proud of your work. You have been faithful over a few things so I will put you in charge of many things."

The man with the two talents gave his report. He reported that he took his talents to the market and turned his two talents into four talents. The man said, "Great, I'm proud of your business savvy. You have been resourceful with a few things so I will put you in charge of many things."

Then came the newest servant. The man asked him, "What did you do with your talent?" The servant said, "I was fearful of disappointing you or losing your money so I hid the talent underground. Here it is." The businessman said, "You knew I wanted a profit and you did nothing to attempt to get me a profit. You could have at least earned interest on the talent." The servant was then thrown into the darkness.

The point is you do not want to waste even one talent. No matter your station in life you can create your own opportunities based on how well you perform with the resources you are given. I do not want what happened to the third servant to happen to you. That is why regardless of your job or opportunities you should take full advantage of each opportunity, no matter how small. If you do not do this you could be just like the servant in the story who missed out on what could have been a huge break in his career.

After-Work Activities

If overtime work is needed and the financial gain is significant, take the overtime. However, you need to be careful because if the overtime starts to take away from your personal relationships you will need to make a point to decline the overtime. Remember there is more to a job than a paycheck. There is more to life than making money. I do agree that we all want to make more money, but money cannot replace your spouse, kids, or friends.

Remember that what you do after work influences your job performance. Your life is made up of interrelated parts. I believe that is why you should maintain a personal educational program of some sort. This type of self-improvement will prepare future opportunities for yourself. Along with your self-improvement program you may consider developing new marketable skills and experiences by volunteering for committees, extra projects, and/or civic organizations. Work hard on these activities as a way to define and perfect your new skills.

How to Deal with Feedback or Criticism

When you get feedback or criticism you will want to know how to get the most out of it. Useful criticism is one of the best ways to make you a better person. When I first wanted to be a public speaker, I joined Toastmasters International. This group gave me an opportunity to learn and practice my public speaking skills. The way it works is you give a speech and they evaluate your speech.

In this evaluation, the evaluator would give me feedback and tips to use in the future. Sometimes this feedback hurt, but the good news is it never killed me. One of the greatest benefits I have received from Toastmasters is not only the feedback, but also the ability to handle feedback even if it was not what I wanted to hear. Feedback is not a personal attack; feedback is a way that professional individuals grow.

Feedback and criticism are good if only for the reason that they force us to look at what we are doing. This often gives us the desire to improve our actions or ourselves. Sometimes we are not aware that what we are doing is not working. Feedback helps us determine what works and what does not work. The fact is if we keep doing what we have been doing we are not going to be any more successful. Feedback and criticism from others is the opportunity to look for new ways to improve our performance. This is why I believe that we should seek constant feedback on how we are performing professionally.

Ask For Feedback

Find out exactly what other people think about what you are doing. If they say, "You stink" do not get mad, but ask them for specifics. Find out why that person thinks you stink, and let them know it is okay to be honest. Occasionally you may find a person who refuses to give you reasons for criticizing you. If this is this case, there are some things you can do. Look for self-assessments that relate to the job and/or task, or find someone else to ask for feedback.

The person who is refusing to give you their reasons for criticizing you may be afraid of your potential for success. Since they are not enjoying life they do not think other people should. I believe that most mean people act this way not because they want to hurt you but because they are hurting. While this negativity is not intentional, it can still have the same effect as if it were intentional.

If someone says you are great, find out why that person thinks you are great. They may be "being nice" to you. This really is not nice, because it is keeping you from growing. If they say you are great, thank them for the compliment, but tell them you would really like to increase your performance. Then ask them for advice on how you can get better. Ask them what you can do to improve and then do it. Follow their advice. If they do not offer you any suggestions, my suggestion would be to ask someone else.

How to get the people you work with to like you and respect you.

Good relations with your co-workers and your superiors will not only help you on the job, but these relationships are a valuable element that make going to work more enjoyable. I have never heard of a person who liked their job because their co-workers hated them. I have heard of people who liked their job because they liked their co-workers. The fact is people want to be liked by other people.

If you treat people the way they want to be treated, they will like you. In this next section I will discuss ideas that will help you treat people the way they want to be treated.

Some of this may be new. Some of it may be old hat. You may agree with some of it. You may disagree with some of it. Either way I want you to use to it, but the key to using it effectively is being sincere. If you are not sincere in your interactions with other people, they will know.

Treat People like People

Everybody enjoys and desires recognition. It is natural. I do not know a person who does not want approval from someone in some form. Many people will work harder for recognition than what they will for money. I believe that recognition is one of the elements that make people like going to work.

However, you should only praise people when they deserve it. If you praise people when they do not deserve it, or if you praise too much, you lose your credibility. Since people will want more praise they will tend to repeat the action that got them the praise originally. Depending upon the nature of the praise, you may be lowering the expectations of that person. Since we all tend to do what is expected, what you are doing to that person is a disservice. You never want to lower people's expectations because you will lower the results of their work and their general output.

Work to increase the expectations of others. This will encourage them to become better and more successful people. This also communicates to the person that you think they are capable and able to do the task. Be careful not to exaggerate your praise. Make sure your praise is always warm and sincere, and always look to find someone doing something right.

My wife once told me that at her then current job, one of the managers sent out an email to all the staff in the organization bragging on the staff that was under that manager at a specific location of the organization. One of my wife's co-workers read the email and said, "Wouldn't it be nice to be praised like that just once." This co-worker had worked in the organization over 12 years and had never been recognized for her daily efforts.

We know that praising people shows approval and recognition for what they have done. When an individual's action has been positive in some way, it is your duty to let that person know how much you appreciate their action. If you do not do this, you may not benefit from their assistance again. I believe that when you do this you should use specific phrases such as:

> ➤ I really appreciate the way you_____
> ➤ Thank you very much for_____
> ➤ You are very good at_____
> ➤ I really want to tell you how much I appreciated_____
> ➤ You were very nice to_____

In addition, when you are treating people like people, remember that everyone appreciates people who are courteous, tactful, polite, and who listen with care. I have never heard of two people listening their way out of a relationship. I have heard of people talking their way out of a relationship but not listening. There are two ways to learn these qualities. The first is by observing others, and the second is by reading or listening to books on the subject.

Don't "Show Up" Others

I am sure you are a person who would not do this, but when a person shows up another person they mistakenly think they are doing this at someone else's expense. The fact is they are doing it at their own expense. This is one of the most costly mistakes a person can make when they are trying to get ahead. When attempting to show up another person, you are only showing what a shallow person you are. No one wants to work with or help people who are constantly trying to out-do them.

I am not sure if it is arrogance, meanness, ignorance or lack of social skills that cause people to do this. The only person who looks bad in these situations is the person doing the showing up and not the person being put down. I believe that if you are better than others are, they will know it, and you should not have to degrade another person to prove that you are better.

I would even say that no matter your talent, skill, or education, if you degrade another person you are not better than that person, because you are not a just person. People admire and respect just people. Putting down or showing up another person for whatever reason will always cost you more than you will gain. The greatest rewards come from treating all people with respect at all times no matter what you think they deserve.

How to Make People Feel Important

All people want to feel important. You do not accomplish anything when you attempt to put yourself in a "superior" position. The only thing you do is show how small you are. A key element to success is making other people feel comfortable around you. People feel important when you give them your undivided attention. You make people feel important when you make them feel valued. Here are some things you can do to make people feel important.

> - Get rid of all interruptions.
> - Make sure you have good eye contact and that you are not playing with objects.
> - Give the other person the opportunity to bring up topics, change the subject, and demand attention.
> - Do not bombard the other person with questions.
> - Offer advice only when it is asked for.
> - Do not give too many intimate personal details.
> - Avoid absolute statements and all or nothing comments such as "That is a terrible song."
> - Relax and help the speaker to relax, too.
> - Do not let the speaker's tone of voice, personal appearance, or manner tune out their message.
> - If possible, prepare beforehand for the conversation.
> - Mentally collect the main points of the conversation, and ask for clarification of the speaker's comments.

When you make people feel important, you are becoming important. You will find the more you make other people feel important the more people will do things to make you feel important. When this happens people will come and ask you to participate on projects because they will respect your opinion and value your input. This will help you to become more successful on and off the job.

KAPS

➢ Getting a job is only the first step.
➢ To be successful on the job you must have a vision and mission to guide you.
➢ Remember to treat people as you want to be treated.
➢ Be positive, determined and persistent.

Bonus Chapter 2

Getting Your First Raise
Or Promotion

If you find yourself in a position where the raises are few and far between, this chapter may be of use to you. I know that many organizations have regular pay increases based on performance. I hope you are working for such an organization. I also know that there are misguided organizations that believe one way to save money is by not increasing salaries.

If you find yourself working in an organization that saves money by refusing or avoiding raises, it is up to you to do something. Typically, that something is asking for the raise. However, before you go ask your unreceptive boss for more money there are some things you should know. You should realize that this is another selling situation. You are trying to sell yourself for a new position or you are trying to sell your boss on the idea that you deserve more money. Knowing this, you should assess the product you are selling (you).

Before you try to get a raise or promotion, ask yourself the following questions and answer them honestly:

- ➤ If you were your boss, how would you rate your job performance?
- ➤ If you were your boss, would you even know who you are?
- ➤ If you were your boss, would you consider yourself a professional by organizational and industry standards?
- ➤ Does your employer know what contributions you have made to increase organizational effectiveness?
- ➤ Do you constantly seek out more responsibility?
- ➤ Do you constantly seek out training even at your own expense?
- ➤ Do you constantly perform well in your present position?
- ➤ Do you stay current with what is happening in your industry?
- ➤ Do you have good relationships with your co-workers and superiors?
- ➤ Can you be specific and quantify your accomplishments?

If your work performance is not adequate, you do not deserve a raise. If you are not making positive contributions for the organization, you do not deserve a raise. If you do not seek more responsibility, you do not deserve a raise. If you are not current with new changes within your industry, you do not deserve a raise. If you are not able to get along with your coworkers, you do not deserve a raise.

When you are asking for a raise you need to remember that before you can get you have to give. Do not be like the farmer who said, "Lord, if you give me some crops this year I promise that next year I will plant." Just because you have been with an organization for a long time does not mean that the organization owes you anything unless you have been getting results.

The rest of this chapter will be dedicated to this question: "who does the promotion -- the employer or the employee?" I believe that the employee does the promotion. You owe it to yourself to do a great job and to put everything you can into your job. If you do this, you will get a raise. If you do this, you will get a promotion. If you do this, you will be a success. If you do this and are not able to find higher salaries and higher positions with your current employer, believe me when I say that you will be able to find these things with a different employer.

Go the Extra Mile

Going the extra mile works because it makes use of the law of compare and contrast. Since most people never go the first mile, when you go the second mile it makes you an asset for the organization. The truth is it does not take any more effort to go the second mile than it does the first. As a matter of fact, the people who constantly go the second mile will find themselves with more energy because they are working with a definite purpose. Even if you do not like your current position or organization, by constantly going that extra mile you will be able to leave your current situation much sooner.

One way to go the extra mile is to seek more responsibility and to constantly take on the tougher assignments. This will make work both challenging and rewarding. Be proactive about this. Do not be afraid to take on all the responsibility you can handle. I should warn you not to overdo it, but try to find additional responsibilities in addition to your assigned work. The greater your responsibilities, the more you are an asset to the organization.

Increase Your Interests, Skills, and Talents

The more you know, the more valuable you are. You owe it to yourself to finish your degree or if you have a degree to get your advanced degree. You can do this by going to night classes. Remember while formal education is important, do not forget that self-knowledge will make you a fortune. This is why you should constantly read books, listen to audiotapes, or watch videos that will give you the additional information, inspiration, and motivation necessary for success.

Increase your interest in various activities. This will help you become well rounded. Your participation in various activities and the group involvement that comes with this will help you grow. This will also give you a network that will help you move forward with your career and life. Remember that nobody ever becomes successful without the help of others. So along with increasing your interests, skills, and talents you should constantly network with individuals inside and outside of your organization.

Know Your Organization

Find out everything you can about your organization. Understand the industry. Understand the culture of your organization. Understand why people do what they do in your organization. Examine the implicit and explicit norms of your organization. There are unwritten rules at your organization; do you know them?

Listen for stories about heroes at your organization. Determine the qualities of your organization's heroes and develop those qualities in yourself. At the same time determine the qualities of your organization's villains and avoid those qualities. Seek to gain an understanding of why your organization does what it does. At the same time, take time to understand, study, and learn the positions of your fellow workers and the value of those positions. Understand what they do and why they do it. Always try to increase your knowledge about your organization.

While it is more important to know the informal culture at work, take time to understand your organization's formal written policies, especially towards salaries, raises, and promotions. The organization uses these written policies as reasons for not giving raises or promotions. You may have to be with the organization a specified length of time to get a raise. Find out how long and act at the right time. If you are getting the maximum salary for your position, you may have to ask for a promotion or a re-classification.

Know Your Boss

Treat your boss like a person, even if your boss does not treat you like a person. This is because the way you treat a person directly affects the way that person treats you. While this is true, the way another person treats you should not determine the way you treat that person. Get to know your boss and learn what it takes to earn *idiosyncrasy credits* from your boss.

Idiosyncrasy credits are things that you need in order to gain additional leeway in adhering to group norms. Idiosyncrasy credits are given to a group member for valuable contributions to the group. What is valuable is in the eyes of the person giving the credit? When determining what Idiosyncrasy credits are for your organization, do not let your organization's mission statement mislead you.

The organizational leaders may not actually reward what is stated in the mission statement. Take the time to find out what is really rewarded in the organization and then do what it takes to get those rewards. Then when you have adequate credits, ask for a raise and the boss should be more receptive. When asking for a raise consider your timing. Consider your bosses mood. Consider what is happening to the organization in the marketplace. Even if you are turned down it is better to be turned down when the timing is right than when the timing is off. Chances are good that if you ask at the wrong time the boss will remember and have a negative image of you much longer than if the time was right. You should also make an appointment with your boss to discuss your raise and try to avoid a Monday or Friday appointment.

Market Yourself

Make sure your accomplishments are seen. There is nothing wrong with letting others know what you have accomplished, as long as you don't brag. If the opportunity arises for recognition, take it, and let others know what you have done for the organization. A great idea is to keep a record of your accomplishments in a journal. When you ask for a raise you will need specifics and you can refer to your journal for an accurate account of your actions. Also, keep all your recommendations, awards, certificates, and other relevant information in a file.

Be Ready to Negotiate

If your boss talks to you about the potential for a raise, they have actually started the negotiating process. This is good because it means that you are being considered for the raise. When you negotiate the raise you need to be able to justify the raise; you should be able to tell the person what you want, your acceptable range, and you should be ready to be creative in the negotiation process. After all, there is more to work than earning a paycheck.

Justify the Raise

When you ask for a raise be ready to tell specifics about your accomplishments and how the accomplishments have had a positive impact on the organization. Show them how much you saved the organization or how much the organization has profited as a result of your work. Research the market and gain an understanding of what your skills are worth for another organization in the same area. Present this information to the decision makers in a very non-aggressive manner. Let them know you like working for them and you want to continue to get results for the organization.

Sell them on the idea that your raise is an investment in the organization. Sell them on the fact that your value to the organization has increased. Please do not mention anything about your personal needs or desire for the extra money, and be prepared to handle rejection. If you are rejected, ask for specific reasons why you did not get the raise or promotion. There may be policy issues such as time on the job. There may be economic issues like a slow market. If the reasons are valid it is okay to agree with them and develop a plan to overcome those objections. If those reasons are invalid tell them, but do not give ultimatums unless you are ready to back them up.

If the reasons are irrational, remember that job jumping is a viable career and success strategy. If the organization is not going to reward your efforts, find an organization that will. You may not have gotten the raise because the organization is planning a layoff, plans to outsource your position, or just does not care about you. None of these reasons is good enough to stay with the organization.

Clearly Explain What You Want

If you want more money or a better position, you need to be able to clearly identify what you want. Develop a realistic career/business plan that will show the value for them if they give you what you want. Tell the person exactly what you want in terms they will understand. For example you want to be able to say:

> ➢ I want more responsibilities.
> ➢ I want a better office.
> ➢ I want a clearer career path.
> ➢ I want more time off.
> ➢ I want this position.
> ➢ I want _____.

Know the range.

How much money is realistic to ask for? It depends on your situation. You should research salary information for similar positions. Find out what other people in your position make, find out their responsibilities, and see how this relates to you. To be effective you need to document your research. To document your research you can check the employment classifieds, talk with colleagues in other firms, check out employment websites, and check with your local college career services department. Your goal is to find the salary range for a person with your education, background, and years of experience.

Know what you want and what you will accept. You should have your bargaining position fully worked out before you sit down to negotiate. This means knowing three important figures:

> **The Dream** This is the top end salary for people in your position. This is what the highest paid people are paid. This figure is the most you can hope to get because of the market conditions.

> **The Bottom Line** This figure is the least that you need to accept to stay with the organization. If you plan to leave the organization, I would either have a job already lined up, or not tell them that you plan to leave. If you have a job lined up you can say, "I need $52,000 or I will have to start with XZY Company at the end of the month." If you do not have a job lined up, I would take their offer and then start looking for an organization that would invest in you and what you are really worth. Don't tell them of your plans because if they think you are going to leave soon they will not give you as much or any additional money.

> **The Actual** This is a realistic figure that you have a good chance of getting. You should feel comfortable with this amount and your employer should feel comfortable. The goal is dependent upon your situation but it is probably somewhere between the maximum and minimum figures.

Be Creative

There is more to work than earning a paycheck. If you are not able to get the money you want, try to negotiate for other things. If you like where you work, do not make this decision based solely on money. Here is a partial list of things you may be able to negotiate for and remember that this list is not comprehensive:

> Ask for additional vacation time.
> Ask for a more flexible schedule.
> Ask for tuition assistance.
> Ask for lower insurance premiums.
> Ask for a better office.
> Ask for a better computer.
> Ask for rewards such as oil changes for your car, massages for yourself, or country club memberships.
> Ask for trade and organizational memberships.
> Ask for time off to attend those meetings.
> Ask for an increase to your 401k.
> Ask for your spouse to go on corporate retreats with you.
> Ask for a company car or allowance.
> Ask for free parking.
> Ask for a clothing allowance.
> Ask for books, audio programs, or videos that relate to your job.
> Ask for more training at the organization's expense.
> Ask for anything that will help you enjoy your job more.

When you try to get a raise or promotion it is important to remember that you get those things the same way you get a job. That is by solving problems for your employer. When you first got your job, you were hired to solve some sort of problem. You were a solution to a problem. When you want a raise or promotion, you still need to be providing solutions.

Even if your employer is not giving you the rewards you deserve, you still owe it to yourself to do a good job. The best time to leave any job is when you are on top. You do not get to the top or stay at the top by being mediocre. Constantly doing the best job you can do will always get you better positions and more money, even if it may not be with your present employer.

KAPS

- ➤ The employer doesn't do the promoting; the employee does.
- ➤ You earn a promotion or a raise by what you put into your time at work and not the amount of time you spend at work.
- ➤ Asking for a raise is a selling and negotiating process.
- ➤ Be willing to discuss benefits other than money.

Bonus Chapter 3

Employment Solutions for 40, 50, and Beyond

According to the AARP, there are currently more than 30 million men and women age 50 and older in the labor force. This number is expected to rise as the Baby Boomers continue to age. Still employers are reluctant to make use of this valuable resource. Age discrimination is illegal, but it does not keep it from happening. If you are in this group, you are aware of this.

When it comes to getting a job, there is more than age discrimination. In some cases, individuals in this age group have not had to practice their job-hunting skills for decades. The job market is different today. People do not expect to go to work for and to retire from a particular organization as they did 30 years ago. Organizations and people assume that job jumping is a viable career strategy.

There are still more obstacles for individuals in this age group. According the AARP, once these individuals are unemployed, they have limited employment opportunities; re-employment after job loss declines dramatically at older ages. Of the nearly 1 million workers age 55 and older that are displaced, only 53 percent are able to find new jobs. The bad news is many of those who did not find jobs became "discouraged workers" who gave up.

Breaking the Age Barrier

That is the bad news. The good news is that no matter your age you can become successful. There are many individuals over the age of 50 that are breaking the age barrier. Some of my favorite examples are:

➢ Lee Iacocca, Chrysler's former CEO
➢ Senator John Glenn, the oldest man to go into space
➢ Dr. Debakey, open-heart surgeon
➢ Mother Teresa, who won the Nobel Peace Prize at age 69
➢ Hulda Crooks, who in her nineties became the oldest woman to climb Mount Fuji; she started climbing in her 70s
➢ Zig Ziglar, motivational speaker—not full time until his 40s
➢ William "Bud" Adams, retired at 92 from a position as prison guard that he started at age 77

This list could go on and on, but you get the point. The good news is as a person in this age group you can duplicate the results of the individuals who are able to find jobs. In this chapter, I will tell you what these people did to get results. I will also tell you what people I have known have done to get results. In the past few years, I have been fortunate to meet many people in this age group that started new careers.

I have known people who have each defied the odds, continuing to grow well beyond the age of 50 or 60. I have known people to return to college to finish their degrees. I have known people to return to college and finish their degree and go on to get their masters. I have known people in this age group to start their own business and make it a success. I know that you can be one of those people.

Lee Iacocca says that growing older does not mean you "run out of visions." On the contrary, he says, "When you're over 50, don't start planning your retirement, plan the next third of your life." Retirement is something that was started by a king in the Middle Ages as a way to get his opponents out of power. Iacocca says that retirement is not just about getting ready financially to do nothing. It is about planning to make a difference. How do you do this?

You do this by planning the next 20 years of your life the same way you would tell a college graduate how to plan his next 20 years. Right now, you and the college graduate have two things in common. You both want a job, and you both have the next 20 years to look forward to.

Select the Right Mentors

Mentors will always be a valuable resource. John F. Kennedy had a mentor. Lee Iacocca had a mentor. Chances are great that earlier in your life, you had mentor. Now may be the time to get another mentor. Let me ask you a question, "What if you find a mentor who is younger than you are? It does not matter if your mentor is younger. What matters is if your mentor can help you get a job or acquire the skills necessary to move forward with your life.

If your mentor is younger than you are, you can each that individual some of the effective strategies you have learned over a lifetime. If this person does not want to learn, do not force them. Avoid letting your ego get in the way of you making good decisions. I understand you may have a need to give something and if this person is not willing to accept it, give that something to a nonprofit group who will appreciate it.

Develop Supportive Networks

Develop a network of supportive friends that will provide the support and advice needed to find a job in today's market. These people need to be positive and results focused. If you surround yourself with dream stealers, they will steal your dreams. If you surround yourself with dream builders, your dreams will become a reality.

This network will become a valuable resource for you. These people will help share job leads and job ideas. These people will give you advice. These people will be there to cry with you. These people will be there to rejoice with you. This may mean that you need to look beyond your current sphere of influence. This may mean that you need to go church. You may need to find a self-help group. This may mean that you may need to start your own self-help group. There is one group that I have always found supportive and that is Toastmasters. Look in your town's yellow pages or look them up on the Internet at www.toastmasters.org

Speaking of networks, you need to continually network. Over half of all jobs are filled because someone knew someone. To assist in networking, consider joining the chamber of commerce, or volunteer your job skills with a local non-profit organization. You might even want to join the Society of Human Resources, even if you are not interested in human resources as a career. This will put you in a situation where you can meet people who are in charge of the hiring process.

Learn New Tricks

It is never too late to get a degree, to earn an additional degree, or get an additional certification. If not having a degree has been holding you back do something about it and get a degree. I have known many individuals who have gone back to college and finished their degree. As a matter of fact in my graduate class there were at least three people over the age of 40. In my undergraduate classes there were a number of people over 40.

All of these people had the same thing in common. They had gone as far as they could with what they knew. They had to get additional information before they could move forward. This next phrase is going to be hard to read but here it is: *age is not an indicator of knowledge.* I know many people would like to believe it is, but it is not. I do believe that age provides experience, and experience causes one to gain knowledge, but just because you are older does not necessarily mean you are wiser.

If you already have a degree and you want to change careers, consider getting a master's degree in the field you want to enter. Most graduate programs just require a degree and it seldom has to be in the same field. Chances are great that you have been out of school for so long you would still have to take the same pre-requisites even if you had that degree. The truth is there is more prestige that goes with having a graduate degree than an additional undergraduate degree.

The purpose of going back to college or gaining additional training is twofold. The first purpose is for you. When you do this, you are growing. When you do this, you are acquiring new skills. When you do this, you are investing in your greatest asset— yourself. The other reason to gain more training is to prove to your prospective employer that even though you have lived longer than most of the other candidates, you are willing to grow and adapt.

Who's Stereotyping Who

No one wants to admit that they have stereotypes, but we all do. Stereotypes are powerful, and stereotypes influence how we interact with other people. If you stereotype someone as being someone who discriminates, you are going to act as though you are being discriminated against, whether or not you have been. It then becomes difficult to distinguish when it really happens and when it does not. I do believe age discrimination really happens and this chapter is my response to it, but I do not believe you should act as if it happens in every job interview.

When you carry this negative stereotype, it will impact your performance in your job search. This stereotype causes anxiety and leads to inaccurate perceptions about the situation. This leads to miscommunication. Miscommunication leads to missed opportunities, and missed opportunities can lead to failure. This is all because the anxiety created by the negative stereotype subconsciously influences the way this person treated you because they can sense you do not feel comfortable around them.

We know that stereotypes create expectations about various situations. We know that stereotypes cause us to make inaccurate predictions about the results we get. They actually fulfill our expectations and if we have negative stereotypes, we will get negative results. This means if we develop positive stereotypes, we will get positive results. Because of this, stereotypes are a form of self-fulfilling prophecies. How does this impact the stereotypes we have of ourselves?

The Strongest Stereotype

One of the strongest, if not the strongest stereotype you have is the stereotype you have of yourself. Think about the stereotypes you have about yourself. What excuses are you giving for not pursuing the career you want? I understand that there is a certain level of comfort in maintaining these beliefs. That is why it is called staying in your comfort zone. However, as long as you hold these stereotypes and beliefs about yourself, the only thing you are doing is hurting yourself.

Much like this brave old knight named Sir Workalot. This knight worked for years and went on many adventures. He had trained well. He had even read this book. His armor was full of clichés and good sounding reasons for not moving forward. This knight could tell other knights what they needed to do to enter the Forest of Fortune and to gain their rewards, but he was unable to pursue those same victories for himself.

In this forest was the Dragon of Defeat. Some people said that this dragon was real. Other people said this dragon only existed in the mind. Either way the knight was afraid of this dragon. Legend said that this dragon would defeat the old knights by breathing fire phrases such as:

- ➢ You're too old.
- ➢ You can't teach an old dog new tricks.
- ➢ You should have finished college 20 years ago.
- ➢ Nobody wants an old fool like you around.
- ➢ Your time has passed.
- ➢ I can't believe you would even apply for this job.
- ➢ Wake up to reality: you're old.
- ➢ You are a failure.

As a result of this fear, the Knight never went into the forest to find his treasure. Instead, he decided to live on the edges of the forest. He decided to play it safe. He decided the dragon could not defeat him if he never faced it. The Knight was wrong. The fact is the Knight was defeated because he never faced the dragon. If you are like this Knight all you have to do to slay the dragon is to face the dragon, and when you do you will find that the dragon only existed in your mind.

Of course, this is a fictional story with fictional excuses, or is it? What dragons are keeping you from getting the job you want? The dragons you have are just as real as the dragon in this story. It will hurt you just as much as it hurt the knight for you to face your dragons. If you do not face your dragons, you will get the same consequences as the knight. If you face the dragon, you will get the rewards that the Knight only dreamed of. If this knight had gone into the forest he would have realized the only power the dragon had was the power the knight gave to the dragon. If you continue your job search, you will realize the same thing.

The simple fact is if you believe that those dragons are real then they are. If you believe that those dragons are not real then they aren't. The good news is either way you are right. The news gets better when you decided the dragons are not real. When you believe this you will realize the only obstacle between you and what you want to accomplish is a lack of belief.

The Power of Beliefs

This brings us to the importance of beliefs. The fact is whether you think you can or can't is up to you. Beliefs are power. Beliefs shape our opinions of the world and what we can do. I like to believe you can do whatever you put your mind too. I believe that for myself, and I believe it for you.

I believe when trying to find a job at any age you need to believe that you are the best candidate for the job. If you are 40, 50 or beyond there are certain beliefs that you need to develop for yourself. These are beliefs that should give you an advantage in the job-hunting game that no one else can have and they are:

> **Experience**- You have knowledge, insights, and understanding. This makes you an asset for any organization. You should know what works and what doesn't work. You should not have to reinvent the wheel. At the same time you need to be flexible to new ideas and to new technologies.

> **Knowledge**- Even if you do not have a degree you can demonstrate that you have gained knowledge over the years. Show the prospective employer how they can benefit from this.

> **Self Confidence**- You have years of practice at developing self-confidence. If your self-confidence has not been that great, that's okay, because you do not need to tell anyone. If you look and act as if you have confidence, you will develop self-confidence. If you keep reading books like this, you will develop self-confidence. Confidence is important because when you have confidence in yourself others will have confidence in you as well.

> **Enthusiasm**-Just because you have a few years behind you doesn't mean that you cannot get excited about your work. If you find a job that you can and will be enthusiastic about you will have the energy to get the job done. Enthusiasm is catchy; if you go into a job interview enthusiastic about the job no matter the job, chances are better that you will get the job.

> **Work Ethic**- Your experience in the job market will allow you to work harder and smarter than younger people. You have had more time to perfect your work ethic and do not hesitate to make this known

> **Motivation**- I am sure you are self-starter. Let the prospective employer know this. Do not act like you need the job because you need money. Act like you need the job because you are a motivated individual. Typically, people do not hire people because they need a job. They hire people because they have a problem they want solved. Indicate that you are motivated to solve their problems.

Start at the bottom

I know you do not like to hear this anymore than the young crowd, but to get the job you want you may need to start at the bottom and work your way up. The fact is there are a number of entry-level positions in the market. If you are not having luck finding a job at your previous level, be prepared to start at the bottom. I do believe, however, that it is okay to start at the bottom only as a last resort.

I hope that your experience and knowledge will help you move up. If it does not help you, you can take comfort in the fact that it is easier to find a job when you have a job. Even if the entry-level position does not offer any growth prospects within that organization, it will offer prospects outside of the organization. By taking an entry level or part time position you are indicating that you are willing and able to work.

Go Out on Your Own

If the thought of starting over doesn't appeal to you, consider starting your own business. Your maturity, thoughtfulness, experience, knowledge, risk tolerance, and ability to think long term are all assets in this endeavor. However, you will want to do research before you invest your money into a business. I would recommend that you take an entrepreneur class from a local college or other institution.

Colonel Sanders was a little gray headed when he started his business and became quite successful. Dave Thomas was in his fifties. Jack Smith of Jack's Music started his music store after he retired from his previous job of over 25 years. The point is you can start your own business too. It may take a little time to get the rewards but if you work hard enough they will come.

Practical Advice for 40, 50, and Beyond

There are some job-hunting realities I would like to discuss for individuals in this age group. The first is job hunting is hard at any age. When you are younger, you worry about lack of experience. When you are older, you worry about age discrimination.

I do not believe that someone who is 40 is not responsive to changes in the environment. I do not believe that someone who is 50 cannot be trained to do new things. I do not believe that someone who is 60 should retire. I believe people can continue to grow, as long they want to grow. I believe people should work as long as they want to work.

My beliefs are not important to the people in charge of hiring. I am convinced that many people involved in the hiring process are not good decision makers. I believe that the business owners, CEOs, or other organizational leaders should make the hiring decisions. However, this is not the case and the result is the people hiring tend to hire individuals that have a certain look or other qualification to get the job.

To combat this you should do all you can to get into contact with the real decision maker in the organization. Do some networking, get to know this person and let them know that you would be an asset to the organization. I talked in an earlier chapter about some networking techniques that should be useful to you.

When applying for a job I think you should use what is called a functional resume. On this resume do not put the dates you graduated from college unless it was in the last 10 years. I would use this instead of the chronological resume because the chronological resume lists your job by date. With the functional resume, you can go further back in time without revealing how far back you go.

Another practical tip is to use new techniques for job hunting. If you are not familiar with the Internet, you should take the time and learn about it. As a part of becoming familiar with the Internet, I would read articles on the web about job hunting and look for sites that relate to your season in life. I believe you should read this book cover to cover. After you read this book, read Todd Bermont's book 10 Insider Secrets to Job Hunting Success. After you read that book find another book to read.

Conclusion

You can do it! No matter your age or obstacles, you can get a job and the job you want. If you believe you can get the job, you will be able to get the job. As a mature job seeker, you have certain advantages and selling points that younger job seekers do not have.

If you have assumptions or beliefs that are holding you back you should change those beliefs. Even though there is a certain level of comfort in holding on to the ways things used to be, you get a job by the way things are or are going to be. 40, 50, or beyond is too young to retire. It is too young to be useless. It is the right time to put your experience, education, and ability to use.

KAPS

➢ There are many individuals over the age of 50 that are breaking the age barrier, and you can be one of them.
➢ The greatest stereotype is the stereotype you have of yourself.
➢ The only way you can slay your dragon is by facing your dragon.
➢ Your beliefs are power.
➢ You really can do it!

Appendix: Additional Sources and Resources

- ➤ Researching the Organization
- ➤ Job Interview Preparation
- ➤ 65 Traditional Interview Questions
- ➤ Behavioral Interview Questions
- ➤ Interview Evaluation
- ➤ Self-assessment of Interview
- ➤ Evaluating your compensation and benefits package
- ➤ Evaluating Job Offers
- ➤ Resume Check List
- ➤ Key Resume Phrases and Words
- ➤ Additional Resume Categories
- ➤ Actions Verbs That Sell
- ➤ Sample Resumes
- ➤ Sample Cover Letters
- ➤ Cover Letter & Resume Grammar

RESEARCHING THE ORGANIZATION
15 Questions to answer when you research any organization.

1. How old is the organization?
2. What are the organization's products and services?
3. Where are its plants, offices, or stores located?
4. What is the price of its stock?
5. Is the organization privately or publicly held?
6. What are the organization's plans for the future?
7. What is the organizational mission statement?
8. When and where was the organization founded?
9. Who are the officers of the organization and what are their functions?
10. What are some popular corporate stories at the organization?
11. How large is the organization? What is its industry rank?
12. What were the organization's sales last year? What are the sales this year?
13. What is the turnover rate for the organization and for the position for which you are applying?
14. What problems have they faced in the past or perhaps will they face in the future?
15. What is the organizational culture like? Will I fit into that culture?

15 Places to Find Answers to These Questions
1. Dun and Bradstreet's Million-Dollar Directory
2. Ward's Business Directory
3. Standard and Poor's register of Corporations, Directors, and Executives
4. Thomas Register of American Manufactures
5. Hoovers Online. www.hoovers.com
6. Security and Exchange Commission's *Edgar* web site www.sec.gov/edgarhp.htm
7. Value Line Investment Survey
8. Business week
9. Wall Street Journal
10. Company Websites
11. Search engines such as google, yahoo, infoseek, msn, dogpile, or any of the many others
12. Chambers of Commerce
13. Public Libraries
14. The Better Business Bureau
15. Newspapers

Remember that research is critical to your job-hunting success. If you don't do the research for the job, your competition will. Do you think someone who cared enough to learn about the company or someone who didn't will get the job? The truth is employers like it when prospects research the organization and they expect you to know something about the company you want to work for.

JOB INTERVIEW PREPARATION
A Check Sheet For The Interview

- ➢ Have you researched the potential employer?
- ➢ Do you have a copy of the company's annual report?
- ➢ Have you studied it?
- ➢ Have you visited the company's web site? What did you learn from the site?
- ➢ You are prepared to discuss the company's competitive environment.
- ➢ You have copies of the competition's company materials so you can speak intelligently about the industry.
- ➢ Have you prepared a SWOT analysis and assessed what the company's major challenges are and how you can help them?
- ➢ Do you know someone who works at the organization and have you talked to him or her about the corporate culture?
- ➢ Are you educated on the company's products and/or services?
- ➢ Have you identified the qualifications that the organization is seeking with this job hire?
- ➢ Do you understand the job you are applying for?
- ➢ Have you talked to someone with a similar position?
- ➢ You are prepared with stories that will demonstrate your strengths, weaknesses, and learning experiences.
- ➢ You can show how events in your background have been a learning experience, which has prepared you for this new position.
- ➢ You can discuss your personality, leadership, and management style.
- ➢ You have read and prepared answers to the most commonly asked interview questions.
- ➢ You have reviewed the dress for success guidelines and have picked your outfit at least a day in advance.
- ➢ You know how long it will take to get to the interview.
- ➢ You have additional copies of your resume and references.
- ➢ You have a pen & notepad to take notes.

After the interview

- ➢ Leave an extra copy of your resume with the interviewer.
- ➢ Record what you can remember about the interview.
- ➢ Wait a week and call to see if they have made a decision.
- ➢ Send a follow-up letter.

65 TRADITIONAL
INTERVIEW QUESTIONS

Here is a list of sample interview questions that can be expected from a traditional interview. When preparing for a job interview you must spend time developing and rehearsing answers to these questions. You may want to practice with a friend or someone else that will give you honest feedback on your answers. Remember the goal is to strike a balance between sounding natural and spontaneous and being completely prepared and knowing all answers in advance.

1. Why did you apply for this job?
2. Why did you leave your last job?
3. What do you know about this job or organization?
4. Why did you choose this career?
5. How do you plan to achieve your career goals?
6. Can you explain the gaps in your employment history?
7. Why should I hire you?
8. What would you do if…? (Usually about a work-related crisis)
9. How would you describe yourself?
10. What would you like to tell me about yourself?
11. What are your major strengths?
12. What are your major weaknesses?
13. What type of work do you like to do best?
14. What are your interests outside work?
15. What type of work do you like to do least?
16. What accomplishment has given you the greatest satisfaction?
17. What was your worst mistake?
18. What would you change in your past life?
19. What courses did you like best or least in school?
20. What do you see yourself doing five years from now? Ten years from now?
21. What do you want to find rewarding about your career?
22. What is more important, money or work?
23. How would you describe yourself? How would others describe you?
24. What motivates you?
25. What is your greatest accomplishment?
26. Why did you select your college or university?
27. Why did you choose not to go to college?
28. Why did you pick your major field of study?
29. What plans do you have for future education?
30. What do you know about our organization?
31. Do you work well under pressure?
32. Are you willing to travel or relocate?
33. What is more important to you: the work you do or the paycheck?
34. What is one mistake you made and what did you learn from it?
35. Is there a geographical location that you prefer?
36. What extracurricular activities do you take part in?

37. What did you learn from your extracurricular activities?
38. How would you describe your ideal job?
39. What are two or three things that are important to you about your job?
40. Why are you interested in this position?
41. What attracted you to our organization?
42. What are your ideas on salary?
43. Are you interested in sports?
44. What was your class rank in high school?
45. Do you believe your grades reflected your ability?
46. Do you work better alone or on a team?
47. How do you handle criticism?
48. What do you think are the characteristics for success in this job?
49. How did the previous employers treat you?
50. What did you learn from your previous jobs?
51. What would your previous employers say about you? Would they give you a recommendation?
52. How long did it take you to get your degree?
53. Why did you never finish your degree?
54. How well do you get along with others?
55. What's one of the hardest decisions you have ever had to make?
56. How well do you adjust to new situations and change?
57. How do you handle conflict?
58. Do you work well with others or do you prefer to work alone?
59. Are you seeking employment in an organization of a certain size? Why?
60. Were you in the military? What was it like?
61. Did you ever change your major? If so, why?
62. How long do you plan to work with us if you get the job?
63. What would your ideal manager/leader be like?
64. What have you accomplished that shows your initiative and willingness to work hard?
65. If you were in charge of finding someone for this position, what qualities would you look for? Do you have those qualities?

SAMPLE BEHAVIORAL INTERVIEW QUESTIONS

The behavioral interview method is becoming more commonplace. The reason is it relies more on the interviewee's experience and expertise than their ability to sell themselves. This is important for a skilled interviewer because hiring decisions should not be made based on how well someone can make up answers, but hiring decisions should be made based on how well someone can develop and demonstrate solutions.

During a behavioral interview you will be asked how you would handle specific situations like dealing with a difficult customer, co-worker or leader. This type of questioning gives the interviewer the opportunity to examine the thought process behind the decisions and choices you make. The key to answering these questions is to ask yourself why you approached the situation the way you did. In addition to this you will need to understand what the organization expects from individuals in the position you are applying for.

Here is a list of sample behavioral-based interview questions separated by traits that employers look for in successful job candidates:

ADAPTABILITY
  - ➢ Tell me about a situation in which you have had to adjust to changes over which you had no control. How did you handle it?
  - ➢ Tell me about a time when you had to adjust to a classmate's or colleague's working style in order to complete a project or achieve your objectives.
  - ➢ How was your transition from high school to college? Did you face any particular problems? How did you handle them?
  - ➢ Give me a specific example of a time when you had to conform to a policy with which you did not agree.
  - ➢ By providing examples, convince me that you can adapt to a wide variety of people, situations and environments.

ANALYTICAL SKILLS / PROBLEM SOLVING
  - ➢ Describe the project or situation that best demonstrates your analytical abilities. What was your role?
  - ➢ Tell me about a time when you had to analyze information and make a recommendation. To whom did you make the recommendation? What was your reasoning? What kind of thought process did you go through? Why? Was the recommendation accepted? If not, why?
  - ➢ Tell me about a situation where you had to solve a difficult problem. What did you do? What was your thought process? What was the outcome? What do you wish you had done differently?
  - ➢ Describe a time when you anticipated potential problems and developed preventative measures.
  - ➢ What steps do you follow to study a problem before making a decision? Why?
  - ➢ Give me a specific example of a time when you used good judgment and logic in solving a problem.

- ➤ Give me an example of a time when you used your fact-finding skills to solve a problem.
- ➤ Tell me about a time when you missed an obvious solution to a problem.

COMMUNICATION
- ➤ Tell me about a recent successful experience in making a speech or presentation. How did you prepare? What obstacles did you face? How did you handle them?
- ➤ Have you ever had to "sell" an idea to your classmates or co-workers? How did you do it? Did they accept your idea?
- ➤ Give me an example of a time when you were able to successfully communicate with another person even when that individual may not have personally liked you (or vice versa). How did you handle the situation? What obstacles or difficulties did you face? How did you deal with them?
- ➤ Tell me about a time in which you had to use your written communication skills in order to get an important point across.
- ➤ Please discuss an important written document you were required to complete.
- ➤ Tell me about a time when you had to use your presentation skills to influence someone's opinion.

CONFLICT MANAGEMENT
- ➤ Describe a situation where you had a conflict with another individual, and how you dealt with it. What was the outcome? How did you feel about it?
- ➤ Describe a time when you were faced with a stressful situation that demonstrated your coping skills.
- ➤ Tell me about a recent situation in which you had to deal with a very upset customer or co-worker.
- ➤ Tell me about a time you were able to successfully deal with another person even when that individual may not have personally liked you (or vice versa).
- ➤ What is your typical way of dealing with conflict? Give me an example.

CREATIVITY
- ➤ When was the last time you thought "outside the box" and how did you do it? Why?
- ➤ Tell me about a problem that you've solved in a unique or unusual way. What was the outcome? Were you happy or satisfied with it?
- ➤ Give me an example of when someone brought you a new idea that was odd or unusual. What did you do?
- ➤ Describe an instance when you had to think on your feet to extricate yourself from a difficult situation.

DECISION MAKING
- ➤ Tell me about a time when you had to make a decision without all the information you needed. How did you handle it? Why? Were you happy with the outcome?
- ➤ Give me an example of a time when you had to be quick in coming to a decision. What obstacles did you face? What did you do?
- ➤ What is the most difficult decision you've had to make? How did you arrive at your decision? What was the result?

- Tell me about a difficult decision you've made in the last year.
- Give me an example of a time when you had to make a split second decision.

GOAL SETTING
- Give me an example of an important goal that you have set and tell me how you reached it. What steps did you take? What obstacles did you encounter? How did you overcome the obstacles?
- Tell me about a goal that you set that you did not reach. What steps did you take? What obstacles did you encounter? How did it make you feel?
- How do you determine your goals and the steps necessary to accomplish your goals?
- Give me an example of a time when something you tried to accomplish failed.

INITIATIVE
- Describe a project or idea (not necessarily your own) that was implemented primarily because of your efforts. What was your role? What was the outcome?
- Describe a situation in which you recognized a potential problem as an opportunity. What did you do? What was the result? What do you wish you had done differently?
- Tell me about a project you initiated. What did you do? Why? What was the outcome? Were you happy with the result?
- Tell me about a time when your initiative caused a change to occur.
- Describe a time when you set your sights too high (or too low).
- What was the best idea you came up with during your professional or college career? How did you apply it?
- Give me an example of when you showed initiative and took the lead.
- Tell me about a time when you had to go above and beyond the call of duty in order to get a job done.

INTEGRITY/HONESTY
- Discuss a time when your integrity was challenged. How did you handle it?
- Tell me about a time when you experienced a loss for doing what is right. How did you react?
- Tell me about a business situation when you felt honesty was inappropriate. Why? What did you do?
- Give a specific example of a policy you conformed to with which you did not agree. Why?

INTERPERSONAL SKILLS
- Give an example of when you had to work with someone who was difficult to get along with. How/why was this person difficult? How did you handle it? How did the relationship progress?
- Describe a situation where you found yourself dealing with someone who didn't like you. How did you handle it?
- Describe a recent unpopular decision you made. How was it received? How did you handle it?

- What, in your opinion, are the key ingredients in guiding and maintaining successful business relationships? Give me examples of how you have made these ingredients work for you.
- Give me an example of a time when you were able to successfully communicate with another person even when that individual may not have personally liked you (or vice versa). How did you handle the situation?
- Tell me about a time when you had to work on a team with someone you did not get along with. What happened?
- Describe a situation in which you were able to use persuasion to successfully convince someone to see things your way.

LEADERSHIP
- Tell me about a team project when you had to take the lead or take charge of the project? What did you do? How did you do it? What was the result?
- Describe a leadership role of yours. Why did you commit your time to it? How did you feel about it?
- What is the toughest group that you have had to get cooperation from? What were the obstacles? How did you handle the situation? What were the reactions of the group members? What was the end result?
- Give me an example of a time when you motivated others.
- Tell me about a time when you delegated a project effectively.
- Tell me about a time when you were forced to make an unpopular decision.
- Please tell me about a time you had to fire a friend.

PLANNING, ORGANIZATION AND/OR TIME MANAGEMENT
- Describe a situation that required you to do a number of things at the same time. How did you handle it? What was the result?
- How do you prioritize projects and tasks when scheduling your time? Give me some examples.
- Tell me about a project that you planned. How did your organize and schedule the tasks? Tell me about your action plan.
- Tell me about a time when you had too many things to do and you were required to prioritize your tasks.

TEAMWORK
- Describe a situation where others you were working with on a project disagreed with your ideas. What did you do?
- Tell me about a time when you worked with a classmate or colleague who was not doing their share of the work. How did you handle it?
- Describe a situation in which you had to arrive at a compromise or help others compromise. What was your role? What steps did you take? What was the result?
- Tell me about a time when you had to work on a team that did not get along. What happened? What role did you take? What was the result?

PROBES / FOLLOW-UP QUESTIONS
- What steps did you take?
- What action did you take?

- What happened after that?
- What did you say?
- How did he/she react?
- How did you handle that?
- What was your reaction?
- How did you feel about that?
- What was the outcome/result?
- Were you happy with that outcome/result?
- What do you wish you had done differently?
- What did you learn from that?
- How did you resolve that?
- What was the outcome of that?
- Why did you decide to do that?
- What was your logic?
- What was your reasoning?
- Where were you when this happened?
- What time was it?
- Who else was involved?
- Tell me more about your interaction with that person.
- What was your role?
- What obstacles did you face?
- What were you thinking at that point?
- Lead me through your decision process.
- How did you prepare for that?
- Why? How? When?

Remember the interviewer is not your friend or coworker. How you answer pre or post interview questions will effect how the interviewer perceives you and will be used to evaluate you as a candidate for the position.

THE TOP 25 QUESTIONS TO ASK EMPLOYERS

Myth: Having the right answers to the interview questions will get me a job.
Fact: Interviewing is more than answering the right questions. It is asking the right questions.

1. Does your organization encourage further education or training?
2. What plans do you have for expansion?
3. What opportunities are there for growth in this organization?
4. Is this a new position? If not, why did the last person leave this position?
5. How did you get started in the organization?
6. What other position would you like to have in the organization?
7. What do you like best about your position/organization?
8. What advice would you give someone entering the industry?
9. What skills would I need to be successful in this position?
10. How long has the position been vacant?
11. What is the organizational atmosphere/culture like?
12. What would a day on the job be like?
13. Who would be my coworkers and what would they be like?
14. What is the dress code?
15. Where do you see the organization in the next five to ten years?
16. When will a decision be made about who will get the job offer?
17. Will you notify me? Or may I contact you later?
18. Can I provide you with any relevant information in the future?
19. Who will I be reporting to? What are they like?
20. How long is the training process? How will I be evaluated?
21. Is travel required for this position?
22. What is the housing like in the geographical area I will be working?
23. Where does this position fit in the organizational structure?
24. How many employees does the organization have in this position?
25. I am interested in this position; what do I need to do next?

INTERVIEW EVALUATION

Organization Name: _____ Date and Time: _____

Interviewer's name and position: _____

Title:_____

Phone: _____ Contact _____

Job Source:_____

Organizational Mission and Vision: _____

Organizational Values: _____

Can I support their mission: Yes or No _____

Can I support their values: Yes or No _____

Interviewer personality (what did I think of the interviewer?): _____

Title of Position I interviewed for: _____

Primary Responsibilities: _____

Secondary Responsibilities: _____

Immediate supervisor(s) and/or leader(s): _____

Title: _____

Initial Response to immediate supervisor or leader: _____

Will I be able to follow that leader: _____

Who will my co-workers be: _____

What are my co-workers like: _____

Will I be able to work with my co-workers: _____

What did I learn about the organization: _____

What I liked about the organization: _____

What I did not like about the organization: _____

My qualifications for this position are: _____

My potential weaknesses for this position are: _____

What would I like about this job? _____

What I wouldn't like about this job: _____

Is this job my dream job: Yes or No _____

Salary Negotiations: (Has the organization offered a job yes or no. If not, do not discuss salary) _____

Bonuses/Benefits: _____

If I am interested what is my next step: _____

SELF-ASSESSMENT OF INTERVIEW

Strengths of the interview: _____

Weaknesses of the interview: _____

What I should have done differently: _____

Do I want this position: _____

What should I do next if I want this position: _____

Follow-up letters to: _____

Follow-up phone calls: _____

Other: _____

What I should emphasize in the next interview or follow-up:

EVALUATING
COMPENSATION AND BENEFIT PACKAGES

Salary

Base Salary _____

Signing Bonus _____

Commission _____

How soon would there be a possibility of a salary increase? _____

When will the next review be? _____

Will the employer sign a one-year contract with certain employment provisions? _____

Performance Bonus

Specific Criteria _____

When paid? _____

Other Compensation Benefits

401 K Plan _____

Profit Sharing _____

Pension Plan _____

Child Care Tax Savings _____

Deferred Compensation _____

Travel reimbursements _____

Non-tangible benefits _____

Equity Participation

Is Stock available? _____

Stock Options _____

Vesting Requirement _____

Price per share - when will it be set? _____

Employee Stock Purchase Plan

> How long until you can participate? _____

> Purchase benefits? _____

Vacation/ Travel Sick Time

Vacation

- ➢ First year _____
- ➢ Second year _____
- ➢ Third year _____
- ➢ Fourth year _____
- ➢ Five years and beyond _____

Holidays observed _____

Overtime / Compensation time for long work weeks _____

Flexible Time _____

Maternity and Paternity Leaves? _____

Family leave Policy _____

Sabbatical _____

Personal days or holidays _____

Other Leaves of Absences _____

Other Benefits / Perks

Discounts on Health Clubs _____

Discounts on other memberships _____

Discounts at select retailers _____

Annual Physicals Included _____

Severance pay _____

Out-placement assistance _____

Educational Allowance (academic) _____

On the Job Training _____

Non-academic training (seminars/workshops) _____

Academic training or tuition reimbursement _____

Parking _____

Free lunches _____

Status of break room _____

Oil changes _____

Travel _____

Moving expenses _____

Coffee _____

Soft drinks _____

Snacks _____

Dry cleaning _____

Distance from home _____

Personal Phone Calls _____

Expense Account _____

Tickets to Sporting Events _____

Tickets to Movies _____

Tickets to Culture Events _____

Car Allowance _____

Laundry Service _____

Clothing Allowance _____

Evaluating Job Offers	Job 1	Job 2	Job 3
Salary			
Benefits			
Other Compensation			
Commute			
Opportunity to advance further			
Will I have to travel?			
How well will I get along with my supervisor and co-workers?			
Organizational Culture			
Vacation Benefits			
Health Care			
Organization stability, reputation			
Are the company products exciting?			
What hours will I work and how many?			
Will this make use of my skills and talents?			
Do I have to relocate?			
Confidentiality issues with previous job?			
What do my mentors, friends, and family think of this job?			
Organization's industry rank?			
Is this job what I really want to be doing with my life?			

RESUME CHECK LIST

Resume Headline or Lead-in (Objective or Profile)
- Do you use business language that is action/results oriented?
- Do you have a specific job title that you are seeking?
- Do you show how you can solve the employer's problem(s)?
- Do you clearly define what type of responsibility you can handle?
- Do you indicate how your contributions will specifically benefit the employer?
- Does it arouse attention?
- Is it easy to read?

Professional Qualifications
- Does this section highlight each of your major strengths?
- Are all of the qualifications/achievements related to the career objective?
- Is there appropriate usage of key action words?
- Have you described your qualifications in a way that the reader clearly understands the benefits of your achievements to the organization?

Experience
- For each job listed, have you listed the Job title, Function and Employer's name?
- Have you updated the language of your resume to include updated jargon that is widely used in your targeted industry?
- Will the reader understand the level of responsibility that you have experienced in other positions from reading the information?
- Does this section talk more about accomplishments than responsibility?
- Do you quantify your accomplishments by using specific examples?
- Don't be timid about listing non-paid accomplishments that you may have achieved for a non-profit or civic organization.

Education
- Does the section begin with your highest academic achievement and work backwards?
- Did you include other training (even if it is non-academic) that might be relevant?
- Have you listed classes that you audited that might be relevant?
- Have you listed credits that might be irrelevant?

Professional Organizations and Community Activities
- List only those items that have specific relevance to your career objective
- Did you list any organizations that do not present a professional image?
- Does it highlight organizations that will give you prospective employer an advantage with your contacts and business relationships?

➤ Does it refrain from personal information?

Overall

➤ Does the resume look great? Have you highlighted or boldfaced titles, subtitles and other important information?

➤ Is there enough white space - does the text flow for easy reading?

➤ Has the resume been checked by you and at least two others for spelling, punctuation, syntax and grammar?

➤ Does the body of the resume complement the career objective?

➤ Does the resume focus on what the organization is seeking?

➤ Don't include references on the resume.

➤ Would you consider this resume to be an excellent sales tool for your performance and past accomplishments?

When you are ready

➤ Print it as needed on a laser or laser quality printer if you have one.

➤ Avoid paper colors other than white or ivory.

➤ Always modify your resume so it is position and/or organization specific.

Remember

➤ A resume should never be longer than two pages; it is ideally one page.

➤ If you have worked for a well renowned organization, use a resume format that highlights that fact.

➤ If you had interesting assignments, then highlight experiences.

➤ Use "power" and "action" words, simple sentences and check your punctuation and spelling, remember you only have one chance to make a first impression.

KEY RESUME PHRASES AND WORDS

The following phrases and words should help your resume to be the marketing tool it needs to be. These phrases indicate how your experience, expertise, and education can solve problems for your new organization. It does this by conveying involvement, accomplishments and your pursuit for excellence. These phrases and words work in your favor because when used properly they make your resume easy to read.

Interaction with...
Established...
Edited...
Initiated...
Managed...
Maintained...
Instrumental in...
Remained as...
Honored as...
Recommendations accepted by...
Adept at...
Assisted with...
Coordinated...
Delegated...
Directed...
Developed...
Consulted...
Budgeted...
Evaluated...
Installed...
Instructed...
Negotiated...
Planned...
Presented...
Proven track record in...
More than _____ years experience...
Successful in/at...
Knowledge of/experienced as...
Initially employed...
Proficient/competent at...
Sales quota accountability...
Served/Operated as...
Direct/Indirect control...
Assigned to...
Resulted in...
assistance...Acted/Functioned as...
...to ensure maximum/optimum...
Worked closely with...

Acted as liaison for/between...
Formulated...
Handled...
Implemented...
Assigned territory consisting of...
Promoted to/from...
Recipient of...
Innovation resulted in...
...amounting to a total savings of...
Administered...
Analyzed/Assessed...
Arranged...
Counseled...
Conducted...
Demonstrated...
Advised...
Delivered...
Drafted...
Gathered...
Improved...
Investigated...
Organized...
Performed...
Recommended...
Experience involved/included...
Expertise and demonstrated skills...
Experienced in all facets/phases...
Extensive training/involvement...
Specialize in...
Temporarily assigned to...
Reported directly to...
In charge of...
Familiar with...
Contracted/Subcontracted...
Provided technical
...on an ongoing/regular basis...
Accomplished...

In addtion to those phrases I have complied a few examples of skills and descriptive lines that you should feel free to use or modify for your own situation.

Organizational Skills

- Performed data entry duties with excel and access.
- Attained highest sales for the month of _____ by selling $$$$ amount of product.
- Operated under time constraints and proficiency requirements.
- Received associate of the month for paying attention to detail and accuracy.
- Successfully used multi-line telephone.
- Learned the value of accuracy and efficiency by…
- Employed multi-tasking skills to react to changes in a fast-paced environment.
- Perfected time management and planning skills by successfully maintaining full-time academic status while working _____ numbers of hours a week.
- Protected the integrity of confidential, privileged information, and large cash transactions.
- Handled late accounts assertively and effectively by…
- Successfully handled credit cards, checks, and depository security issues.
- Accurately maintained park cash operations during working shifts.
- Successfully met production deadlines on a daily basis.

Teamwork Skills

- Gained a reputation for being a team player by …
- Received Team Player award for …
- Entrusted to work and uphold protocol within corporate office among high-level executives by …
- Served as a liaison between team employees and management.
- Work with team members to design a process to accomplish…

Public Relations and Interpersonal Skills

- Dealt with diverse customers on a constant basis, promoting my excellent communication and customer service skills.
- Constructively handled difficult situations.
- Developed and maintained an extensive network of contacts and clients.
- Established and maintained good rapport with over 20 colleagues and managers.
- Developed crisis management skills during health emergencies.

Leadership and Management Skills

- Recuirted, trainined and supervised X-Number of personnel in _____
- Conducted timely performance apprisals
- Supervised bi-weekly scheduling X-Number of departmental team members

ADDITIONAL RESUME CATEGORIES

To improve your selling position try adding **RELEVANT** information to your resume and/or cover letter that focuses on special experience, knowledge or skills that you have and are ready to put to use:

    HONORS
    TRAVEL
    PROFESSIONAL AFFILIATIONS
    INTERNSHIPS
    EDUCATION
    INTERESTS
    QUALIFICATIONS SUMMARY
    PUBLICATIONS
    TRAINING
    TECHNICAL SKILLS
    VOLUNTEER ACTIVITIES
    SKILLS
    PRESENTATIONS
    SUMMARY
    PURPOSE
    RELATED EXPERIENCES

ACTION VERBS THAT SELL

A

Accelerated
Accomplished
Achieved
Acquired
Activated
Active in
Adapted
Addressed
Adjusted
Administered
Advanced
Advertised
Advised
Aligned
Allocated
Analyzed
Answered
Applied
Appraised
Approved
Arbitrated
Arranged
Ascertained
Assembled
Assimilated
Assisted
Assure
Attained
Attended
Audited
Augmented.

B

Bargained
Billed
Bought
Brought
Brought about
Budgeted
Built

C

Calculated
Called
Changed
Clarified
Classified
Cleaned
Closed out

Coached
Collected
Collaborated
Commanded
Commended
Communicated
Compared
Complied
Completed
Composed
Computed
Conceived
Conceptualized
Condensed
Conducted
Conserved
Consolidated
Constructed
Consulted
Contacted
Contracted
Contributed
Controlled
Coordinated
Correlated
Corresponded
Corroborated
Counted
Counseled
Created
Critiqued
Cultivated
Culminated

D

Dealt
Debated
Designed
Detected
Determined
Developed
Devised
Diagnosed
Directed
Dissembled
Discovered
Discussed
Dispensed
Displayed
Disproved
Dissected
Distributed

Diverted
Documented
Doubled
Drafted
Dramatized
Drove

E

Earned
Edited
Educated
Elaborated
Eliminated
Employed
Enforced
Engineered
Enhanced
Enlisted
Equipped
Established
Estimated
Evaluated
Exceeded
Examined
Executed
Expanded
Expedited
Experimented
Explained
Expressed
Extracted

F

Fabricated
Facilitated
Fashioned
Filed
Filled
Financed
Fixed
Followed up
Forecasted
Formed
Formulated
Found
Founded
Functioned

G

Gained
Gathered
Generated

Governed
Graduated
Graphed
Greeted
Guided

H

Handled
Heard
Helped
Hired
Hope
Hosted

I

Identified
Illustrated
Imagined
Implemented
Improved
Improvised
Increased
Influenced
Informed
Initiated
Inspected
Inspired
Installed
Instilled
Instigated
Instituted
Instructed
Insured
Integrated
Interface
Interpreted
Interviewed
Introduced
Investigated
Invoiced

J

Joined
Judged
Juggled
Journalized
Justified

K

Key
Kept
Knowledgeable

L

Led
Learned
Lectured
Lifted
Loaded
Lobbied
Located
Locked

M

Machined
Made
Maintained
Managed
Manipulated
Mapped
Marketed
Mastered
Mediated
Memorized
Minimized
Modified
Monitored
Motivated
Moved

N

Negotiated
Networked
Neutralized
Nurtured

O

Observed
Obtained
Offered
Opened
Optimized
Orchestrated
Ordered
Originated
Overcame
Oversaw

P

Participated
Perceived
Perfected
Performed

Persuaded
Piloted
Pioneered
Planned
Played
Positioned
Predicted
Prepared
Prescribed
Presented
Prevented
Printed
Prioritized
Processed
Procured
Produced
Programmed
Projected
Promoted
Proofed
Proposed
Protected
Proved
Provided
Publicized
Published
Purchased

Q

Qualified
Quality
Quarterly
Questioned

R

Raised
Ran reacted
Read
Realized
Reasoned
Recapped
Received
Recognized
Recommended
Reconciled
Recorded
Recruited
Rectified
Redesigned
Reduced
Reevaluated
Referred

Refined
Regulated
Rehabilitated
Related
Remembered
Rendered
Renovated
Reorganized
Repaired
Replaced
Reported
Represented
Reproduced
Researched
Resolved
Responded
Restored
Retrieved
Revamped
Reviewed
Revised
Revitalized
Revived
Risked
Routed
Rushed

S
Saved
Scanned
Scheduled
Screened
Secured
Separated
Served
Serviced
Set up
Shaped

Shifted
Simplified
Solved
Sorted
Sparked
Spearheaded
Spoke
Staffed
Staged
Stimulated
Stocked
Streamlined
Strengthened
Stressed
Stretched
Structured
Studied
Succeeded
Summarized
Superseded
Supervised
Supported
Surveyed
Synthesized
Systematized

T
Tabulated
Talked
Taught
Tended
Tested
Took
Traced
Tracked
Traded
Trained
Transferred

Transformed
Translated
Traveled
Trimmed
Tripled

U
Uncovered
Unified
Unraveled
Updated
Upgraded
Used
Utilized

V
Vacated
Validated
Verified
Visualized

W
Wielded
Widen
Wired
Withdrew
Won
Worked
Wrote
Wrestled

Y
Yielded

Z
Zeroed
Zoomed

Jason McClure

www.jasonmcclure.com

54 Valley St
Little Rock AR, 72205
501.909.9600

Sample Functional Resume that I used to get a job as the
Training Manager for The Peabody Little Rock

MISSION: To use my experience, education, and abilities, to achieve organizational goals as a training and development manager at the Peabody of Little Rock.

QUALIFICATIONS

Computer Literate	Organized	Time Management
Skilled Public Speaker	Motivated	Results Oriented

EDUCATION

MA: *Master of Arts in Interpersonal and Organizational Communication*, UALR, Little Rock AR, expected graduation 9/02
BBA: *Marketing*, UCA, Conway AR, 5/99
Audited: 12 Hours of MBA courses at UALR as a graduated assistant

CAREER EXPERIENCE

TRAINING & SPEAKING: Prepared and facilitated the following trainings: Listening the Neglected Skill, Stress Management, Suicide Awareness, Unlimited Selling, How to Know if Your Clients are Getting it, Ready, Aim, and Hire: How to Hire Right, Supportive and Defense Climates, and Working in a Team Environment. Achieved ATM status with Toastmaster's International by giving 20+ presentations; currently working towards Accredited Speaker status. Develop training programs for the SCIL Center at UALR. Currently work as a contract trainer for HuCom Training Solutions.

COMPUTER EXPERIENCE: Proficient with most Microsoft Office programs, FrontPage, Print Shop, Microsoft Picture IT, HTML 4.01, SPSS, Banner, most other windows based programs, and web publishing software. Webmaster for www.SuccessSpeakers.com, www.AmericasSuccessCoach.com, and www.JasonMcClure.com

LEADERSHIP: Lead team members and recruited interns for the SCIL center at UALR. Duties included developing training programs and work projects. Served as Vice-President of Education for Toastmaster Club 4901, which included conducting "Better Club Series" training, attending leadership conferences, and member development.

WORK HISTORY

> UALR, Speech Communication Dept, Testing Services, and Distant Learning MBA Outreach Program: Graduate Assistant, 2000-2002
> Williams/Crawford: Campus Rep for TACO BELL, 1999-Present
> HuCom Training Solutions: Training Consultant, 1998-Present

PROFESSIONAL ORGANIZATIONS

> ASTD: Member of American Society for Training and Development, Little Rock AR, Chapter
> Little Rock Regional Chamber of Commerce
> Toastmaster International, Club 4901, Little Rock Ar

SUMMARY: An experienced and self-motivated opportunity finder, that sets and achieves long-term goals, wants to create and develop new programs that will help others grow.

SAMPLE CHRONOLOGICAL RESUME

NAME
Address
Telephone
E-mail

OBJECTIVE   Briefly describe the position that you are applying for.

CAREER
EXPERIENCE

List work experience in chronological order, starting with the most recent position including title, company, tenure of the job, and brief description of duties.

Example:

Office Manager (part-time) HuCom Training Solutions
Little Rock, Arkansas 1995-1999
Duties: Managed computerized inventory system. Maintained company records, including payroll and sales

EDUCATION

List diplomas and degrees earned, starting with most recent or highest level achieved.

Example:

University of Arkansas at Little Rock, Little Rock, Arkansas
Bachelor of Business Administration, May 2000
GPA in major 3.6/4.0 (Do not list GPA if less than 3.0)

SPECIAL SKILLS

List additional competencies that support or enhance your selling position.

Example:

Proficient in Microsoft Word, Excel, Access, PowerPoint
Competent in Spanish

HONORS AND ACTIVITIES

List any honors, awards, scholarships, and memberships in professional, honor, philanthropic societies, or civic organizations.

Example:

Dean's List, 3 semesters
Member, Lambda Pi Eta, Communication Honor Society
President, Marketing Club

REFERENCES   Available upon request

SAMPLE COVER LETTER

John Beaker
603 Park Avenue
Greenville, MS 38745
May 10, 2001

Ms. Joan Smith   RE: Job Title
Any Company, Inc.
123 New Street
Phoenix, AZ 38732

Dear Ms. Smith:

As a recent graduate of State University with a well-rounded marketing background, I would like the opportunity to put my skills, experience, and knowledge to use in an entry–level position at your organization.

I received my Bachelor of Business Administration degree in Marketing in May 2002. In addition to my marketing courses, I have learned a great deal about the advertising industry as an active member of the Future Advertisers of America Club. Through my internship with XYZ Marketing Company, valuable knowledge and work experience was gained.

To further discuss how my qualifications might meet your needs, please contact me at (555)545-4646 to schedule an interview.

Sincerely,

John Smith

Enc. Resume

SAMPLE COVER LETTER

The Peabody of Little Rock   **RE: Training**

#3 Statehouse Plaza
Little Rock, AR 72201

I hope you are having a great day, I am writing in response to the ad in last Sunday's Arkansas Democrat Gazette. I will make this letter short, because I understand you are busy. I am excited about the opportunity at the Peabody of Little Rock and if I understand the job requirements, I believe that there is a compatible match between your needs and my experiences. They include:

Your Needs:	**My Offerings:**
BS/BA or equivalent	BBA in Marketing and I have completed my course work for my Graduate Degree at UALR in Interpersonal and Organizational Communication.
Self motivated with excellent communication skills	I am a motivational speaker/trainer, member of Toastmaster's International. I can be counted on to work on tasks independently and on a team.
Experience office management	I have worked at UALR as a Graduate Assistant supervising interns and conducting evaluations along with developing work schedules and projects in the Speech Dept.
Expertise with Microsoft Office	I have taken a course in Microsoft office and I have work experience with excel, power point, word, and access.
Experience coordinating training and/or special events	As Vice-President of Education for Toastmaster's International Club 4901, I organize contests and conduct Successful Club Series training/seminars. As a campus-marketing representative for TACO BELL, I organize events for sponsorship by TACO BELL. As a graduate student in the MAIOC program, I have mastered effective workshop development, and communication strategies necessary to be successful in this position.

I hope I have clearly stated how my abilities will benefit the Peabody of Little Rock; I look forward to meeting with you to discuss my experiences and how they can equip your organization.

Thank you,
Jason McClure
501-909-9600

COVER LETTER & RESUME GRAMMAR

One of the best ways to separate yourself from other individuals applying for the same position is to ensure that your resume and cover letter are free of errors. Learning to use written grammar effectively will have a positive impact on the way individuals will judge you, affect your career, and thus have a great effect on your earning power.

Frequently Misused Words

Affect/Effect

Affect means to have an influence on or cause a change in.

Effect means to produce a result or bring about.

Example:

Your work performance can affect you whether or not you get a promotion.

My work performance effected the organization in a positive way.

Among/Between

Among is used when referring to a group.

Between is used in connection with two persons or things.

Example:

I was responsible for dividing workloads among my team members.

I divided the paycheck between my savings account and checking account.

Aggravate/Irritate

Aggravate means to make worse.

Irritate means to exasperate or inflame.

Example:

My poor performance during the interview aggravated my chances at getting the job.

A poorly written resume will irritate the interviewer.

Adverse/Averse

Adverse means contrary to one's interests or welfare; harmful or unfavorable.

Averse means having a feeling of opposition, distaste or aversion.

Example:

If you do not proofread your resume it will have an adverse effect on your job search.

I hope my averse feelings towards the interviewer did not show.

Continual/Continuous

Continual is an action that occurs with pauses and intermissions.

Continuous is an action that occurs without pauses.

Example:

My old car continually breaks down.

The waves of the ocean are continuous.

Complement/Compliment

Complement means to complete.

Compliment is a flattering remark or expression of esteem.

Example:

When you get a job you will complement the department.

When you meet the interviewer you might want to give them a compliment.

Disinterested/Uninterested

Disinterested means to be impartial, showing no preference or prejudice.

Uninterested means to lack interest.

Example:

The interviewer must be disinterested in a person's age when they are interviewing them.

I left my last job because I was uninterested in the position and company.

Eagar/Anxious

Eager means to be enthusiastic or excited.

Anxious means to be worried or full of anxiety.

Example:

I am eager to find my dream job.

I am anxious about the downsizing of my company.

Expand/Expend

Expand means to increase or enlarge.

Expend means to spend or to consume.

Example:

I am right for this position because I was able to expand my sales by fifty percent.

I need to find a job before I expend my savings.

Farther/Further

Farther refers to physical distance.

Further refers to degree or extent.

Example:

To get the job I really want I will have to drive farther to work.

To become a lawyer I will have to further my education.

Imply/Infer

Imply means to throw out a hint or a suggestion.

Infer means to take in a hint or suggestion.

Example:

The interviewer implied that the applicant was not qualified for the job.

I inferred from my last write up that my manager was not happy with my job performance.

Its/It's

Its is a possessive pronoun that never takes an apostrophe.

It's is a contraction of it is.

Example:

Its parts are missing.

It's your responsibility to find your dream job and make it a reality.

Lay/Lie

Lay means to put or place something.

Lie means to rest or recline.

Example:

Please lay your resume on my desk.

I asked the interviewer if I could lie down because I was sick.

Less/Fewer

Less is used for quantities.

Fewer is used for individual units or numbers.

Example:

If you do not get a job you will have less money.

Your resume has fewer mistakes than the last time I read it.

Stationary/Stationery

Stationary means something is still and/or fixed.

Stationery is letter paper.

Example:

The building is stationary.

Please put your resume and cover letter on nice stationery.

UNDERSTANDING SUBJECT VERB AGREEMENT

- ➤ The subject and verb must agree in number.
  - o A singular subject requires a singular verb.
  - o A plural subject requires a plural verb.
- ➤ When two or more subjects are joined by **and**, use a plural verb.
- ➤ When two or more singular subjects are joined by **or** or **nor**, use a singular verb.
- ➤ When subjects differ in numbers the verb should agree with the subject closest to the verb.
- ➤ When using nouns such as: much, someone, everyone, each, everybody, nobody, every, one, and another use a singular verb.
- ➤ When using nouns such as: few, both, many, several, and others use a plural verb.
- ➤ When a group is acting as one unit, use a singular verb.
- ➤ If the members of the group are acting separately, use a plural verb.

UNDERSTANDING CAPITALIZATION

- ➤ Capitalize the first word of each sentence.
- ➤ Capitalize all official titles when they precede personal names.
- ➤ Capitalize both the full names and shortened names of government agencies, bureaus, departments, services, etc.
- ➤ Capitalize academic degrees that follow a name. Also capitalize academic titles and religious titles when they precede a person's name.
- ➤ Capitalize trade names.
- ➤ Capitalize official names of buildings, streets, and public places.
- ➤ Capitalize days of the weeks and the months of the year.
- ➤ Capitalize holidays and holy days.
- ➤ Capitalize official documents.
- ➤ Capitalize streets, roads, and highways.
- ➤ Capitalize the sections of country or of a continent.
- ➤ Capitalize bodies of water.
- ➤ Capitalize special events.

UNDERSTANDING PUNCTUATION

When and how to use commas
- ➢ Use a comma to separate long independent clauses in a compound sentence.
  - ○ The interviewer tried to interest me in the position, but I insisted that I would invest my career elsewhere.
- ➢ Use a comma to set off a long introductory phrase or clause from an independent clause that follows.
  - ○ Not willing to settle for less than my dream job, I refused to consider any other job.
- ➢ Use a pair of commas to set off words and group of words inserted within a sentence.
  - ○ The interviewer did not say that, as you would know if you had listened carefully, nor did the interviewer even hint at it.
- ➢ Use commas to divide elements in a series.
  - ○ In my previous job I was responsible for establishing new accounts, maintaining old accounts, and communicating with management.
- ➢ Use a comma to set off parenthetical information
  - ○ Mr. McClure, the key note speaker, arrived on time for the event.
- ➢ Use a comma to set of the name of anyone you are addressing directly.
  - ○ It was a pleasure to interview you, Rebekah, now I want to offer you the position.
- ➢ Use a comma between consecutive adjectives instead of *and*.
  - ○ Sue loved her modern, well designed office.

When and how to use semicolons
- ➢ Use a semicolon to separate a series of phrases that already contain commas.
  - ○ The panel interviewers wanted to hire different applicants: John Smith, Sales; Jane Doe, Accounting; and William Smith, Operations.
- ➢ Use a semicolon when two complete thoughts are linked by a transitional expression such as however, therefore, accordingly, consequently, and moreover. Place the semicolon in front and a comma behind.
  - ○ The manager agreed to give the applicant the job; however, the applicant must demonstrate their ability to do the job.

When and how to use colons
- ➢ Use a colon after the salutation in your cover letter, follow-up letter, and other business letters.
  - ○ Dear Ms. Smith:
- ➢ Use a colon to introduce a list with an expression such as for example, namely, that is, or following:
  - ○ "There are three kinds of lies: lies, damned lies, and statistics." –Mark Twain

ISBN 141200538-8

9 781412 005388